WILDWATER

WILDWATER

The Sierra Club Guide to
Kayaking and Whitewater Boating

Lito Tejada-Flores

DRAWINGS BY CAROL INGRAM

Sierra Club Books   San Francisco

Copyright © 1978 by Lito Tejada-Flores. All rights reserved. No part of this book may be reproduced in any form or by any electronic or mechanical means including information storage and retrieval systems without permission in writing from the publisher.

Library of Congress Cataloguing in Publication Data

Tejada-Flores, Lito.
Wildwater.

    Bibliography: p.
    Includes index.
    1. White-water canoeing.
    2. Canoes and canoeing.
    I. Sierra Club.   II. Title
    GV788.T44   797.1'22   77-28189
    ISBN 0-87156-209-X

Book design by Jon Goodchild
Printed in the United States of America

10 9 8 7 6 5 4 3 2

Grateful acknowledgment is made for permission to reprint selections from *Heaven My Blanket, Earth My Pillow* by Yang Wan-li, translated by John Graves.
N.Y.: John Weatherhill, Inc., 1975.

Pour Hélène qui sait
comme Héraclite
que $\pi\acute{\alpha}\nu\tau\alpha$ $\rho'\epsilon\hat{\iota}$.

CONTENTS

Part Two
The Whitewater Scene

WILDWATER MAGIC

What is wildwater?

Wildwater is a tumbling mountain stream, barely deep enough to float a boat, choked with boulders, lined with spruce and pine, dropping down out of the high country in an alternation of crystal pools and sparkling rapids. . . .

Wildwater is a wide, muddy-brown torrent surging between red sandstone walls through desert canyons, tons of water towering up in twenty-foot waves, exploding back onto itself in a chaos of foam. . . .

Wildwater is both these extremes and everything in between: a free-flowing river, a rapid dancing leaping river, a gentle sinuous laughing river, a fierce river, an endless succession of rivers, all different.

Wildwater sport is even more. It's the river plus you, the river runner, and the combination is magic.

The word itself comes from the German expression *wildwasser fahren* (loosely, wildwater travel or wildwater running), which is what the sport of running rapids has been called in the eastern Alps since its invention there. In America the term wildwater has often been used to designate one type of boating competition, but it never totally caught on, and today this type of competition is far better known as *down-river racing* (by analogy with down*hill* racing on skis). Wildwater, however, is far too fine an expression to lose, and so in this book we use the term wildwater to sum it all up: river and rapids, boat and boater, excitement and adventure.

Just what is this wildwater magic that every boater has experienced but that is so hard to put into words? Rivers themselves have always been objects of power and reverence, inspiring symbol and myth and, alternately, love and fear. But river running introduces something new: the drama of being somewhere you manifestly don't belong, of balancing on that razor's edge where you're neither out of control nor ever really in control, of playing with forces so much greater than your own that you just can't win—and then, at least temporarily, winning when you stop fighting the river and for a moment become part of it.

Wildwater boating is a classic wilderness adventure sport, like mountaineering or wilderness skiing but different from either. Its quality of motion does recall skiing, especially powder skiing—another adventure in a fluid medium. But it is far more serious, potentially at least more hazardous, and requires a greater commitment. One thing that the neophyte wildwater boater soon discovers is that there are some places, some rapids, where you just can't stop—the river takes you and you're committed to go all the way through this stretch, rightside-up or upside-down, in your boat or out of it. In this sense of commitment, wildwater boating does resemble the tenser moments of a good climb—those scary leads where once you've started you just can't back down. But the climber is a slow fellow indeed compared to the boater in rapids; on the river, decisions, obstacles, waves, holes come one after the other in lightning-fast succession and the boater's reactions must be quick, dynamic, flowing. Although the experienced wildwater boater uses eddies to pause here and there, he still cannot inch his way down a rapid the way a rockclimber may inch his way up a cliff. Like the river itself, thé boater must cast loose and flow.

The kind of river running that comes most easily to mind when we talk of wildwater sport is descending whitewater rivers in light paddled craft, primarily kayaks and canoes, although many a wildwater adventure is to be had in oar-powered dories or rubber rafts (*not* outboard-powered rafts!). Most of this book is devoted to river running in kayaks, and the reasons for this emphasis, as well as criteria for choosing your own wildwater craft, are explained in detail in Chapter 1, *To Paddle or to Row?* But the kayak is an ideal craft in which to get your first taste of wildwater magic. With a kayak you play a kind of David-and-Goliath game against elemental river forces in a light, elegant, and seemingly fragile craft, making your peace with foaming water, sudden drops, and curling waves through subtlety and technique.

What else? Much of the attraction of wildwater sport comes from its basic improbability: how unlikely, almost impossible, it seems that one should be able to comfortably and safely go down these wild-looking rapids. There's the kinesthetic element, literally poetry in motion through a changing mix of water, spray, and air. All the qualities of pure sport are there: subtle movements, powerful ones, a whole array of techniques to master and then apply. It is a thinking, reacting sport where strategy and split-second timing are both important; an individual sport in which nobody can run that rapid for you, yet a sport that develops strong bonds, since your very life may depend on your companions' quick action—a sport for the whole person.

But there is something else. Wild rivers, whitewater rivers, are extraordinarily beautiful. Esthetics are the final ingredient in what I've called wildwater magic. From rock-walled gorge to gentle valley, the landscape that slips by along the river's banks as seen from the river is like no other. The water itself has a thousand surprises: mother-of-pearl waves, cascades of rainbow-hung foam, boiling cauldrons of frightening white energy, still reflecting pools where each paddle stroke seems a sacrilege, liquid figures and fantasies an artist wouldn't have dared to invent.

All this and more lies ahead, around the corner, in the next canyon, the next rapid. So back in our boats now and let's go. Out of the eddy with a couple of long easy strokes, out into the current. And now we can hear it, faintly, still out of sight, a whisper of falling water that may turn into a roar . . . Wildwater!

In Razorback rapids on Stanislaus River
Kayak capsizing in cascade of foam
Roll up to the surface surrounded by wingbeats
Bright yellow butterflies cover my boat
Crystals of water crash against cliffside
Gray limestone rock green willow bank
Cool twisting canyon sunlit and calm
Carries me onward wide-eyed with wonder
Surrounded by beauty before and behind me
Too much for one person to bear by himself

PART ONE

WHITEWATER & WHITEWATER TECHNIQUE

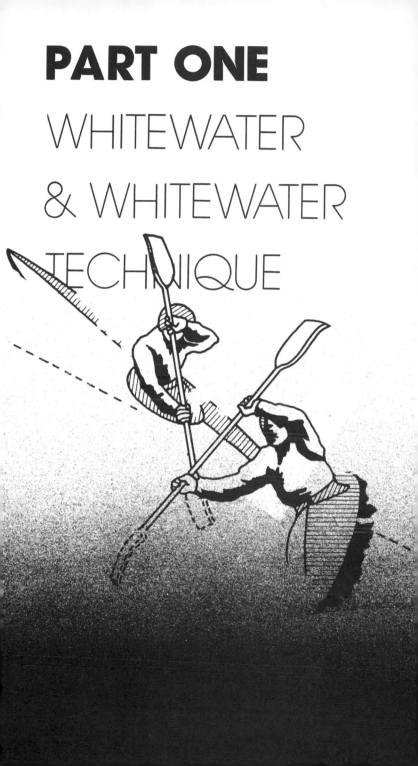

CHAPTER 1

TO PADDLE OR TO ROW?

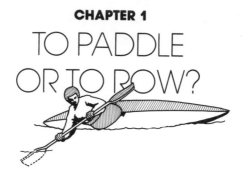

The very first choice in whitewater boating is that of a boat. Will it be the single-place kayak, agile and nimble, that can maneuver as though it were part of the river itself, yet can also be so ornery and tippy that the beginner frequently compares it to a bucking bronco? Or the rubber raft, slow and ungainly, not dancing but easing its way steadily and securely through the rapids? Or one of several other choices, ranging from decked-over fiberglass canoes, single and double-place, to the so-called inflatables, small kayaklike craft that are neither sporty nor tippy? The choice of boat is important, for it will determine the whole character of your wildwater adventure.

A little background will be helpful in making this decision. When we think of whitewater craft, we automatically eliminate open canoes on the one hand, and such nonboats as inner tubes and air mattresses on the other. Whitewater is for real, and part of the attraction of whitewater sport (like that of mountaineering or wilderness skiing) is its potential danger. People run rapids not simply because they are dangerous, but rather because coping with danger, eliminating or reducing it to acceptable levels through skill and judgment is an added attraction of whitewater sport. Let's make this point particularly clear: Anyone who heads down a river known to have rapids in an inner tube or on an air mattress is neither recognizing the potential hazard that exists in all whitewater nor dealing with it. For the old swimming hole, yes, for whitewater, no. Likewise with the open canoe. Despite romantic legends about French Canadian *voyageurs* and their Indian guides shooting rapids in early birchbark canoes, the open canoe is *not* recommended for whitewater touring. It is, of course, a legitimate river craft, and in the hands of a skilled paddler an open canoe can negotiate easy rapids successfully. Nonetheless, water which would be almost trivial for even a novice kayaker represents the limit, the ultimate in paddling difficulty for open canoeists—constantly threatened by capsizing in any big waves, and once capsized, facing the prospect of an awkward rescue. For this reason, we rule out open canoes as whitewater craft, leaving them where they belong, on gentle rivers and open lakes.

Quite different is the decked-over whitewater canoe, a delightful and specialized craft which we shall also ignore in this book, but for quite different reasons. The single-place whitewater canoe (it goes by the designation C–1) looks rather like a kayak to the uninitiated. It is a streamlined fiberglass shell, somewhat beamier (wider) than a kayak, and it invariably has a round cockpit hole in the deck rather than the kayak's teardrop-shaped one. The significant difference is in the way the C–1 is paddled: the boater kneels rather than sits in the cockpit and uses a single-bladed paddle. Compared to the kayaker the canoeist has better visibility of the river ahead because he's kneeling, not sitting, but for the same reason he has slightly less stability and much less comfort on long trips. The whitewater canoeist also has slightly more maneuverability in some circumstances due to his subtler paddle strokes, but much less power than the kayaker, who uses a double-bladed paddle. Most importantly, however, whitewater canoeing is *hard,* technically hard to learn and master, much more difficult for the beginner than kayaking. Indeed, the natural progression seems to be that an experienced kayaker often wants to take up whitewater canoeing or C–1 in search of an extra technical challenge, an added dimension of sport, rather than for any practical reasons. In fact there seem to be no practical reasons at all to prefer a C–1 over a kayak.

Because kayaking is so much easier to learn and in many ways is more suitable for longer touring, we are going to ignore the whitewater canoe in this book. May the partisans of this sprightly craft forgive such a slight; they would be the first to recognize that it is not a beginner's boat. (And everything I've said about the C–1 goes double for the C–2, the two-place whitewater canoe, where the problem of coordination between two partners in turbulent water raises the boaters' art to another level altogether.)

What's left? The basic choice is whether you want to paddle or row. Are you going to take up the kayak or go downriver on a raft? Both kayak and raft are a permanent part of the wildwater scene, but which is for you? As the table of contents shows, this book is biased toward the choice of a kayak, and toward kayaking as the very essence of the wildwater experience, but this choice is still not for everyone.

The basic difference between kayaking and rafting is that between being a participant and a passenger. This is not to say that the rafter has no work to do. Rowing can be hard physical work, but the size of the raft and the length of the oars seem to separate the rafter from the water. (And of course, there's always room on a rubber raft for real passengers, just along for the ride.) In contrast, the kayaker, from the very first, is more intimately involved with the river he's running; the kayaker seems to work directly with the water, with its shapes, its forces, its flow. Instead of riding high and dry above the surface of the river, you are right down in it, sitting in the water, the bow of your kayak seeming for all the world like an extension of your own legs in front of you. You feel, in a kayak, that *you* are riding the rapids just as physically as your boat is and, as you gain both confidence and skill, you will start to feel yourself becoming a part of the river. This sense of identification and involvement with the river is just not available to the rafter, no matter how thrilling his ride down the rapids may be.

This leads to a bit of reflection on the special aspects of whitewater touring as a wilderness experience. Put aside for a moment the limiting definition of wilderness as nature without man, far from the madding crowd, and instead take wilderness as nature *beyond* man—beyond our scope, scale, and above all beyond our ability to subdue it. When the boater in his fragile kayak drops down the smooth glistening tongue of water into the first foaming waves of a new rapid, he is entering a world of forces and flow so elemental, so far beyond the normal scope of over-controlled urban life, that this boater is going to have a wilderness experience even if there is an asphalt highway a hundred yards away —and an intense wilderness experience at that.

To the ancients, water was one of the four elements—together with earth, air, and fire—defining and forming our universe. To the modern geologist, wildwater is one of the great shapers, carving gorges and valleys, changing the face of the planet. The wildwater experience, running rapids in small boats, puts us back in touch with these elemental forces, metaphorically and emotionally. The closer we are to the river itself, the more intense our wilderness experience will be. And far more than any raft, a kayak gets us close to the water.

Having justified in some measure my prejudice in favor of kayaking as a richer and more intense experience, let me hasten to add that the sport is not for everyone. Kayaking is not terribly difficult to learn, nor is it a sport for superathletes, but there are certain limiting factors, physical and psychological. Kayaking is harder than skiing, for example, although not much harder. You must be in fairly good physical condition and should certainly be able to swim well—a skill you're sure to use at first. You must also be a fairly calm person who can accept full responsibility for your own safety and function well under stress. Unlike the mountaineer, the kayaker must depend on himself, not on his companions, for safety. When your boat tips over in rapids, it's up to you to recover. You must do something, even if it's only popping off your spray cover to release yourself from the boat (hopefully you'll soon know how to roll yourself and your boat back up). You can't remain passive, because if you do nothing at all you'll drown. It's as simple as that. This is not meant to scare you, but to make you aware at the outset that kayaking must be taken seriously if it is to be safe as well as fun. But if you are really at home in the water, if you love both water and swimming, if you have never felt afraid of water, then kayaking should be for you. Getting started in kayaking is another matter, with a club or with friends, at one of the few good kayak schools, or even by yourself. All are possible, and, starting in Chapter 3, we'll tell you how.

But suppose kayaking doesn't seem like your cup of tea. Perhaps you're not ready for the commitment of time and energy; perhaps, to be perfectly honest, you're a little hesitant about the intensity, the involvement, the scariness of kayaking, and yet you still want to participate in the wildwater scene, to run rapids but with fewer thrills. Or perhaps you have a family that you want to take with you on your whitewater adventures and you can't imagine your children kayaking down frothing mountain rivers (quite rightly, as kayaking is no sport for young kids). Perhaps photography is your bag and you don't think you'll have much opportunity to shoot the wild rivers on film while shooting rapids in a kayak. For these or other equally legitimate reasons, kayaking isn't for you. What, then, are your boating alternatives?

Rafting is generally more secure and less intense. A good raft properly outfitted for whitewater will get through the most amazing rapids despite a host of boatman's errors. Rafts are hard to capsize, and they provide a wonderful moving platform from which to enjoy and photograph the river and the countryside that glides by on either bank. Also, rafts have the advantage of not being cramped, so they can carry a lot of gear. For this reason, on longer trips kayakers usually seek raft support to carry extra duffle and food. Rafts and kayaks thus form an integrated party for multi-day trips that would be impossible for kayakers alone.

Nor is it particularly hard to row whitewater rafts. Although they are heavy and look quite clumsy and unmaneuverable, the real trick is to put them in the right spot at the start of a rapid and then let the water (which has a lot more force than you) do most of the work, often simply carrying the raft along in the proper course. Rowing rafts in whitewater is an art, but not as much of an art as paddling a kayak, since the rafter never really tries to "play" with the water, but merely concentrates on "getting through" smoothly. That is why I devote so much less space to rafting techniques in this book. Before turning to Chapter 7, *Boating Alternatives*, readers with an interest in rafting should read the river lore sections of Chapters 4 and 5 for a basic introduction to the varied phenomena of whitewater. Later you may want to go back through the kayaking chapters for the discussion of some special on-the-river situations which you can easily apply to rafting.

Rafts do have a few negative points for the would-be whitewater boater, namely their expense, their bulk and weight, and the time and effort it takes to equip them for whitewater touring. If you don't want to take up kayaking right away but still want to get your feet wet (so to speak) in an easy way, experiencing most of the excitement of whitewater boating, an alternative to rafting is the inflatable kayak or canoe. This small rubberized contraption doesn't steer very well but it is devilishly hard to tip over. It provides the easiest introduction to running rapids, and offers some of the excitement of kayaking with some of the ease and stability of rafting. Different types of inflatables and their techniques are covered in Chapter 7. But once again, don't neglect the earlier chapters on river lore.

So much for the all-important first choice. Maybe you have already made it, have recognized yourself as one kind of boater or another while reading this chapter. If you still aren't sure, then cast about and see what your local opportunities for rafting or kayaking might be and let that influence your decision. After reading this book (both the material on kayaking and rafting, as well as all the material which applies to wildwater touring in general) you should be able to make up your mind.

But above all, as a beginner, don't be afraid of kayaking. Kayaking is truly a magical sport. Contrary to popular misconceptions, kayaks are not horribly tippy but, with their low center of gravity, rather stable. They are relatively easy to paddle, and you don't need a high degree of expertise to enjoy running rapids in a kayak. Many enthusiastic kayakers never paddle anything harder than Class 3 water, which is very friendly (the one-to-six scale of difficulty is explained in Chapter 5). These kayakers don't feel they are missing anything by not tackling harder rivers. Whitewater touring in a kayak is not a macho sport where you must constantly test yourself against the river. Make no mistake, in such tests the river will win sooner or later. Instead, the essence of whitewater sport is to flow with the river, to get to know your boat as well as your own skills and limits, to become a part of the riverine scene, not an intruder into it. You may never kayak the Grand Canyon; most kayakers don't. But in all probability you will spend some of the finest moments imaginable in your kayak running rivers. So let's get started—and good boating!

CHAPTER 2

KAYAK EQUIPMENT

Equipment serves the same double function for the kayaker that a rope does for the mountaineer. It not only opens the door to a new environment, it is also designed to keep you safe and secure when this environment—whitewater—gets hostile, as it often does. Even putting aside questions of performance, safety considerations alone dictate that the kayaker assemble a really first-rate kit of gear.

But kayak equipment is quite expensive, especially for the newcomer to the sport who hasn't yet been truly bitten by the whitewater bug. In this chapter I attempt to offer some practical advice—not merely which kayaks, paddles, and the like are best for which boaters, but almost as important, how to get the very most for your equipment dollar, where you can save money, and where it would be unwise to try to do so. You'll need a lot more than a kayak before you can go kayaking: paddle, spray skirt, life-vest, helmet, and in many rivers some kind of special clothing for warmth.

Boats

Your kayak is the heart of the matter, and that's where we'll begin. The modern kayak is the product of years of trial and error, research and refinement. It is also the result of an emerging fiberglass and plastics technology which, for whitewater at least, has completely replaced the earlier "foldboat" construction (collapsible boats made of wood and canvas). Although kayaks of fiberglass-reinforced plastic (FRP) began to appear in the fifties and have been completely accepted for over a decade, the technical basis of the boat-builder's craft is still changing; new materials and construction techniques appear each year. This steady progress toward lighter, stronger, more resilient boats is likely to continue for years to come. In addition there is a bewildering diversity of shapes and designs, so before you can choose the right boat you should learn something about kayak design—basic principles and different styles of specialized boats.

Design and Construction

All kayaks are more or less streamlined, decked-over craft with a cockpit and seat somewhere in the middle, but certain design features influence their handling characteristics to an overwhelming extent. Obvious features are length, width, and volume; more subtle ones are hull *cross-section, rocker,* or side profile, and the outline of the boat as seen from above (there's no short term for this one).

Everything else being equal, a longer kayak will be faster and will track in a straighter line than a shorter one. Conversely, a shorter kayak will be easier to turn. A wider kayak will be more stable, a narrower one more tippy. Actually, however, definite standards of length and width for racing boats have been set by the International Canoe Federation, and these are universally respected, even for purely recreational kayaks, so there is less variation than one might think in these dimensions.

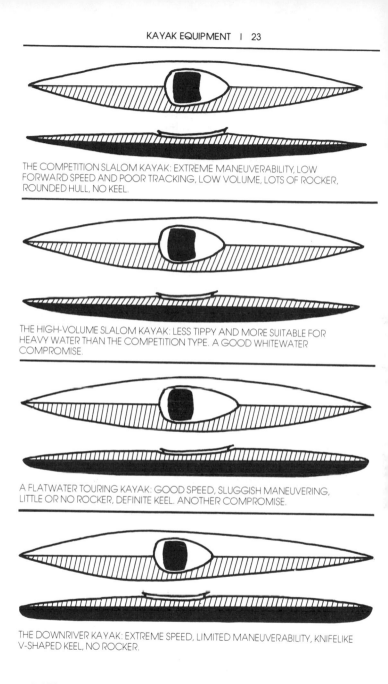

THE COMPETITION SLALOM KAYAK: EXTREME MANEUVERABILITY, LOW FORWARD SPEED AND POOR TRACKING, LOW VOLUME, LOTS OF ROCKER, ROUNDED HULL, NO KEEL.

THE HIGH-VOLUME SLALOM KAYAK: LESS TIPPY AND MORE SUITABLE FOR HEAVY WATER THAN THE COMPETITION TYPE. A GOOD WHITEWATER COMPROMISE.

A FLATWATER TOURING KAYAK: GOOD SPEED, SLUGGISH MANEUVERING, LITTLE OR NO ROCKER, DEFINITE KEEL. ANOTHER COMPROMISE.

THE DOWNRIVER KAYAK: EXTREME SPEED, LIMITED MANEUVERABILITY, KNIFELIKE V-SHAPED KEEL, NO ROCKER.

1. Different kayak designs, their comparative shapes shown in top and side views.

More significant in practical terms is the hull's cross-section. A boat with a V-shaped hull will track forward through the water better than one with a rounded hull. If the V is very deep the kayak will track very well, be tippy, fast, and almost impossible to turn or maneuver. If, on the other hand, the boat has a rounded hull cross-section, it will turn more easily, be slower, and have a tendency to wander rather than track. If the rounded bottom is also designed to be somewhat flat and pancake-shaped (gently dished rather than scooped out), it becomes extremely easy to turn and spin the kayak, and almost impossible to get any straight-line speed.

A basic pattern emerges. We have speed and tracking at one end of the spectrum and ease of turning at the other end. Other design features can also push the kayak in one of these directions or the other. Take the rocker, for instance. The rocker of a boat is the amount its bottom curves upward from the center toward the two ends. A boat with a lot of rocker curves up quickly in a deep rounded arc toward bow and stern, and as a result will turn and spin easily. In a boat with little or no rocker, the bottom (or keel) remains almost level in the water until it reaches the bow or stern. Such a kayak will, of course, be good for speed and tracking, but bad for turning. The shape of the kayak as viewed from above can have similar effects. A long, blade-shaped boat—starting with a very thin bow and tapering back with straight sides to its widest point behind the cockpit—will be fast but nearly unturnable. Its opposite, an oval, balanced shape—widest at the center and tapering in smooth curves toward bow and stern—will be an easy turner rather than cutting straight through the water.

If we combine these various design features so that they all work the same way, we arrive at two extremes, the two basic styles of racing kayak—the downriver boats and the slalom boats. The *downriver kayak* is built for only one thing: speed from here to there with as few detours as possible. It is long and knife-shaped (or delta-formed) with a deep V hull and virtually no rocker. Its counterpart, the *slalom kayak,* is as short as the rules allow, has a flattened-out round bottom, lots of rocker, and a symmetrical shape. As a result it is a delight to turn, far less tippy than the downriver style and paddles almost as well backwards as forwards.

All other kayaks represent a balance between these two extremes. Most folks who paddle whitewater for fun choose something other than an extreme racing machine, tending toward the slalom end of the spectrum to get a livelier, more maneuverable kayak. The difference between most paddlers' boats and extreme racing craft, however, involves one more design feature: volume.

In theory, more volume can be an advantage to the whitewater kayaker, especially in big and rough water. The extra buoyancy of a large-volume kayak will keep the boat from being driven as deep beneath waves or into holes as a smaller one would be. Also, larger boaters need high-volume designs just to keep afloat. Yet the design trend in slalom kayaks in recent years has been to smaller and smaller volume boats. It is over this point that the recreational kayaker must eventually part company with the racer.

A word of explanation is in order here. Why even talk about racing kayaks in a book on whitewater touring? There are a couple of reasons. First, most of the real advances in boat design and construction have evolved out of racing, which is in many ways the cutting edge of whitewater sport. And, second, all the good kayak designers (and it is an art) can only make a living and a reputation by producing specialized racing designs, not merely recreational kayaks. Worse still, whitewater racing is currently in the grip of a very archaic set of rules, developed by the International Canoe Federation, which specify the minimum length (4 m) and width (60 cm) of a slalom kayak. As a result, most of the designers' creative energy these days goes into "beating the rule," that is, building boats that technically qualify, but behave as though they were much smaller than the rule allows. The bow and stern of the newest slalom kayaks have been whittled away until they seem to be mere antennae stuck onto the boat. And to facilitate "sneaking" the bow and stern through the hanging poles which constitute a slalom gate (see Chapter 6), designers have shaved the front and rear decks down almost flush with the water, producing an ultra–low–volume boat. Such superlow decks have also altered the cross-section of the slalom kayak, giving it sharp edges or gunwales. As a result these boats are much tippier, unless perfectly and aggressively paddled. In short, the latest hot slalom designs are *not* the ideal boats if you just want to enjoy yourself running rapids. The sad truth is that they are not really ideal for the racers either, who should be allowed complete freedom in the choice of their craft. (No one, after all, tells a ski racer than he must race on 207 cm skis and nothing else.)

Nonetheless, this racing influence will be with us for some time to come. For most recreational kayakers, therefore, *even beginners,* we recommend a high-volume slalom design. Most of these were hot boats four or five years ago, and although now obsolete for serious competition, they have found favor with river runners in general for their great maneuverability with no sacrifice of volume and big-water security. They are sometimes called *recreational slalom kayaks,* and that's a good description.

But what about the many other compromise designs, especially the so-called *cruising* and *touring* boats? These are generally much longer than the slalom designs most paddlers prefer for general whitewater running, they have less rocker and more keel, and most were designed in Europe for non-whitewater touring on big, long, meandering rivers. Some of these touring kayaks can be paddled successfully in real whitewater, but generally only by more experienced paddlers, and then only with effort. They are specialized boats for long trips on easy water. Far better to stick with the 4–meter slalom kayak of average or bigger volume. Don't worry, it won't bite. In fact, you will make faster progress and develop better technique in a slalom kayak. The only real frustrations you will encounter will be in your initial efforts to paddle it in a straight line. Like a nervous thoroughbred, your slalom kayak will want to take its own course, veering and even spinning in circles at first, but that soon passes. Very light men and many women will even want to consider one of the slighter, pared-down, low-volume competition designs. Since the minimal-length rule for slalom kayaks has the effect of making everyone paddle the same size boat, selecting a low-volume design may be the only way a smaller person can get a boat to fit.

This brings us to a very important subject: your kayak's fit. It is an oft-repeated cliché that one doesn't so much sit in a kayak as wear it. And that's nearly true. Almost any kayak you buy or build must be customized to fit your lower body before you can hope to paddle it comfortably or efficiently.

The standard outfitting of a whitewater kayak includes seat, knee pads, and foot pegs. In most but not all boats the seat is a molded fiberglass bucket seat suspended from the cockpit rim, allowing the boat to flex beneath the boater. The seat should fit snugly around the hips. *Knee pads,* or braces, are little more than pieces of foam glued inside the kayak so that the boater can comfortably brace his knees upwards against the kayak's shell. *Foot pegs* should be adjustable forward and back, and there should be a separate foot peg on either side rather than a single bar running across the kayak which could possibly trap the boater's feet.

The purpose of this outfitting is pretty obvious —to allow the kayaker to brace feet, knees, and hips in such a way as to easily control the angle or tilt of the boat. You don't want to be crammed in like a sardine, so the foot pegs must be adjusted long enough that you can relax your legs, yet close enough that you can press against them at will (jamming your bent knees strongly up against the pads under the deck). Whenever you go kayaking in an unfamiliar boat or shopping for a kayak, you can save a lot of time and bother by adjusting the foot pegs while sit-

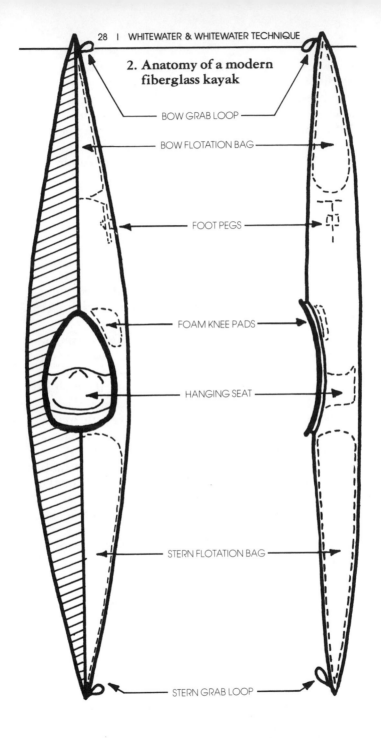

2. Anatomy of a modern fiberglass kayak

BOW GRAB LOOP

BOW FLOTATION BAG

FOOT PEGS

FOAM KNEE PADS

HANGING SEAT

STERN FLOTATION BAG

STERN GRAB LOOP

ting in the boat on the ground, before ever going near the water.

Hip bracing is more subtle. To control your boat, and especially to do an eskimo roll— that is, to right the capsized kayak without leaving it—the sides of the seat must fit very snugly against your hips—and most don't. You will usually have to cut several foam pads and tape them in place until you obtain the desired fit. Small or slender-hipped people trying to roll will fall out of some kayaks before they can even start, so don't neglect the important step of customizing your seat.

Some kayaks have integral knee-brace flanges built into the cockpit rim. This is a nice detail but not essential. Another extra, and a real back-saver on long trips, is a wide backstrap of nylon webbing. This is not standard on many boats, but is worth adding once you have your own.

How about kayak construction? Most boats today are made of fiberglass, but this is just a small part of the story. The fiberglass itself is bonded and held in a resin, generally polyester since epoxy resins, although superior on many counts, are too toxic and dangerous for most manufacturing processes. Fiberglass is terribly strong, but the finished boat needs a combination of strength and flexibility, and certain areas that take more of a beating (directly under the seat and both ends) must be stronger than the rest of the boat. Thus, fiberglass is sandwiched around other materials such as nylon cloth or Kevlar to give it greater tear strength, while different weights of glass as well as varying numbers of layers are used for selective reinforcement. A new method of sucking away excess resin, called "vacuum bagging," results in a nearly optimum strength-weight ratio but is still not in common use, and kayaks made this way tend to be rather expensive. Most kayak companies offer special layups at customer prices, either stronger boats or superlightweight jobs for serious racers. These ultralight kayaks would be demolished by most whitewater boaters, and are not recommended for general use.

One very important exception to the fiberglass rule should be mentioned—the all-plastic boat. Only one such boat, the Hollowform River Chaser, is readily available today. But as of this writing several kayak companies are experimenting with all-plastic boats, and we can expect to see more in the future.

The Hollowform kayak (a high-volume recreational slalom design) is spun-molded in one piece out of a high-density plastic, which has some unique advantages and corresponding disadvantages. It is far tougher than fiberglass, much less likely to tear and puncture upon hitting rocks in the river. On the other hand, once it tears, making a good repair is virtually impossible, whereas fiberglass can be easily and permanently repaired without any special skills or special tools. Again, on the plus side, the one-piece construction eliminates side seams, which are weak spots in fiberglass kayaks (made in separate top and bottom molds, then seamed). The most serious disadvantage of the plastic kayak is its excessive flexibility. For this reason the Hollowform is sold equipped with vertical reinforcing pillars of foam, extending fore and aft from the cockpit. In a fiberglass kayak such reinforcement is only needed when the boater begins to play in big powerful waves and holes, but in the Hollowform it is a necessity since a large wave could easily collapse the front deck if unreinforced, injuring or trapping the boater's legs. Unfortunately, at least in this author's opinion, vertical reinforcement is not sufficient to make the Hollowform completely safe. If a kayaker broaches (crashes sideways) on a rock in strong currents the boat can still bend laterally at the center and *wrap* around the rock, trapping the boater and possibly drowning him. It's happened. The most insidious aspect of this danger is that the Hollowform's resistance to impact makes it extremely useful in constricted rocky streams, the very situations where one is most likely to broach and wrap. You can eliminate this danger in a Hollowform by adding further lateral bracing to stiffen the entire cockpit area—why take a chance?

Another, as yet largely unrealized, advantage of the plastic kayak is its potential low cost. The actual manufacturing process is much simpler than with fiberglass, once the molds have been designed and made, so that large-scale production could result in very low prices indeed. When the Hollowform River Chaser was first introduced, it was a real bargain. But recently its price has been raised to roughly that of fiberglass boats (why?), so price is no longer the deciding factor.

Buying or Building

Learning in a borrowed kayak is great, provided that it fits you reasonably well. And if you are taking an introductory course offered by a local sports store, whitewater club, or one of the few kayak schools in the country, kayaks and other equipment may be provided for the duration. But unlike skiing, one just can't go out and rent a kayak every weekend. Pretty soon you'll want your own boat.

Basically the choice is whether to buy a new one, buy a used one, or build your own. Building your own kayak can even be fun, although it is a terribly messy job and requires both patience and a certain do-it-yourself attitude. It also requires special molds, and unless you know someone, or, more likely, a paddling club that owns molds and will rent them, better forget it. We'll go into this option in more detail further on and just note here that for one reason or another most kayakers buy rather than build their boats.

New commercially made boats are quite expensive: from $275 on up, with many of the best kayaks priced at $350 or more. (Please bear in mind that all prices given as examples here are approximate and based on mid-1977 levels. They are, of course, subject to change and nearly always in one direction—up.) When considering cost, you should remember also that the rest of your kit—the necessary minimum of paddle, spray skirt, flotation bags, vest, and helmet—can easily run you another $100 or more. So we're talking about an initial outlay of $400 to $500. This total is enough to frighten a lot of folks away from the sport. Fortunately, there are cheaper alternatives.

Once someone becomes an avid whitewater paddler, the small technical advantages of a fine new boat may well become very important, even indispensable. Thus many boaters will sell their old kayaks not because the boats are worn out, but only because they feel themselves ready for a newer, hotter model. Your main task in buying a used kayak is to make sure that you're getting a boat in serviceable condition, not a dog. Reject boats with an excessive number of patches, sloppy, crude-looking patches, cracked side seams, or a "soft" tail (which results from hitting too many rocks). On the other hand, as a beginner, don't be too fussy about extra weight, cosmetic defects, or the lack of a sophisticated special layup utilizing Kevlar or "S-glass" or the like. Nor is it important for a beginner's boat to be designed by one of the big-name European designers such as Lettman or Prijon. A good fit is more important than pedigree, and almost any moderately large-volume slalom-length boat will do just fine. And don't neglect somebody else's homebuilt in this category.

The secret to finding used kayaks at reasonable prices is making contact with the local community of whitewater paddlers (if there is one). You're going to need and want experienced friends to boat with, if at all possible, and such people can steer you toward bargains in boats. You should be able to find a good used kayak for $100 to $150 if you're determined. By far the best place to pick up a used boat is at a major slalom race. Competitors are always upgrading their equipment, and there are always good deals to be had at big whitewater races. Just remember not to get too extreme a low-volume model. If in doubt, ask several good paddlers about whether the kayak you're considering is too radical a design for you.

When it comes to commercially made new boats,

there are really almost no bad ones. The various companies differ a lot regarding design and construction philosophy, but they all make good boats. Perhaps the two best known manufacturers in the country today are Hyperform and Phoenix. Hyperform has the American license for Lettman and Prijon designs, often regarded as the state of the art. But we must repeat our caution about the latest racing designs. The boats Hyperform calls its Rec/Slalom (recreational slalom) models, the Lettman Mark 1 and Mark 4, would probably be suitable for the greatest range of whitewater paddling and paddlers. Phoenix, too, makes a complete range of boats from extreme racing models through oversized touring craft. Their larger slalom boats, such as the Savage and the Cascade, are ideal for most whitewater boating.

Dick Held whitewater boats are almost as well known as Hyperform and Phoenix, and there are a host of smaller companies that produce really fine kayaks. These include Idaho's Natural Progression kayaks, Easy Rider kayaks of Seattle, Seda boats from Chula Vista, California, and many others. One of the very first kayak manufacturers, Klepper, which produced foldboats in Europe during the pre-World War I era, is still active, although no longer a leader in the American market. Typically, many of the smaller companies are able to experiment with, and excel at, the more esoteric construction systems involving hard to handle epoxy resins and space-age materials such as Kevlar and S-glass. One such company, Eddyline, has recently become famous for its superbly constructed vacuum-bagged kayaks. However, these are so expensive that they just would not be a reasonable buy for beginners. It's certainly safe to assume that more small manufacturers will spring up as the sport grows, and that they will develop the most exciting innovations. Interestingly, the all-plastic kayak discussed earlier was not first introduced by one of the established kayak manufacturers.

In the last analysis, your choice of a boat will probably come down to whatever is locally available.

That's quite all right; as a beginner or novice kayaker you simply don't have to worry about getting the very best. Later, as an experienced paddler, you will be able to make a more sophisticated choice based on your own personal style of paddling.

To return to the build-it-yourself option, if you are even tempted by this solution, you would do well to buy a copy of the *Boatbuilder's Manual* by Charles Walbridge. This concise 70-page pamphlet is clearly written and will save you many hours of frustrating trial and error and endless mistakes. If you can't find a copy locally, write to Charles Walbridge, Penllyn, PA 19422. This pamphlet will answer every question you can think of. To put homebuilt boats in perspective, remember the following. You can save at least half the cost of a store-bought kayak by building your own, maybe more. But taking into account the time and trouble it will take, the only real reason to build one is for your own satisfaction, which, of course, can be considerable. But if your only concern is cost, then it's far better to opt for a used kayak.

Paddles

A kayak paddle is a long, double-ended, double-bladed affair. The first question people ask on seeing one is always, Why are the two blades at different angles? Indeed, the two blades of any kayak paddle are always set at right angles to each other. The purpose of this *feathered* blade arrangement is really quite simple: while one blade is being pulled back through the water in a power stroke, the other one is slicing forward through the air sideways rather than head-on. As a result, the blade in the air encounters almost no air resistance—a significant factor, as you will discover the first time you try paddling against a strong headwind. Were the blades of your kayak paddle not feathered, such a headwind could almost stop you cold.

But the blade configuration of a kayak paddle is

stranger yet. Most paddles have either curved or scoop-shaped blades so they can cup and grip the water better. The concave side of such blades is called the *power face* and is obviously the one you stroke with. However, since the blades are already perpendicular to each other, something quite curious happens when they are curved. The paddle becomes either right- or left-handed, which paddlers call *right-control* or *left-control.*

When paddling, one hand is always fixed on the shaft and controls the blade angle, while the other hand rotates around the paddle shaft as it turns. Right- or left-control refers to the hand that controls the angle of the paddle. The terms have nothing to do with being right- or left-handed.

Suppose you are pulling the right blade through the water. When the stroke is finished, you lift this right blade and make a small adjustment with your right wrist in order to place the other (left) blade in the water at a good angle. If the scoop of the left blade is now pointing backwards toward you, you are using a right-control paddle. But if you find yourself taking that left-side stroke with the back, or non-power, face of the paddle, your paddle is left-control and must be used in a different way. Confused? Very likely, as this is one of the most difficult aspects of

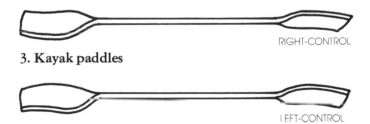

RIGHT-CONTROL

3. Kayak paddles

LEFT-CONTROL

kayaking to put into words, so take a look at figure 3, which should help to clarify this point. In any case, the mysteries of right- and left-control paddling will be explained in detail in the next chapter. It's best to get a right-control paddle, simply because there are more of them around and you will be able to trade paddles or use someone else's without having to change your style.

What about straight-bladed paddles? They have no power face and so can be used by either a right- or left-control paddler. Beginners are always tempted by the apparent simplicity of this solution and usually want to purchase a flat or straight-bladed paddle right off. Resist this temptation. The reason that curved paddles are more popular is simply that they work better. With the power face of a curved blade you will achieve a stronger stroke with less effort, and it will be an advantage, too, when you learn to roll your kayak.

Having dealt with the more mysterious aspects of kayak paddles, we can get down to basics: what length, what materials, what brands, and of course, what price. In truth, there are as many paddles as kayaks on the market today, and the choice is, if anything, more confusing. They come in all lengths from around 205 cm to more than 220 cm, but the longer paddles are used almost exclusively for extra speed on flatwater or for downriver racing. For general whitewater paddling, one seldom sees a paddle longer than 212 or 214 cm. And the choice is reduced still further by the fact that finding anything other than the typical 210 cm paddle is often impossible, even in good whitewater shops. Theoretically, someone with a taller torso and longer arms should use a longer paddle than a short-bodied, short-armed kayaker. But there is no general agreement as to the perfect length and no method for determining it. A small weak person might find the extra leverage of a long paddle too much to overcome, yet one of our paddling friends, a petite, hardly muscle-bound girl, prefers to hold her paddle closer to the center so as to increase her leverage! By the time you become an expert you will have developed some very personal ideas about paddle length, but at first the standard size paddle will do just fine.

Construction is something else again. Basically

paddles are either wooden or fiberglass, but among the latter there is a wide variety of materials and techniques, and perhaps a greater spread in quality. Wooden paddles, beautifully laminated of hard and soft woods, are less common. They are lovely to look at, a delight to use, and getting more expensive every year. It's hard to explain why experienced paddlers favor wooden paddles. It comes down to the virtually indefinable feel of a beautifully crafted object in your hands. A well-made fiberglass paddle might duplicate all the "specs" of a wooden one (although most don't) and still not feel quite as alive in the paddler's hands. Perhaps, too, in a sport beginning to be dominated by space-age materials and esoteric industrial processes, we simply treasure fine wooden paddles as a throwback to an earlier, more human age. For whatever reason, once you have used a fine wooden paddle you're not likely to go back to anything else. While European imports, such as Kober and Azzali paddles have the biggest reputation, American wooden paddles by Mitchell, New World, and Aquarian also qualify as functional works of art. Most wooden kayak paddles cost around $75, and no one will be surprised when they top $100. The only real disadvantage of wood is that you must take special care of the finish from season to season if you want your paddle to last. They are not at all fragile, but it's a shame to beat them up unnecessarily, and for this reason they are not really recommended for beginners and novices.

Fiberglass paddles offer great strength and durability and are generally less expensive, although the best ones are not cheap. Most fiberglass paddles have round fiberglass vaulting-pole shafts, which makes them a bit more awkward to grip than the oval-shaped shafts of wooden paddles. An oval shaft, at least in the handgrip area, is sometimes called an *indexed shaft*, and is particularly useful when the paddler is upside-down in the water, setting up for an eskimo roll, since the oval shaft provides a way of relating your hand grip to the position of the paddle blade. Many kayakers using round-shafted paddles tape a bicycle handgrip to their paddle shaft to obtain this indexed effect, but this seems an awkward compromise at best.

Fiberglass paddles cost from $40 to $60, and as a first paddle they are a good investment. They will take quite a beating in rocky streams where the beginning boater sometimes seems to be jousting with boulders. Two fiberglass paddles deserve special mention. The Hurka, at about $60, is a very sophisticated example of molded Kevlar/fiberglass technology that virtually eliminates all the heavy-feeling, awkward qualities of more typical fiberglass paddles. It is shaped like a classical European wooden paddle and is doubtless much stronger. The Illiad, at $65, is the very epitome of the awkward, clunky fiberglass paddle, with an oversized round shaft that some people find hard to grip; yet this paddle has a great reputation. Strong and well-made, it has extra-long flat blades that are preferred by some big-water addicts for stronger braces in violent heavy water. It is essentially a rugged oversized paddle for brutal, oversized western rivers.

My final advice on kayak paddles is to avoid flimsy, knock-apart paddles and the few very, very cheap ones available. You get what you pay for, and it's a mistake to spend all your equipment dollars on a fine kayak and neglect your paddle. Remember, as one kayak-instructor friend always tells his students, your paddle is a tool, not a club.

Essential Paraphernalia

A kayak and paddle do not a well-equipped kayaker make. To complete your outfit, you need a number of very important small items. They are not really extras, for you cannot safely kayak without them, at least not in whitewater. For your own safety you will need an adequate helmet and a life jacket. To render your boat watertight and unsinkable, you will need a spray skirt to seal the cockpit around you, and a set of flotation bags. The choices here are not as varied and complex as those of kayak and paddle, so we can cover these essential accessories in short order.

For the Boat

To keep arctic water out of their skin boats, the earliest kayakers sealed themselves into their cockpits with extensions of their skin parkas or cuffs made of hide which could be laced tight around the paddler's waist. Today the neoprene *spray skirt* (or spray deck or splash cover) does the same job, only better, since unlike the Eskimo version it does not trap you inside the kayak should you tip over and be unable to roll back up. The spray skirt really looks like a short skirt or a simplified ballerina's tutu when you put it on. It is a piece of neoprene cloth (the same material that wet suits are made of) formed roughly like the pointed oval of a kayak's cockpit, with a vertical round cuff set in it which fits around the kayaker's waist and torso. The outer edge of the spray skirt fits over the rim of the cockpit and has an elastic shock cord sewn into it to keep it snug. The neoprene material is elastic enough to stretch over the cockpit rim as well as to fit snugly about the paddler's waist. Finally, the spray skirt has an all-important tab or *ripcord* of some sort (often it's a ping pong ball tied to a cord) projecting from the front end of the spray skirt. This enables you to pop the whole thing off the kayak underwater if you have to make a wet exit.

Spray skirts are also made of waterproofed nylon cloth, but frankly these are not worth purchasing. They cost a little less but are too troublesome to justify the savings. The main advantage of neoprene is that the small deck of the spray skirt stays very taut and unwrinkled and as a result sheds nearly all the water that hits you, but nylon spray skirts tend to accumulate large puddles unless you hike them up every few minutes. Neoprene models are perhaps safer as well, since they are easier to pop off the cockpit rim. You will eventually get a neoprene spray skirt anyway,

so why not start out with one? Nowadays, good neoprene spray skirts cost about $25, and there is not
much significant difference among various brands.
The very best ones have a double layer of neoprene in
the small of the back to pad against the rear of the
cockpit—a great feature for anyone who has a relatively bony back with prominent vertebrae. If you are
trying to save money, there are do-it-yourself spray-
skirt kits available which almost cut the cost in half.
You won't even need a sewing machine, as neoprene
is sealed with a special glue rather than thread. It's
quite easy.

The other item you'll need for your kayak is a set
of airtight *flotation bags*. Kayaks, you see, sink. At least
fiberglass ones do when they fill up with water. And
since every kayaker is forced out of his boat into the
river occasionally (and beginners rather often), you
need something to fill up the dead space in the bow
and stern so that the kayak won't sink while you're
swimming it to shore. Even if kayaks floated, and the
all-plastic models do, flotation bags would still be necessary to fill up the space inside and prevent water
from filling the boat. Water is so heavy that a kayak
filled with it becomes almost unmovable, and by the
same token, more likely to trap you should you be
pinned between it and a rock.

Standard flotation consists of two fairly heavy-
gauge polyethelene or vinyl bags contoured and ta-
pered to fit into the ends of your kayak. The small bag
goes in front of the foot pegs, the large one behind the
seat. Several ingenious variations on normal flotation
are also available. Various companies make combination flotation *and* waterproof storage bags, with a separate sealed expandable compartment for keeping
clothes and gear dry; a real boon to serious touring
kayakers. And also there are so-called *split-flotation
sets*: four thin bags rather than two fat ones, designed
to fit on either side of vertical reinforcing pillars under
the front and rear decks. Split flotation is a must with
the plastic River Chaser kayaks, but otherwise is probably not needed until you reinforce your kayak for

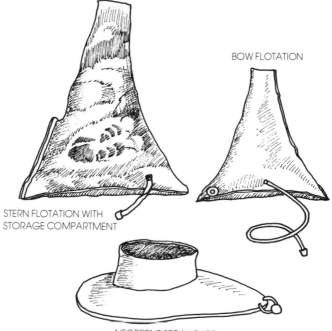

BOW FLOTATION

STERN FLOTATION WITH
STORAGE COMPARTMENT

NEOPRENE SPRAY SKIRT

4. Spray skirt and flotation bags

playing in waves and holes (advanced boating maneuvers which can bury a kayak's nose beneath powerful water). Standard flotation sets cost around $15, split flotation sets around $20, combination storage/flotation bags around $30.

For You: Helmets and Life Vests

Kayaking bare-headed and with no life vest would probably feel marvelous, but sane kayakers never do it. You're simply too vulnerable, especially your head. Unlike whitewater rafters, kayakers need helmets because when your kayak tips over you find yourself in the awkward position of acting as a human keel, still traveling along with the current, head hanging down and highly exposed to submerged rocks. Even if you get out of your boat immediately, you will be exposed for a certain time. The experienced kayaker tends to remain beneath his boat even longer, setting up his paddle in position for a good eskimo roll back to the surface. Obviously, one good blow against a rock could knock you unconscious and you would drown. So the rule is, Never kayak a whitewater river without a helmet, period!

There are a number of choices. A few lightweight models specially designed for kayaking are imported from Europe. These are popular with racers for their extreme lightness, but many American boaters have found that they don't really offer enough protection against a hard blow. Hockey helmets are popular with some kayakers, as they give good protection for the temples and forehead without covering the ears— good for hearing and for letting water drain out quickly. Perhaps the most satisfactory helmets on all counts are those designed for rockclimbing and surfing. Essentially these are more or less lightweight, stripped-down versions of the modern energy-absorbing motorcycle helmet. They should have a snug chin strap, adjustable headband and suspension, and a crushable, energy-absorbing lining. The ideal is such a rockclimbing-type helmet with slots or holes cut in it to allow easier draining of water. It's hard to find a satisfactory helmet for less than $20, and $30 is more likely. Lest you think such money ill spent, however, just examine the helmet of a more experienced kayaker. The number of scratches and small dents should tell you how common it is to actually hit rocks underwater. Fortunately, most such encounters aren't too serious because of the somewhat protective *hydraulic cushion* formed by flowing water against the rock.

Just as important as your helmet is your *life vest*. Books and articles on river running often refer to these nifty articles as "personal flotation devices," or PFDs—which is somewhat like calling the garbage man a sanitary engineer—and go on to list all the Coast Guard specifications such "devices" have to meet in order to be officially approved. Out of a passionate dislike for bureaucratic prose, I will stick with the more common *life vest*, and only note in passing that I've never seen such a vest in any reputable sports shop that was *not* USCG approved. So it all comes down to fit, price, and availability.

Kayaking vests are rather distinctive looking. They generally have vertical tubes containing long, thin foam panels that provide the flotation. Because a long jacket would bind against the spray deck and hamper movement when paddling or rolling, kayak vests typically have a drawstring at the waist and some provision for flipping the lower part of the vest up above this drawstring. This makes a double row of buoyancy tubes around the kayaker's middle, which may look a bit odd but gives far more freedom of motion. Beware of flimsy imitations which look as if they won't last—they won't. Especially make sure the zipper is a heavy-duty one, preferably plastic, since lightweight metal ones won't survive two trips. When wearing your vest, make sure all loose ends are tucked away, drawstring neatly done up, and so forth, so that nothing can trap you in your kayak or get snagged on a sharp object in the river. This type of life vest can be had for around $25, but the best made ones I've seen are the Seda models for $35.

Did we answer the obvious question: why life vests? Not to keep one from drowning, although hopefully they will do that too, *in extremis*. Actually we wear life vests to aid in swimming through rough water, should we miss our roll and be forced out of the kayak (this is a fairly common occurrence with novice boaters until the eskimo roll is truly mastered). There's more than enough to do, trying to tow one's kayak and paddle ashore, without worrying about staying afloat, and in heavier water a good vest will keep you from being pushed far beneath the surface by any waves or holes you may encounter. In the biggest water, however—the huge rapids found on the Grand Canyon and other western desert rivers, and even on smaller rivers at flood stage—the traditional kayaking flotation vest is inadequate, and a real honest-to-

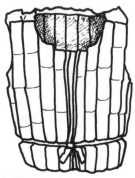

TYPICAL KAYAKER'S LIFE VEST

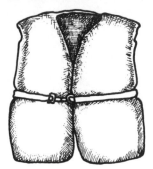

"TYPE I" LIFE VEST FOR HEAVY WATER

LIGHTWEIGHT
KAYAKING HELMET

ROCKCLIMBING HELMET   MORE PROTECTIVE KAYAKING HELMET

5. Kayaking helmets and life vests

goodness heavy-duty "Mae West"-type life vest is
almost always worn. These bulbous ugly things (so-
called *type I vests*) are usually made of orange cotton
stuffed with kapok, and are not designed for paddling
comfort, or indeed for anything other than keeping a
body afloat in rough water. They usually provide about
33 pounds of buoyancy and can be rented or borrowed for the few trips where they are really needed.
Such vests are not recommended for most kayaking,
but are invaluable when you've just been forced out of
your boat amid 20–foot waves. 33–lb flotation jackets
are sometimes available in the traditional kayak style.
And the lighter standard vests can be rendered more
buoyant by sewing more nylon-covered foam panels to
the back and chest.

Clothing and Warmth

All the equipment discussed so far has been essential. Now we enter a realm of options. If all whitewater kayaking were done on sunny days and in warm streams the kayaker's clothing could be limited to a bathing suit and a pair of sneakers (to protect the feet both from the foot pegs of the kayak and from sharp stones on river banks and bottoms). This is fairly often the case in high summer, and such unencumbered boating is a delight indeed. In other situations, the unclothed or underclad boater is in real danger. So we need to consider, When do you need to stay warm, and how do you do it?

The Problem: Cold

In a nutshell, the problem is cold water and what it does to the human body. In fact, a condition known as *hypothermia* (a severe shocklike reaction to extreme loss of body heat) is one of the most serious objective dangers in whitewater river running; it is treated in detail in Chapter 8. But long before it becomes a medical problem, chilling from cold water can plague the kayaker. It begins when you are too cold to enjoy yourself. Soon afterward you may find yourself without the strength and energy for vigorous paddling, and you may experience reduced coordination, timing, and efficiency while you are paddling. Such reactions to cold can make a trip miserable for you as well as for companions who must wait for you. But they can also bring you perilously close to a survival situation.

Wet cold is different from dry cold, and in some ways more serious. Any cold will accelerate the onset of fatigue and sap one's strength, but a wet body loses heat even faster through evaporation. And this sort of heat loss is further increased by any breeze or wind passing over the skin. Afternoon breezes blowing upstream are a common phenomenon on many rivers (just when you're getting tired, too), and the kayaker's own speed through the air is not negligible. These factors add up to a potentially rough situation that must be recognized and dealt with long before things get out of hand. I even suspect that many whitewater accidents not directly attributable to cold are in fact the indirect result of diminished judgment or sloweddown physical responses caused by exposure to cold water and wind.

The problem of cold is further complicated by the diversity of individual reactions. When we speak of people being "warm-blooded" or "cold-blooded" in everyday life, we are often describing important physiological differences. Some people are insulated by layers of fatty tissue (without necessarily being fat) and can bear far lower temperatures than their skinny counterparts. Differences in metabolic rate and a host of other complex factors make it impossible to state an exact rule about how much immersion in water of such-and-such degrees is actually dangerous. Then too there is the question of technical proficiency with the kayak. You're not likely to suffer any adverse effects from cold water unless you're in it. So the expert, who can roll up in all situations, may not need much protection from the cold, even if the river water is bitterly chilling. On the other hand, the beginner, who winds up swimming to shore every time his kayak tips over, might need a wet suit in much warmer conditions.

The best advice for beginners and novices is to take the problem of warmth seriously, and in general overdress rather than underdress for the conditions. Even experts take the consequences of a swim in cold water very seriously and they often wear some protective clothing even when it's not absolutely necessary. A rule of thumb might be: When the water is 50 degrees or colder, wear a wet suit. But again, many people should wear one when boating warmer water, and those people who chill very quickly should probably never boat without one.

The Solution: Protective Clothing

Wet suits—the same neoprene rubber suits used by scuba divers—are really the only effective solution for extreme cold-weather, cold-water boating. Unfortunately, they also have some drawbacks, so for borderline situations that aren't really cold enough to absolutely demand wet suits, kayakers tend to wear lighter and looser clothing.

Let's begin with minimum protection and see how to adapt it to progressively colder situations. The *paddling jacket* is like a short anorak with no hood. It is made of waterproof nylon, with tight closures (elastic, velcro, or neoprene) at neck and wrists, and is tucked *into* the spray skirt. It's not tight fitting and gives marvelous freedom of action for paddling. Although it keeps a lot of water off you, its real function is not to keep you dry but rather to protect you from the wind, as even the slightest breeze accelerates heat loss through evaporation from bare skin. Paddling jackets cost around $25 and range from overdesigned models with waterproof pockets to the simplest possible nylon shell, which works just fine. Even in sunny summer weather many boaters bring their paddling jacket along to wear in the late afternoon when upstream breezes are likely to blow up and lengthening shadows from canyon walls start to change air temperatures.

Many experienced kayakers slip on a wool sweater under their paddling jacket for really cold conditions. Wool, of course, will keep you warm when it's wet, and even in heavy rapids a sweater will get only slightly damp under a good paddling jacket. Nor will your sweater be soaked underwater in the time it takes to set up for a good eskimo roll. But there's the rub—if you can't yet roll your kayak, and in consequence take a couple of long swims, you will wind up wearing a soaking sweater all day, which in addition to offering only marginal protection is no fun at all. So the sweater and jacket combination is only really effective for moderately skilled kayakers who don't crash—much.

If you're a beginner, you're definitely in for your share of swimming, and if you want to stay warm, some kind of wet suit is the only answer. The most complete protection is the full wet suit, which experi-

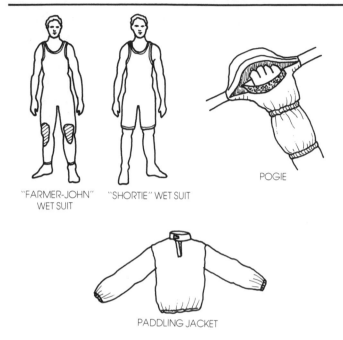

"FARMER-JOHN"
WET SUIT

"SHORTIE" WET SUIT

POGIE

PADDLING JACKET

6. Wet suits, paddling jacket, and pogie

enced paddlers tend to avoid until absolutely necessary because of its tight, constricting fit at the shoulders. The effect of paddling while wearing a long-
sleeved wet-suit jacket is something like stretching a
strong rubber band with each stroke; the elastic resistance to shoulder and arm movements is hardly
noticeable at first, but can add up over the course of a
long day's paddling. But there's no way a wet suit can
have baggy shoulders and still be effective, since it actually works by trapping a small amount of water next
to the skin where it can be warmed up. For this reason
the full wet-suit top is usually reserved for only the
very coldest conditions.

Fortunately there are other options in the wet-suit
area. The simplest and cheapest is the neoprene tunic,
an armless wet-suit top which pulls on over the head.
It completely covers and protects the torso without in

any way restricting paddling movements, and is thus a great light solution for experienced paddlers. But it may be insufficient protection for the neophyte who does a lot of swimming.

Between the pull-over tunic and the full head-to-toe wet suit, we find an amazing variety of shapes, styles, and possible combinations of neoprene gear. There is the "shortie" wet suit, with legs that end above the knee and either short or no sleeves. This abbreviated one-piece suit will provide adequate warmth in a lot of situations, but is not so heavy or so hot that you will be tempted to leave it home in marginal weather when you just might need it. There's no sense in having a superb, totally protective wet suit that always stays in the closet because it's a pain to put on.

If you want more protection than the shortie suit gives, then consider full-length "farmer-john" wet-suit pants. These pants extend upward as a tunic to cover the shoulders but leave the arms free for paddling. With a sweater and paddling jacket over a farmer-john wet suit, an experienced kayaker can paddle in nearly any conditions. (By the same token, wearing a paddling jacket over a *full* wet suit extends even that suit's range in the very coldest conditions.) The only possible disadvantage of farmer johns is that your legs may get too warm in the kayak, but if you know how to roll, you can always tip over in the river to cool off. The expert kayaker's legs really don't need protection as they should be safe and dry inside the kayak; in very cold conditions good boaters who don't plan on swimming wear sweat-suit pants or jogging warm-up pants inside their boats.

The beginning kayaker needs the most protection from cold water, but kayak equipment is expensive enough initially without running out to buy a special wet suit. So look around. If you have a wet suit of any kind, use it at first even if it's not perfect. Otherwise try to borrow one that fits. If all else fails, and most of your kayaking takes place in fairly cold rivers, then go out and buy yourself a wet suit.

For real fanatics who kayak in every condition (as long as the river isn't iced up), we must mention a fabulous invention—the *pogie*. Neoprene gloves and mittens don't give adequate feeling for subtle control of the paddle, but pogies have solved this problem. They are cufflike mitts attached around the shaft of the paddle itself. The paddler sticks his bare hand into the pogie and grips the shaft inside this warm, oversized mitt. Pogies are made of neoprene or waterproof nylon and fasten with velcro tape bands. In the coldest water they are literally indispensable if you want to keep paddling for more than a few minutes.

But enough talk about equipment. River running is for action-oriented folks, not gear freaks, and, indeed, the only reason for placing the equipment chapter at the beginning of the book is that a good deal of this information is essential for what follows. (See Appendix B for names and addresses of major equipment manufacturers.)

Now it's time to put this equipment to work. Your apprenticeship will be demanding, but it need not be either long or frustrating, and every time you take out your kayak, you will learn something new. An exciting prospect.

CHAPTER 3

STILL WATER

It's not at all unreasonable to teach yourself how to kayak; in fact most good kayakers have done just that. It can only help, of course, to have an experienced friend, a good paddler who will be a good model for you to copy, but since this isn't always the case, we are going to talk about the first steps as though you were doing it on your own.

But before we even get our feet wet, let's look ahead to what the river has in store for us. In the first place, it's far better not to start on the river at all. A pond or a swimming pool—any flat, quiet water—is preferable to a moving current, as there is a lot to be learned before we point our kayaks downstream. In this chapter we'll cover the basic paddle strokes essential to moving about in any kind of water, and then go on to begin working on the kayaker's most important single maneuver: the *eskimo roll*. The roll is to kayaking what the rope and belay are to mountaineering and rockclimbing—basic security. It will take time to master, but only after you have achieved *some* sort of roll can you begin to learn advanced techniques with real confidence. In later chapters you'll first learn something about moving water, maneuvers where your own paddling interacts with the force of the current; then we'll move on through real rapids and some very specialized maneuvers into the world of truly wild water.

Learning to Paddle

To get started you'll need your equipment, but not all of it. We don't intend to be paddling in anything more than a backwater or a pool at this point, so we won't need any protective gear. Bring your boat, paddle, and spray skirt, and in addition to your bathing suit, a pair of old sneakers to protect your feet from the foot pegs. Once at your practice spot, put your spray skirt on before even dealing with the boat. If it's made of neoprene you may have to really wriggle and pull to get it on; coated nylon spray skirts go on easier but aren't as watertight. The waist band should fit quite high (halfway up the torso to the armpits), making the spray skirt more snug across the cockpit so it will shed water more easily. Having dressed for the part, we're ready to learn some basics.

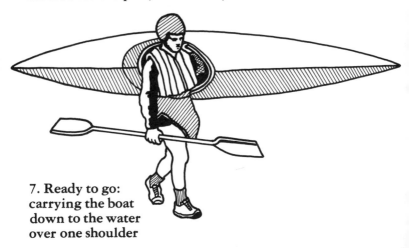

7. **Ready to go: carrying the boat down to the water over one shoulder**

Entries and Exits

Ease your boat into the water parallel to the edge of the pool or to the bank of the practice pond or lake (remember, if possible, no moving water yet). The first problem, and don't laugh because it really can be a problem, is getting into your boat. The oval hole of the cockpit is so small that if you just innocently try to step in, you'll probably find yourself in the water with your kayak upside-down beside you. There is a time-honored method for getting into a kayak—not merely a beginner's method, but one that all kayakers use, and it goes like this: Lay your paddle across both boat and bank so that the middle of its shaft goes across your boat just behind the rear of the cockpit and the near blade of the paddle is flat on the ground. Suppose the nose of the kayak is pointing left as you look out at the water; in this case, grasp *both* the paddle and the rear of the cockpit with your right hand, holding the two firmly together. Now, facing the front of the boat and reaching behind you, grasp the paddle shaft with your other (left) hand, and use the braced paddle as a kind of handrail to support yourself while you put first your right leg, then left, into the boat and wiggle yourself down into the seat. If your kayak is pointing the other way, use the other hand; in either case it is the outer, or away-from-shore, hand that grips the back of the cockpit and paddle.

Next, feel with your feet for the foot pegs (the clever novice will have already adjusted them to the correct length while sitting in his boat on shore, thinking of river trips to come). Now you are ready to snap the spray skirt into place over the cockpit rim and paddle away. Begin in the rear, using both hands to hook the elasticized edge of your spray deck over the lip of the cockpit as far forward as your waist on either side. Then, grabbing the front of the spray deck (where a tape loop or ping pong ball will be attached as a kind of ripcord), pull it straight forward and hook it over the apex of the cockpit rim. The ripcord *must* be on the outside, not stuffed down into the cockpit.

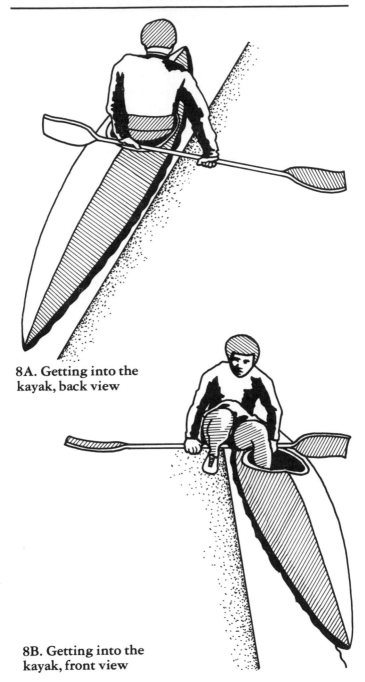

8A. Getting into the kayak, back view

8B. Getting into the kayak, front view

9. Fastening the spray skirt over the cockpit rim

With most of the spray cover secured, it's now an easy matter to flip the remaining front sides into place. You're in.

At this point, before you paddle more than a couple of strokes, you're going to have to get wet. Please put up with this and do it; it's very important. The problem is, Now that you're in your boat, how do you get out? The conventional exit is easy. All you do is reverse the steps of getting in, putting your paddle behind the cockpit and bracing it on shore as a kind of handrail to steady the boat while you get out. But we're talking about a different kind of exit now, a wet exit.

Once the spray skirt is firmly in place, most beginners feel a bit uneasy, as if they were somehow sealed into the boat. That's the idea—or at least to seal the water out. But what happens when you tip over? It's obvious that the kayaker's body hanging downward under the water will act as a kind of keel or ballast, keeping the boat stable in this unpleasant upside-down position. Until you learn how to roll back up, there is an easy way to get out of the boat underwater, called a *wet exit,* that is well worth practicing.

Having pushed off from the side of the pool or shore, just sit a moment in your kayak and collect your thoughts. You are going to take a deep breath and then let your body fall over to one side until the kayak capsizes and you find yourself underwater. When you do, hold your paddle in one hand and reach with the other hand for the tape (or cord or ping pong ball) attached to the front of your spray skirt and pull. One good jerk should cleanly release the spray deck from the boat, and by relaxing your thigh and leg muscles you will simply fall out of the boat. Actually your body will do a kind of upside-down somersault out of the boat, but you won't feel that when you do it. Just fall out, and as you come to the surface keep your free hand on the boat so that you will still have control of both kayak and paddle.

Sound simple? It is. But before you try it, two more points. You should be practicing in a pool with no dangerous underwater rocks to bash your head on; in the river this will not always be so, hence the absolute necessity of wearing a good helmet. But while a helmet will protect the top of your head, it won't help your face in an argument with a rock. Therefore, right now, from the very beginning, get in the habit of bending or leaning forward toward the deck of the kayak as you tip over. This bent-forward position will not only protect your face, but also, your body will not stick as far down in the water, reducing the likelihood of hitting anything. And later on this same position will help you get set up to roll.

Second, once you come to the surface, move immediately to one end of the boat and grab onto the grab loop, using it to tow the boat to shore. The boat will be upside-down and you should leave it that way, rather than attempting to turn it rightside-up in the water. Even if your boat has no flotation bags, a certain amount of air will be trapped under the kayak, making it easier to handle. You will want to keep it upside-down so you can empty it out before you get back in. Moving to the end of the boat is a good habit to form early for later days on the river. In a river situation you will move to the rear, or upstream end, of the boat and, holding the grab loop with the same hand as the paddle, swim the boat to shore—always staying behind, or upstream, of the boat. This is to avoid the possibility of being pinned between your own boat and a rock—a simple and terribly important rule.

Emptying the boat of water can be simple or frustrating. Probably the easiest way is to remain in the water yourself while pushing the far end of the boat up onto the shore (or the side of the pool), preferably onto a rock or grassy hummock or other such surface approximately a foot and a half higher than water level. Then simply raise the near end (keeping the boat upside-down) and most of the water will slosh forward out of the cockpit. You won't get it all out the first time, so now lower your end, sloshing more water out, then raise it again and so forth several more times, until the boat is almost empty of water. Flip it over and you're ready to start again. Some strong paddlers like to invert the boat on their bent knee and rock it back and forth to empty it, but this is only possible if there isn't much water in it to start with. Water is quite heavy.

One final thought on getting out of your boat underwater: You always will. Even if, in the excitement of capsizing in a full-blown rapid, you completely forget about the ripcord at the apex of your spray skirt, you can still push your way out of the boat, and the spray deck will come off fairly easily. You won't be trapped! One kayaking friend who was a bit apprehensive about finding herself upside-down underwater used to get out of her boat so fast as it started to tip over that somehow she would never get her hair wet. Nobody could see how she could do it, but she did.

So relax and enjoy it. The only reason to practice the wet exit *at least once* before doing anything else is that it will really improve your confidence to experience how easy it is to get out of a capsized kayak.

Forward: Power and Sweep Strokes

Now it's time for some paddling. You got wet and it didn't hurt, and you're probably more eager than ever to start moving your kayak around. As you read this chapter (succeeding ones too) you will find all the maneuvers described as though you were actually in your kayak, paddling, though of course you're probably home reading this book. Describing the maneuvers from an actual kayaker's point of view will help you form a graphic image of what goes on in the water. But there is one very good way for you to practice in your own living room, if you wish, while you are reading. Sit in an ordinary straight chair, paddle in hand, and try the different strokes as you read about them. In a chair you will be high enough off the ground that your paddle blade can move through the air to either side exactly as it does in the water. Don't feel foolish about doing this; it can save hours of practice in your kayak. Just make sure there are no breakable objects nearby that your paddle might swipe.

Another point: All that follows assumes that you have a right-control paddle. Most paddles *are* right-control, and if you start paddling with a left-control blade and ever lose, break, or forget your paddle you will have a terrible time replacing it with another one on the spot. Furthermore, right or left-control paddling seems to be merely a conditioned habit, not a physical preference like writing with a right or left hand.

To begin, like Alice, at the beginning, let's paddle forward in a straight line. There are some very fine points to straight paddling, but they will come later. All you have to remember now is to hold the shaft of your paddle firmly with the right hand and loosely with your left. In this way, after you have completed a full stroke on the right side and you are reaching forward with the left blade toward the water, all you have to do is *cock,* or tilt back, the right wrist (letting the paddle shaft rotate freely in you left hand) and the

10. Exaggerated view of the paddler's "cocked" right wrist while taking a left-side stroke. *Note:* Except when practicing in a swimming pool, the kayaker should *always* wear both helmet and life vest! In some of these illustrations, however, the life vest is omitted for greater visual clarity.

left blade will enter the water at the correct angle for
a good pulling stroke. You will soon see that if you
forget to make this cocking-back adjustment (like
opening the throttle on a motorcycle handlebar) the
left blade will slice ineffectually into the water. The
trick is to make the necessary adjustment always in
the same way, with the same hand and wrist (in this
case the right one), so that it becomes an unconscious, automatic habit. And it will, too, in a very few
minutes. So now without any more explanation or
theory, why not go out and paddle around for a while
and see how it feels?

No doubt you found the boat a bit unruly at first.
At times, especially in a slalom-model kayak, your
boat seemed to make up its own mind to turn either
right or left, and you were unable to do anything
about it. Even if it didn't turn completely in circles,
you may have had a very hard time holding it on a
straight course as you paddled back and forth across
the pond or pool. To smooth this out now and really
gain command of your boat you'll need to learn a little more about forward strokes.

Don't think that there is anything elementary
about straight paddling. It's one of those subtle skills
that fools us by its apparent simplicity, like straight
bouncing on a trampoline, or holding an airplane in
level flight. It's so simple it eludes us. Actually mov-

11. The power stroke, or basic forward
stroke, viewed from the side.

ing across flatwater in a straight line results from a
subtle alternation or blend of two forward strokes—
the basic power stroke and the sweep stroke. The
power stroke sends you straight ahead and the *sweep
stroke* turns you while you move ahead. As you work
on these strokes, your control of your kayak will improve remarkably, but it may take a few seasons
paddling, or a good coach, before you ever perfect
these "simple" strokes.

The power stroke is a sophisticated version of
what you've already been doing. Although it is really
a continuous flowing movement, we talk about three
parts—the paddle's *entry,* the *power phase,* and the
recovery—and naturally these three phases are repeated on each side. To begin the stroke on the right
side (the entry), reach forward with your right arm
fully extended, left arm quite bent and raised so that
the left hand is actually about shoulder level and close
to your head. In this reaching position drop the paddle blade completely into the water close to the side
of your kayak and about as far forward as you comfortably can.

The second, or power phase, is a lot more than
just pulling the paddle blade toward you alongside
the boat. It is actually a push-pull action in which the
left hand pushes forward at the same time as the right
hand draws the completely immersed paddle blade

back. This power phase ends when the blade of the paddle has about reached your hips. At this point no further backward movement of the blade will do any good. Why? Because every paddle stroke relies for its effect on digging into relatively motionless water and getting it moving. As the water caught by the paddle starts moving toward you, you and your boat also start moving toward it; but once the water you are scooping has attained any real speed, then you are no longer pulling yourself forward but just scooping water past you. This is why prolonging the stroke is of no use and why the final (recovery) phase has to start when the paddle blade reaches your hips.

For the recovery, lift the paddle smoothly from the water with an upward flexing of your right arm, while your left arm completes its forward push or extension, and there you are: ready for the paddle's entry on the other (left) side. The only difference in the left-side stroke is that the right wrist must perform its controlling maneuver, cocking back toward your body as the paddle enters the water, and must in fact maintain this angle throughout the stroke to keep the blade angle correctly perpendicular to the direction of pull.

If it sounds complicated, don't be alarmed; the power stroke is far harder to describe than it is to perform. Remember, the three phases blend smoothly into one continuous stroke. Perhaps the most important point for the beginning paddler is that the upper arm is not passive, but pushes forward, contributing almost half the power of the stroke and saving a lot of energy over a long distance. The correct position of the arms is a refinement that will come with time.

There is one more aspect of this most basic stroke that we haven't yet touched on. So far we've talked only of the arms, while good paddlers use their whole body. As you reach forward with the right arm, your torso twists slightly to the left in a kind of wind-up or preparation for the stroke. During the power phase (while pushing with your left arm and pulling with

12. **The power stroke, front view.** Note that the left arm is extended forward completely but still does not cross over the center line of the kayak.

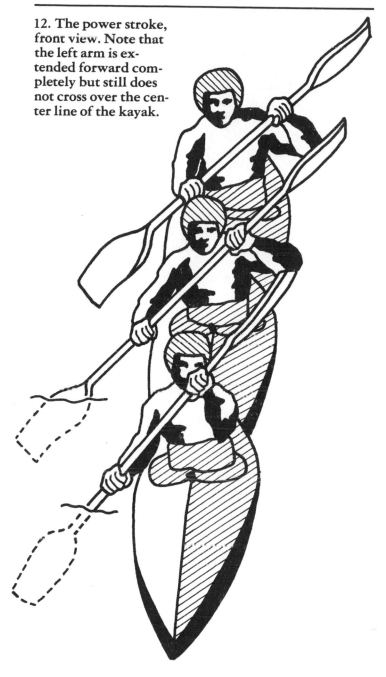

your right), the whole torso actively twists or swings back to the right. Careful—this is not an exaggerated, but a subtle movement, which lends power to the action of your arms. In no case does the kayaker bob his body violently from right to left. It's not that kind of a movement at all, just a sort of helping follow-through with the whole torso. The upper hand should never even cross over the center line of the kayak as it extends or pushes forward.

To get the last ounce of power from every stroke, some kayakers recommend an extension of the leg against the foot peg with every stroke (right stroke, right leg). This supposedly stabilizes the hips so one can paddle more effectively with the whole upper body. But such refinements take time. For now, the main thing is not to achieve good form, but to become conscious that there is such a thing, and to start acquiring it before really sloppy habits develop. Just as in tennis and skiing, a bad habit once learned is nearly impossible to break.

The power stroke alone won't get you where you want to go. You need to turn, and even more important, you need a way of correcting the kayak's course

13. The forward sweep stroke

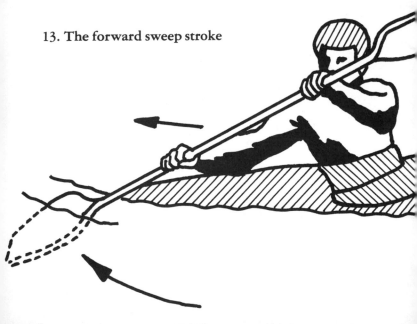

whenever the nose starts to wander, as it always does. You see, every forward stroke on one side of the kayak will have some tendency to make the boat turn its nose toward the other side. (Since you can't get directly beneath the boat with your paddle, your strokes are always off center, and this veering off is the result.) In a kayak this is not as serious as in a canoe, where one always paddles on the same side. And actually, in a kayak each succeeding stroke tends to cancel out the slight turning effect of the previous one with an equal but opposite turning reaction of its own. What the sweep stroke does is take this turning effect and exaggerate it by exaggerating the stroke itself.

Basically the sweep stroke is nothing more than a wide arcing stroke of the paddle that starts close to the boat at the bow, sweeps widely away from the kayak in midarc, and curves back in toward the boat at the stern. To sweep, simply put the paddle in the water as for a normal stroke and pull it back and out in a wide circle rather than parallel to your boat. To obtain as wide a sweep as possible you must use your arms much like the arms of a compass as it describes a circle. There are a couple of fine points. To do a sweep stroke on the right, for example, your right arm will stay virtually extended throughout the stroke (see Figure 13), helping the paddle move in an arc away from the side of the kayak. The left arm, in order to follow the sweeping movement, will doubt-

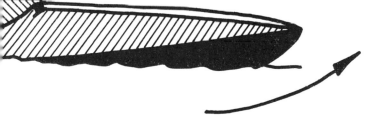

less cross over the kayak, expecially at the end of the stroke, and that's fine. The biggest novelty of a good sweep stroke, however, is the fact that you will no longer be sitting straight upright in your kayak, but instead will be leaning over, tilting the boat toward the side on which you're sweeping, and to some extent leaning, or *bracing* yourself on your moving paddle. This is not yet a real bracing stroke (which will become so important later) but it does require a certain commitment. The idea is simply to lean out on the paddle as you sweep it to one side or the other. At first this leaning will be hesitant and barely perceptible. It's hard to believe that a paddle moving through the water can actually support you. Of course, it can, and as you discover this you can commit your body a little more to each sweep stroke. Don't overdo it, just lean out a bit more to the side you're sweeping on to give a larger radius and more power to your stroke.

Now that you know what a sweep stroke is, the question is, How do you use it? A good sweep will create a strong turning movement. Sweeping on the left turns you to the right, and vice versa. Three good sweep strokes on the same side should turn your kayak a full 360 degrees. Using it is generally the best way to change direction (especially when paddling on flatwater) as it is also a forward stroke and thus doesn't eliminate or "kill" any of your forward speed. That is, you keep on going forward while you're changing direction. But usually you don't just sweep your way around, either. Typically the sweep stroke is combined with forward power strokes. For example, to turn left while paddling forward, you alternate sweep strokes on the right with straight power strokes on the left.

In addition, the sweep stroke is just the thing for making major corrections in your course when that slalom kayak starts to get ornery and follow its own path. In fact, it works for making quite subtle corrections as well. You don't have to make a full sweep stroke every time. Any forward stroke can become more or less of a sweep stroke, more or less of a

power stroke, depending on how much the path of
the blade curves out from the long axis of the boat.
Straight-line paddling, therefore, is the result of constant small corrections as the paddler adds a little bit
more or a little bit less sweep to each stroke, compensating for any tendency to wander off course before the error or deviation becomes a major one. It's
quite analogous to the way an automobile driver must
make a lot of tiny movements of the steering wheel in
order to keep his car traveling in a straight line. The
experienced paddler makes these tiny sweep adjustments automatically and effortlessly; the beginner
must think about it and often tends to overcorrect,
causing the nose of the kayak to veer away in a new
direction, which in turn must be compensated for,
and so forth. But have patience. This skill is one that
you don't actually have to learn; it just evolves
through practice, as if the boat itself is learning how
to go straight through the water. After several hours
of paddling, things should be going quite smoothly.
When you've had a certain amount of practice on
straight paddling, it's also a good idea to reduce the
amount of power you put into each stroke. With improved technique you should still have just as effective a stroke. This is especially important for big
strong men, who often apply too much muscular
force.

There is one further aspect of paddling that you
ought to experience and play with on your first time
out—how the kayak fits and moves as part of your
body. The first few moments paddling around, even
in a swimming pool, are so exciting that you probably
won't notice if the seat and cockpit are too tight or
too loose, whether or not your knees fit the knee
braces, or anything of that sort. But now take a moment to become sensitive to the physical connection
between you and your boat.

The kayak isn't a solid platform but a flexible
moving one, and almost every motion of your arms or
upper body will elicit some sort of countermotion or
response from the kayak, expecially in a lateral or

sideways direction. As we move on into rapids, you
will want to develop a relaxed dynamic balance in
which, although boat and body are connected, the
connection is not too rigid or stiff. You should be
able to tilt the boat right or left without tilting your
body too far, and vice versa. Your knees play the
most active role in stabilizing or tipping the boat laterally. They should fit comfortably and rather snugly
into the padded knee braces attached to the inside of
your kayak just in front and to either side of the forward cockpit rim. Thus your lower body will be quite
solidly braced inside the kayak with foot pegs, knee
pads, and a snug-fitting seat (which can be made
snugger if necessary by taping foam pads to the
sides). By alternately lifting one knee and then the
other, you can easily rock the kayak from side to side,
tilting it quite far over and back with no danger of
falling over. Try it. The sensation is that your hips are
moving up and down, but actually the knees control
this motion.

Perhaps because of the way the body disappears
into the kayak at the hip level, there has been a lot of
confusing talk about "hip action" in kayaking, especially in regard to the eskimo roll, which we'll tackle
later in this chapter. In most cases when anyone refers to hip movement, or *hip snap,* what they mean is
hip-knee action. The knees, braced inside the kayak,
either initiate lateral movements or lend greater
power to them. For now just experiment, seeing how
far you can tip your kayak from side to side without
capsizing; you'll be surprised. And should you go
over, it will merely whet (yes, the pun is intended)
your appetite to get beyond the wet exit and learn
to roll.

On your very first time out, however, your only
goal should be to get acquainted with your kayak and
learn to paddle more or less efficiently. Before you
can realize this goal, you'll need not just the two forward strokes we've discussed but some strokes to the
rear as well.

Refinements: Back Strokes and Braces

Back paddling is rather easy. It's not done as often as forward paddling, naturally, yet it is an important part of the kayaker's technique, and will be used later in "back ferrying," a great way to avoid rocks. Like any important river technique, back paddling ought to be practiced long before it's needed.

The main thing to remember when back paddling is not to change your grip on the paddle. This means that you will be stroking the water with the "back," or nonpower, face of the blade. (Of course, if you're using a flat-bladed paddle there will be no difference.) Kayakers accept the lowered efficiency of this way of back paddling because they can start, stop, and return to forward motion at will, without fussing with their paddle grip. You can imagine that in whitewater one seldom has time to look down at the paddle blade to see if it's turned the right way. The whole principle of one-hand control (in our case right-control) also remains the same. The right hand and wrist must rotate into a "cocked up" position in order for the left paddle to be in the proper position for its stroke. Fortunately, you probably won't have to think about this, as it becomes a solid habit after the first hour or so of forward paddling.

In back paddling you can also take a tip from kayak slalom racers who must paddle backwards through certain gates. Look back over one shoulder if you want to see where you're going, and keep looking over that same shoulder. Don't bob your head from side to side. You will find it surprisingly easy to back paddle in a straight line, especially considering how hard it was going forward.

The second backward stroke is called the *reverse sweep*. Like straight back paddling, it is done with the back, or nonpower, face of the blade, and chances are you have already discovered it for yourself. It is the beginner's instinctive way of trying to straighten the kayak out once it has begun to veer off course. If your kayak's nose started veering off to the left, you probably tried to stop it by putting your right paddle in the water behind you and pushing outward to "block" the turning effect. It worked too, but it virtually stopped you cold in the water, which is why forward sweep strokes are the preferred way to straighten out your course without losing momentum. Nonetheless this reverse sweep is a useful stroke, as we'll find out in more detail further on. If you start in the stern close to the boat and push the paddle strongly out—really leaning on it—you may discover the so-called *low brace.* You don't really need to brace yourself in flat water, but it's great to discover how a paddle moving at a certain angle through the water can actually support a lot of your weight. Later, in the river, you will get just as much support from your paddle in the water as a skier does from planting his pole firmly in the snow.

Maybe you're wondering why the paddle won't sink when you lean on it. It will, eventually. But as long as it keeps moving at the *correct angle,* it will be supported by the water. Let's try a variation on the reverse sweep, and this time pay special attention to

14. Back paddling

15. The reverse sweep stroke

the angle the paddle makes with the water. Relative to its motion, slant the blade forward and up, at much the same angle that a water ski makes with the surface of the water. We call this a *climbing angle.* Clearly, if the paddle were tilted down and forward it would be pushed beneath the water by its own motion—this would be a *diving angle.* Think of the game little children play by sticking their hands out of the window of a fast-moving car: if the hand is tilted up at a climbing angle it forms an airfoil in the wind and "floats," but if tilted down it dives. This is exactly what hap-

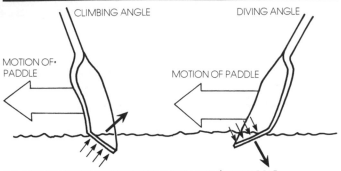

CLIMBING ANGLE   DIVING ANGLE

MOTION OF PADDLE   MOTION OF PADDLE

NET RESISTANCE OF WATER TENDS TO LIFT PADDLE / SINK PADDLE

16. The angle of a moving paddle blade in water: diving vs. climbing

pens to your paddle as it moves or skims across the surface of the water. We will use this principle again and again in kayaking, and all the various bracing strokes, which will become so important later on, depend on it. Occasionally, the paddle itself will not move, but moving water rushing past underneath it will create the same effect. It's all relative; either the

17. A low brace: the kayaker is bracing to his rear on the back or nonpower face of the blade.

paddle moves (in flatwater) or the water moves, or both, but the effect is the same provided the paddle blade is at the correct angle: You can lean and support yourself on the seemingly insubstantial surface of the water. Great!

Now that you understand the principle, try a few more low braces to either side. Starting in the rear, push that paddle blade strongly down and forward through the water, *yet at a climbing angle,* and try to feel all the support it gives you while you progressively commit a little more body weight to the paddle each time you do it. Of course, you must recover to an upright position slightly before the end of your bracing stroke as its support begins to fade, otherwise—whoops!—you'll be upside-down before you know it.

Obviously, if there is a low brace, there ought to be a high brace, and indeed there is. It is a more elegant and in many cases more useful stroke than its counterpart. The primary function of both strokes is to support or "brace" you upright when you start to tip over in whitewater, so it will be a while before you see just how useful they can be. But, of course, they must be learned long before they're needed.

The *high brace* is a combined push-pull action of both arms (just as the forward power stroke was) and it works like this. Hold your paddle chest-high across your body. For a brace on the right, the power face of the right blade should point down toward the water (which it will do naturally if you're paddling right-control). Now reach way out to the right and slap your blade down in the water. With your right hand begin to pull the blade back in, toward the boat; at the same time, with your left hand, push the upper end of the shaft up and out to the right. Your left arm will cross in front of your face as you do so, helping to move your body weight right out over the braced paddle. Why? Well, what keeps the paddle afloat, or braced, is its motion back toward the side of the boat, but your right arm can only pull in so far before it bumps your body. So to prolong and amplify this inward pull on the paddle's blade the upper hand levers the shaft of the paddle outward (using the right hand somewhat as a fulcrum). Take a good look at Figure 18, which should clarify this motion. Naturally, a high

18. A high brace, using the power face of the blade

brace works just the same on the left, except that the left blade must be cocked back somewhat to get the power face to slap flat on the water.

Your first attempts at a high brace will naturally be a bit hesitant. You probably won't lean more than a few degrees out from the vertical. But with practice you can lean further and further out and still lever yourself back upright with the push-pull action of your arms on the paddle. Experienced paddlers can lean right out into the water until shoulder, ear, and chin are wet, and still lever themselves back up using a high brace (an *extreme high brace*). Keep this in mind as a long-term goal.

What next? Of course, you should practice these basic paddling skills. But don't wear yourself out. Paddling a kayak in a swimming pool is really no fun at all, and a small pond isn't much better. And only if you're paddling on a beautiful lake or somewhere with interesting scenery will you really enjoy yourself enough to spend a day, or half-day, practicing flatwater paddling. This would be ideal, because the more basic control you have over your kayak when you start down a flowing river the better. To make this initial practice more palatable, try combining basic strokes in various games and sequences. Sprint twice around the pool clockwise using only sweep strokes to turn the corners, then spin around and sprint back around counterclockwise. Or paddle a zigzag course backward. Or any number of other combinations to make simple paddling more challenging.

But human nature will out. If you're starting to kayak at all it's because you're looking for adventure, and you're probably already impatient to get started down a real river. Many good kayak instructors do prefer to take their students down some small, safe rapids first, before ever teaching them anything about flatwater paddling—both to give them a sense of excitement (what the sport is all about) and to provide motivation for the work necessary to learn good paddling technique. Other equally fine kayak instructors feel it's almost a sin to go near a river until the

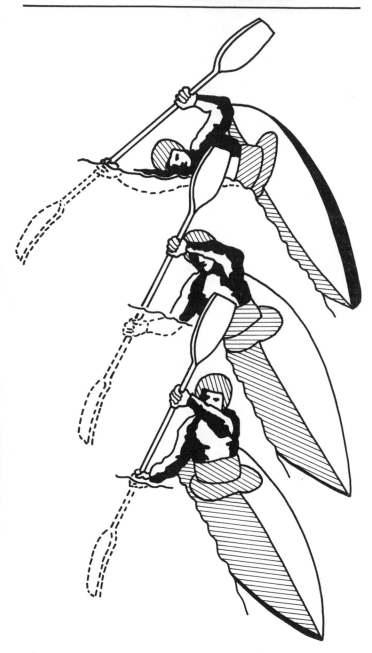

19. Recovering from an extreme high brace

novice has developed excellent paddling technique and can effectively dart in and out of flatwater *slalom gates* (parallel poles suspended just above the water level through which one does various maneuvers). Perhaps the best approach is somewhere in between. The better you handle your kayak in flatwater, the more fun you'll have on your first river trip; but it's not necessary to achieve perfection at each stage before going on to the next one.

At this particular stage we run into a real dilemma: learning to roll and deciding *when* to learn. The *eskimo roll,* or *roll* for short, is the very cornerstone of modern kayak technique. It makes almost everything else possible and gives the paddler a sense of security he can never attain without it. Nor is it a technique for experts or advanced boaters only; *rolling is for everyone.*

It would be great if everyone learned to roll a kayak up *before* running a real river, but most people don't and that's okay. Probably most of you won't either. In that case, be sure to read the next chapter, *Swiftwater,* before going on your first river trip. It discusses the basics of paddling in moving water, a very different thing from our flat calm practice pond, and will save you a lot of trouble, especially if you're not paddling with experienced friends. Your impatience to get going is understandable, but you still must, repeat *must,* start learning to roll as soon as possible. Once you've learned how, you'll find it physically very easy, a matter of coordination, not strength. But learning to roll can be time-consuming and frustrating, and even more than the basic paddling strokes we've just covered, the roll must be learned in stillwater. This is why it will be treated in such detail in the second half of this chapter.

It's especially easy to begin learning to roll if you live in the city, far from the nearest river. In that case you'll be working in a swimming pool, and the challenge of rolling will cancel out the boredom of the pool environment as you wait for that first weekend trip to the river. Potentially timid paddlers, too, will profit from learning to roll right away. The danger of putting off learning to roll is that you will develop a river technique based exclusively on trying never to tip over. You will paddle defensively, and plateau out way below your natural level of ability. So let's stay in our flatwater environment a little longer and really get the job done. The results will be worth it.

Rolling Your Own: The Eskimo Roll

So far you've been learning to kayak on your own. No longer. In order to learn an eskimo roll you will need, at the very least, a patient and willing friend (not necessarily a kayaker) to help turn you back rightside-up whenever you don't make it on your own. But this is also a good moment to discuss the possibility of taking some kind of lessons.

Today there are relatively few organized kayak schools or courses around the country, but in the near future there will doubtless be many more. Beware. Just as in ski schools, there will be as many bad kayak instructors as good ones. Your common sense and intuition must guide you here. If your instructor makes everything seem hard and unnatural, if you fail repeatedly and the instructor is unable to zero in on your problem, then give it up—the class that is—and go back to learning on your own. To repeat, most good kayakers are self-taught, but this said, it's still true that the best point at which to take lessons is when you are ready to learn to roll. Even outside the few kayak schools, some sports shops and some clubs regularly offer "rolling clinics," an afternoon of more or less informal instruction in rolling guided by an experienced paddler. It's well worth taking advantage of these sessions if any are offered in your neighborhood.

In essence, all the many variations of the eskimo roll work like this. The capsized kayaker, upside-down in the water, must first get into a good position to roll up. This means he must scrunch his body up close to the surface of the water, while at the same time getting the paddle in position on the surface for the all-important sweep stroke that follows. Let's call this first phase the *set-up*. Next, the kayaker (still upside-down) sweeps his paddle out from the boat in a wide arc. Just as in our bracing strokes, the angle of the paddle blade as it moves through the water is critical; a climbing angle will keep the blade high in the water, near the surface, and will provide a kind of support (much like a chin-up bar) from which the kayaker can execute the next phase, the so-called *hip snap*. The hip snap is really a combined movement of hips and knees which flips the boat upright. This movement is actually started just after the sweep begins, and the object is to turn the kayak upright, but *not* the kayaker's body, which still remains in the water. The final, or *recovery*, phase is really nothing more than a dynamic high brace with which, at the end of his sweep stroke, the kayaker lifts his body back up, once the kayak has been flipped upright.

Rolling is the single most complex maneuver in all of kayaking, so don't be surprised if this description seems rather complicated. Like any other complex motor skill, rolling a kayak cannot be learned all at once. The different elements must be mastered and linked together in the right sequence, until the entire roll happens smoothly, as one continuous semiautomatic action. If a kayaker had to think about each separate phase, he would never be able to roll up in tough conditions. And don't worry, as formidable as the roll sounds (imagine doing all that upside-down underwater!) many average, ordinary people have mastered it. There is a simplified step-by-step sequence that slowly links it all together. But before we get in the water to try, it's best to have formed a clear mental picture of the whole maneuver, to see where you're going at the end of this step-by-step process.

Here's another way of looking at the roll. The most common mistake that you or any other beginner

20. The eskimo roll

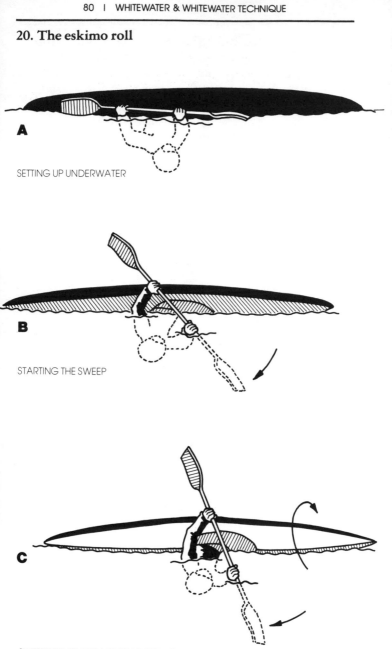

A

SETTING UP UNDERWATER

B

STARTING THE SWEEP

C

SWEEP CONTINUES, HIP SNAP BEGINS

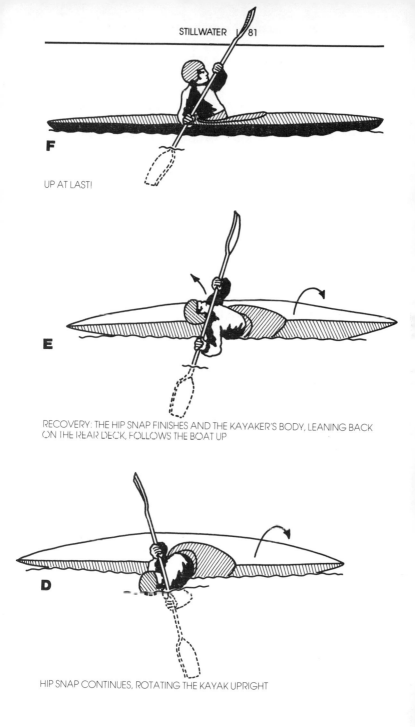

F

UP AT LAST!

E

RECOVERY: THE HIP SNAP FINISHES AND THE KAYAKER'S BODY, LEANING BACK ON THE REAR DECK, FOLLOWS THE BOAT UP

D

HIP SNAP CONTINUES, ROTATING THE KAYAK UPRIGHT

will make is to try to raise your body up out of the
water too early—to be in too much of a hurry to get
that mouthful of air. The reason this is such a mistake
is that the eskimo roll works by a transfer of rotational momentum—big words! But it's the same
principle that lets a falling cat turn over in midair.
Applied to the eskimo roll, it means that what the
kayaker *must* do while partially being supported by
the sweeping paddle is to spin the kayak upright
around its long axis. Then and only then can the body
follow the kayak's motion, and virtually be pulled on
up to the surface. In other words, *roll the boat* and
your body will follow; but try to raise your body out
of the water and the leverage will be too great to
overcome, so you'll tumble back down.

This is where a friend who already knows how to
roll can really help, by demonstrating the movement
so that you can see the whole maneuver before you
get started. Stand on shore or by the side of the pool
and watch from behind as your friend rolls several
times. Put yourself in his place, imagine yourself
doing the same thing, try to visualize the roll as a
whole, and finally, notice how the boat turns upright
before the body comes up every time. Of course, if you
don't have a friend who can roll, you'll have to make
do with our illustrations. Look at them carefully until
you can grasp the whole sequence of events involved
in one roll. Even if you don't entirely understand the
sequence, try to form a mental picture anyway. It will
help once you're underwater, actually attempting to
roll.

Now we're ready for step one. In the whole sequence of moves that constitute a roll, the two most
unfamiliar elements are orienting yourself underwater and the hip snap which flips the boat. We'll begin
by practicing these two elements together. And because we'll spend so much time underwater, a swimmer's nose clip is a good idea to protect your sinuses.
Don't bother about helmet or life vest at first; you
will feel awkward enough without them. Now, launch
your kayak and paddle over to the edge of the pool,

or to the side of a dock or the boat launching float, or—if there is no such sharp edge around—have your friend stand in shallow water holding your paddle sideways just above the water to simulate the effect of a swimming pool edge. (For simplicity, we'll assume that you're in the shallow end of a swimming pool and, again, that you're paddling with right-hand control.)

Come alongside the edge of the pool so that the right side of your kayak is virtually touching it. Lay your paddle aside on the edge of the pool and take a few deep calming breaths. Now, bend forward and tip over to the left side; then, keeping your eyes open, look for the side of the pool, feel with both hands up the wall for the pool's edge, and using that edge as a handhold flip yourself and your boat back upright. Don't worry about doing it right at first; just do it. The idea of this exercise is to get accustomed to functioning underwater. Also, at the same time, try to notice if the cockpit of your kayak fits snugly around you when you are upside-down next to the edge of the pool. If it doesn't you may have to add some foam padding on either side of the seat before going on. There's nothing worse than falling out of your boat before you have a chance to roll.

Now that you're used to tipping over on purpose, let's work on the hip-knee snap which will right your kayak. Take hold of the edge of the pool to your right with both hands and, facing the side of the pool, lower your body down until torso, shoulders, and head are well in the water. In this position, still holding the edge with your hands, experiment a bit with flipping or turning the kayak on its long axis. When the boat is virtually upside down, an outward thrust of the pelvis combined with a strong upward push of your right knee should flip it back up. The whole trick is to use only your hips and knees, and avoid pushing up with your arms on the edge of the pool. To keep from cheating, hold the edge of the pool as lightly as possible, maybe only with one finger of each hand, and try to keep your head completely immersed in the water as you flip the kayak up. Don't hesitate to practice this move twenty or thirty or more times. Although it's easy in itself, we're trying to build up a physical habit, and this happens only through repetition. (if instead of a poolside you are holding a paddle like a rail supported by a friend in shallow water, try also just holding onto your friend's hands; he can tell by how much pressure you put on them whether you're flipping the kayak with a true hip-knee snap or levering up with your arms.)

All right, so far it's easy, what next? Let's go back to the beginning and work on that starting position, the set-up. If you were lucky enough to watch an experienced friend roll several times, you probably noticed that he tucked his paddle neatly at his side, parallel to the boat, before tipping over. But like most good kayakers he probably did not change his grip on his paddle when rolling. Such a roll, with the paddle held in normal position, is often referred to as a *screw roll,* and is ideal because you come up ready to take a stroke. It is actually only one of several possible rolls. It is the most useful, however, and the one we are going to shoot for, though not all at once. To minimize both your struggles and the chance of failure, we will begin with an easier roll called an *extended-paddle roll,* or sometimes a *Pawlata roll* (after Hans Pawlata, the first European to do an eskimo roll). In this roll you do change your grip on the paddle, sliding the shaft forward through your hands. The idea is that by extending the paddle forward you obtain a longer lever arm in the sweep action, and you're very likely to make it up even if you do everything else wrong. Later, by sliding your hands back down the shaft, it is very easy to turn this extended-paddle roll into a screw roll—the motions are identical, only the length of the sweeping paddle will differ. (Although there are some other, very weird ways of rolling up with an extended paddle, we will pass over them in merciful silence.)

We're now ready to try for a complete roll. Move away from the side of the pool and get into position like this: Sitting in your kayak and holding your paddle normally, swing both arms around to your left side so that the paddle is now close to the water and parallel to your kayak. Look at your right wrist. Now roll that right (front) wrist out from the boat a little, just enough so that the outside edge of your front blade is tilting down toward the water. Think about this for a minute. If you moved the blade in this tilted position out from the kayak's side it would be moving at a diving angle to the water and would sink. Yet once you have tipped over, air and water change places, and what is a diving angle from above becomes a climbing angle from below. If, when you begin your sweep from beneath the surface, you remember to roll your wrist this small amount, then

RIGHT

WRONG

21. Setting up for an eskimo roll: correct and incorrect position of the front wrist and paddle blade

your paddle will skim the water and provide support.
Otherwise it will just dive without helping at all. A
subtle but important point which we'll return to
shortly. Now relax your arms and come back to a
normal position.

Next, try the same thing, but once your paddle is
lined up with the boat on the left side, slide it forward
(or your hands back) until your rear (left) hand
reaches the very end of the rear paddle blade. Cup
the bottom rear corner of this blade in your hand, and
once again try to "roll" your front wrist out a bit. You
are now holding the paddle in the correct position for
an extended-paddle roll. To assume your final optimum rolling position, tuck your body forward over
the front deck (a good idea whenever you tip over)
until your head is almost leaning on your right shoulder. Let's call this our *rolling position* (see Figure 22),
and from now on we'll get into this position each time
we want to try a roll.

Wait a minute, don't tip over yet! First be sure to
station your helper, standing waist deep in the water,
just to the right of your kayak beside the cockpit.
And this is what will happen next. You will get in
rolling position and tip over to the left side; once underwater, you will attempt to hold your paddle in the
very same position and feel with it for the surface of
the water, opening your eyes and watching the paddle. At the same time you'll scrunch your body as
high up in the water beside the boat as you can. Since
there's really too much to do the first time around,
your helper is going to grab the paddle and position it
for you—right beside the boat on the surface, with
the front blade flat or at an outward climbing angle to
the water. Then, at a prearranged signal (usually a
sharp rap on the kayak's hull), your friend will move
the paddle out from the boat in a long sweeping arc.
That's right, he'll be doing the work for you. Just try
to feel the way the paddle moves. After this sweep
has started, execute the very same hip-knee snap you
practiced before; and, finally, push your body up with
some support on the paddle—which your friend, of

course, will still be holding and guiding. Because your helper is responsible for so much of the work, you can be sure it's going to succeed. Even if you become completely disoriented on your first try (and it happens) you'll find that your friend can easily lift you back up to try again. Without a helper, every mistake would mean a wet exit, then emptying the boat and starting again.

So where are we now? You've gone through the motions of one complete roll, although with a lot of extra assistance from your helper. Let's repeat this action quite a few more times. Concentrate on an active hip snap and just try to feel the path your arms and paddle follow as your friend sweeps the blade out from the side of the kayak. As soon as you have a sense of what the motion is you will want to try it on your own, while your friend refrains from actually holding or moving the paddle, but just stands by to help if it dives or if you can't come up.

The sweep may well be the most mysterious part of the roll, and it's almost impossible to express in words. When you're sitting on the surface in rolling position with your paddle on your left, parallel to the boat, the paddle almost seems stuck there. There appears to be no way you could actually sweep it out from the boat. And yet, once you're upside-down underwater the movement becomes possible. This is because as soon as you start to move your arms, your hips and the kayak itself begin to twist and roll away from the sweeping paddle, starting the spin which you will amplify with your hip-knee snap. The problem is, which way do your arms move? It's extremely difficult for most people to visualize this arm motion from the surface. This is why we want you to *feel* what happens as your friend sweeps the paddle for you.

If you are beginning to get the feeling, the next step is to try the whole thing by yourself with your friend standing by (only in case you don't make it) but not actively aiding the paddle's movement. To do this he should change sides, standing now on the left, the same side toward which you tip over. In this position

22. Starting position on the surface for a Pawlata or "extended paddle" roll.

he merely has to grasp the far edge or gunwale of the overturned kayak to be able to lever it back upright should your independent efforts not suffice at first. As you try the sweep now, on your own, the most critical point will be positioning the paddle on the surface—the set-up. If the paddle is slanting downward in the water at the moment you begin your sweep, it will simply dive and you won't have enough support to begin your hip snap. So how can you make sure it's correctly set up before trying to roll? Here's a long but important answer.

It's no accident that you've been preparing to roll with your paddle on your left side. This puts the right hand, your control hand, ahead, and it makes the right blade the active one in the sweep phase. Most kayakers paddle right-control and find that using the right-handed sweep stroke is the easiest way to launch their roll. This is because with your right hand fixed you know exactly where that blade is. With the other hand you're never sure. But it's good to double check, making sure that the active right paddle blade is at least flat on the surface before you start to roll up. Do this by reaching up into the air from underwater with the right hand and vigorously slapping the blade down on the surface. This will tell you where the horizontal surface of the water really is. Then if you make that slight correction—the outward roll of the right wrist—your paddle will be at the desired climbing angle to get off a good strong sweep stroke. Later on, in a real whitewater situation you may actu-

ally lose your grip on the paddle momentarily as strong underwater currents try to wrestle it away from you. In such a situation you may have to reach up and feel where the blade actually is before you can hope to set it up correctly for the sweep. So work on becoming conscious of your paddle placement and blade angle when you're upside-down in the water. Slapping the blade down in the water will help, but the whole process takes time. The key point to remember is that unless you set up correctly, you don't have a ghost of a chance of pulling off your roll.

So let's keep practicing, trying to sweep on your own. Chances are your friend will still have to roll your kayak up the last bit, although every now and then things may just click (without you really understanding the difference) and you'll find that you have rolled completely up before your helper had a chance to pull on the boat.

If you are beginning to get the hang of the inverted sweep stroke and you have a reasonable hip snap but are still not rolling completely up, there are several possible explanations. Let's do a little trouble shooting. A good roll should pop you upright before you know what's happened, so if you're not quite making it, or if you're forcing the last bit with a powerful high-bracing push on the paddle, you are probably trying to lift your body up out of the water too early, or else in the wrong place and at the wrong angle. In truth, you never do "lift" your body out of the water; it ought to be pulled out by the momen-

tum you impart to the kayak with your hip snap. But
you do have to let it happen. Try this: As you set up
for the roll, keep your eyes open and fix them on the
active paddle blade (the right blade, ahead of you);
then, as you begin the sweep with that now familiar
up-and-outward reaching of the arms, follow the
movement of the paddle with your eyes for as long as
you can. This will have the effect of keeping your
head down in the water during the whole sweep and
the hip snap.

The first time you watch the paddle in this way
you'll probably come right up, and when you do you
may be surprised to find yourself leaning way back on
the rear deck. This is, in fact, a very advantageous
position, and indeed the easiest rolls, physically, always wind up with the kayaker coming up in an extreme *bent-back* position, arched backward over the
rear deck.

This is such an important point that it will save
your roll even if you do everything else wrong. And
its explanation will give us yet another way of looking
at the roll. Once again, try to visualize the whole
process. We have identified three separate phases
after the set-up: the sweep, the hip snap, and finally
the recovery. But actually these phases all overlap and
blend together in one fluid motion. By sweeping the
paddle on the surface and following this motion
smoothly with the whole upper body, the kayaker
has, in effect, stretched himself out in the water
almost perpendicular to (out to the side of) the kayak.
At the same time, the moving paddle provides a
certain fixed support for the next phase (like a
chin-up bar or the side of a pool). From this support
the kayaker is able to snap hips and knees, imparting
a twist or flip to the kayak itself which will turn it
back over in the water. At this point the kayak has
acquired a certain amount of rotational inertia or
momentum; that is, it wants to keep moving, turning
about its long axis. But the kayaker's body, sticking
out there to the side, is too much for it and only slows
down and overcomes this rotation—unless, that is,

the kayaker *continues* the sweep, bringing paddle and arms all the way back to the rear of the boat and *following this action with his whole torso.* In this way, instead of sticking out to the side to stop the kayak's rotation, the kayaker's torso has moved in close to the "spinning" boat and can be carried upright along with it.

Former physics students will recognize that this has to do with the conservation of angular or rotational momentum, and will remember the famous piano stool experiment, or the action of a spinning ice skater who only spins faster as she moves her arms in close to her body. This is what happens as you continue the sweep back to the rear of the kayak: your body comes in closer to the boat, allowing the turning effort you have begun with your hip snap to become far more effective, strong enough to pull you up after the boat. Of course, the sweeping motion can finish as a high brace, should you need a little more leverage to make it all the way up. But in a perfect roll, you don't really brace yourself up in the recovery phase; you just come up! Once again, to get this effect, concentrate on watching the sweeping paddle underwater; this will keep your head down and bring you up easily on the rear deck.

So how's it going? Some of you will discover a strong roll after only a few tries. Others may spend frustrating hours upside-down without ever really feeling it. But particularly if your helper has a basic understanding of what you're striving for and can give you adequate feedback when you miss one or another part of the roll, you should be getting close to a roll after a couple hours of practice. Be patient; in any case it will take you days and days of practice to really *master* the eskimo roll.

This is our goal—mastering the roll, perfecting its various movements to the point where they are automatic and solid so you come up easily every time. But it will take a good deal of dedication. Many beginners don't achieve a solid roll until they have been boating for months. But every hour spent

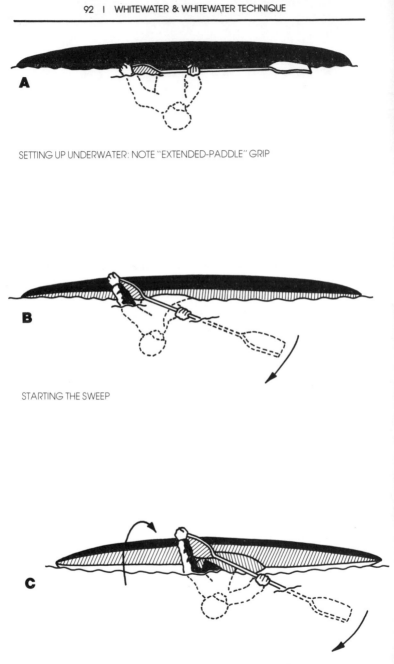

SETTING UP UNDERWATER: NOTE "EXTENDED-PADDLE" GRIP

STARTING THE SWEEP

SWEEP CONTINUES; HIP SNAP BEGINS TO TURN THE KAYAK OVER

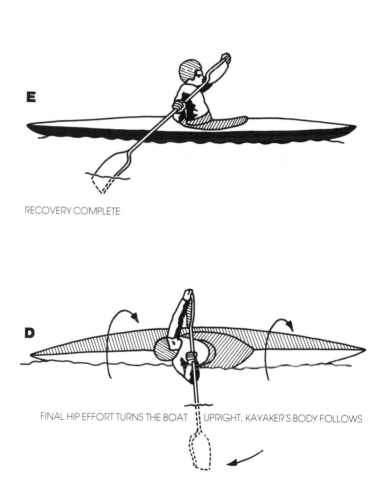

E

RECOVERY COMPLETE

D

FINAL HIP EFFORT TURNS THE BOAT UPRIGHT; KAYAKER'S BODY FOLLOWS

23. The Pawlata or "extended paddle" roll

practicing your roll will be handsomely rewarded by increased confidence and security in whitewater. Stick with it!

Now let's briefly look at the steps that will take you from barely being able to roll with an extended paddle to an effortless screw roll with the paddle held in normal position. The key is repetition, but there's no sense in repeating and reinforcing mistakes. So if your roll works but still feels awkward or if you have to strain and muscle your way up, bracing heavily with the paddle at the end, then make an effort to change what you are doing rather than just repeating a poor roll over and over. Two people working on their rolls together can help one another with analysis and comments, and, better yet, an experienced paddler may be able to pinpoint any problems. If the roll is going smoothly, however, mindless repetition is just great. (After my first river trip, I was so impressed by the rolling abilities of my experienced companions that for a whole week I went down to a local pool every morning and rolled until I could no longer see from the chlorine in the water. The very next weekend, after capsizing in pretty big waves, I found that I had rolled back up before I even knew I was doing it. Those hundreds of practice rolls, day after day, had really paid off.)

As soon as you are confident in your ability to get back up, begin experimenting with a shorter grip on the paddle. Eventually, this will lead from the easier extended-paddle roll to the more sophisticated and useful screw roll. At first, when setting up merely slide your left hand back until it touches the neck of the blade, rather than gripping the very end of the blade. This gives you less leverage than before, but still more than you get with the paddle in normal position. If that works, then try rolling without altering your grip at all. Some of these attempts probably won't work; you'll rise partly out of the water and fall back. In that case just slide your left hand back to the familiar extended-paddle position and try again. This sort of experimenting is very good for you, as it's not uncommon in the river to miss a roll and have to try again. Take your time. Every time you miss a roll you will at least have gotten another breath of air; that's enough to allow you to slowly and patiently set up once more: bend up toward the surface, get your paddle back into rolling position, and feel or slap the surface to make sure the blade angle is correct before trying a second time. If you rush it, your second try will be as bad as your first.

There are a number of other things you can do to improve your roll before you ever get near a moving river. The first is to put some variety into your practice rolls. It has probably occurred to you already that if you do tip over in an actual whitewater situation, it will happen so suddenly that you won't have time to get carefully into rolling position (placing the paddle by your side and so forth). You will find yourself upside-down in rough water with your paddle sticking off at some strange angle. Your very first task underwater will be to pull that paddle in to your side and get into rolling position. So try the same thing in a pool. Crash over in as disorganized a fashion as possible. Or put a little forward motion into things by paddling hard and suddenly tipping over. Spend a little time just staying underwater, learning to defuse that sense of urgency about returning to the surface. Later you may often find yourself in river situations in which you want to stay calmly under your boat for a few extra seconds until you can feel that things are just right for rolling. In the pool, you can stay patiently under your boat while you pass your paddle back and forth from hand to hand over the top of your kayak before you roll up. Another practice game which can get a little rough but can also be a lot of fun is to ask several friends to stand around your boat (in the shallow end of the swimming pool) and simulate the action of rough water, pushing and shaking your kayak, knocking it over when you least expect it, and even shaking it a bit while you're underneath trying to roll. Good experience, but don't overdo it. Practice also with

24. A complete screw roll

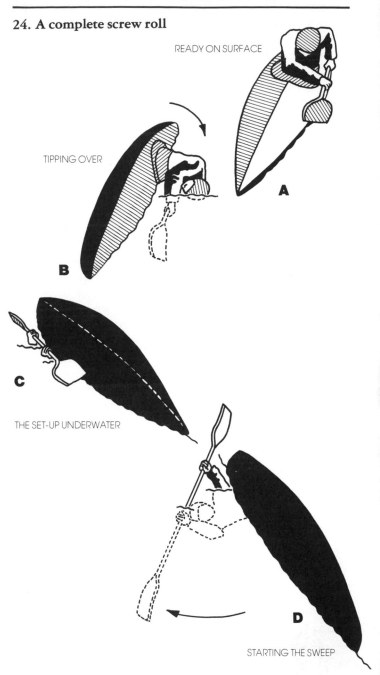

READY ON SURFACE

TIPPING OVER

A

B

C

THE SET-UP UNDERWATER

D

STARTING THE SWEEP

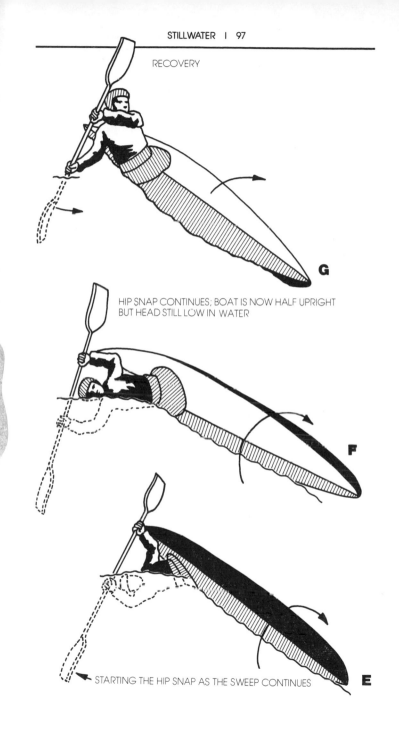

RECOVERY

G

HIP SNAP CONTINUES; BOAT IS NOW HALF UPRIGHT
BUT HEAD STILL LOW IN WATER

F

STARTING THE HIP SNAP AS THE SWEEP CONTINUES

E

your spray skirt half off, with life vest and helmet on—but above all, practice a lot.

In one sense, the process of learning to roll is never-ending. No matter how well you can roll, you can always improve on it. Going from the practice pool to a moving river to the middle of a rapid, and then on to big waves and eventually turbulent holes—each step will be a new experience, requiring a new level of rolling skill. And even the very best kayakers still swim occasionally, very occasionally. The most important task for a beginning kayaker is to get started quickly on the path that leads to a "bomb-proof" roll. At first any sort of roll will do. It can always be improved later. Far too many kayakers have put off trying to roll until eventually they develop a real mental block about it. Rolling is not a superhuman feat, it's not an advanced maneuver for experts only, and, yes, it can even be fun. Once you've had your first taste of rolling, you're ready to learn about moving water, flowing rivers, swiftwater.

CHAPTER 4

SWIFTWATER

Now that your kayak is no longer an unkown, no longer an obstinate unresponsive craft, and basic paddling no longer a mystery, it's time to leave the practice pond and get into a moving river where we belong. This chapter will give you all the information you need to make this transition painlessly. But more is involved than just picking up some new techniques. As you enter this new environment, the river, you'll need a new vocabulary to talk about river features, a new understanding of what the river actually does as it flows between its banks, and of course some new techniques to maneuver comfortably in currents and countercurrents.

River Lore 1

A river is a river is a river. Right? Rivers start in the high mountains as tiny rivulets and flow, eventually, to the sea. We all learned that in school. But how often does the average person go out and study a real living river—walk along its banks, stare at its surface, and wonder about the flow of water beneath? To most of us, rivers are *terra incognita,* or more properly, *aqua incognita.* Becoming a whitewater paddler means getting to know the river, making friends with it. This is an engrossing process that will take you a lot longer than your first couple of trips.

Nomenclature

One must begin somewhere, so let's start with some of the basic terminology used to talk about rivers. Upstream and downstream should present no problems—although many a boater has rolled his kayak up in the middle of big waves and found himself quite unable to say which way was downstream. But how about the *right* and *left banks* of a river? These terms are more confusing, because the right bank becomes the left bank as you turn from facing upstream to face downstream, or vice versa. To eliminate this confusion, the convention is always to speak of right and left as though we were facing downstream (for example, "Half a mile below the old bridge the river makes a sharp turn to the right.") Occasionally you will hear the terms *river right* or *river left,* which mean the same thing—always looking from the direction of the river's flow.

What about this flow? Water levels in most rivers rise and fall drastically according to the season or to the demand for water in the case of a dam-controlled river. The amount of water flowing past a given point in a river at a given time is expressed in somewhat esoteric terms as the number of *cfs*, or cubic feet per second. And although this term sounds quite technical and bothersome, the would-be kayaker had better reconcile himself (or herself) to it, because boaters all across the country describe water levels in terms of how many thousand cfs a river is flowing. It's nearly impossible to visualize or compute the exact meaning of such figures, but they are valuable as arbitrary reference numbers against which you can compare the relative size of the flow in a given stream or river, from your own experience.

The number of cubic feet per second describes only the total volume of flowing water, but another aspect of river flow has a more practical significance. Not all the water in a river moves at the same speed or flows in the same way. For example, even in a smooth and gently rounded river channel with no ob-stacles to break the flow of the water, the current will be much faster in the center than on either side; and even in the center the flow will be faster near the surface than near the bottom. Why? Because of fric-tion, for the ground of the river bed itself exerts a kind of drag on the water flowing next to it. This water in turn slows the level or layer of water next to it, but in a diminishing amount, and so forth (see Fig-ure 25 for a graphic interpretation). If the center of the river channel is relatively deep and the sides are relatively shallow (more friction), then this *differen-*

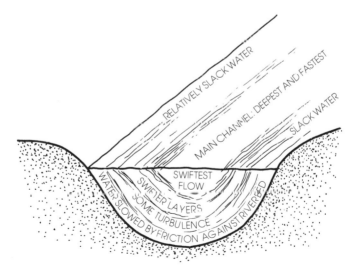

25. Differential flow of water in a typical section of river

tial flow of water is exaggerated—quite swift in the center, almost motionless at the sides. And this, as we shall see, is of utmost importance to the kayaker.

Eddies

Areas of motionless water, water moving much slower than the main current, or in a reverse direction to that of the main current are known as *eddies.* The sides of most river channels therefore offer eddies. A real purist would call the zones of slower flow beside each bank *eddylike slackwater,* and argue that they are not true eddies, even though they are often called eddies. But in any case these zones of slower flowing water are far less important to the whitewater boater than the kind of eddies that are typically formed behind, or downstream, from any obstacle to the flow of water. Such eddies form natural stopping and resting spots for the kayaker, even in the middle of rather fierce rapids.

An eddy formed behind a large boulder has a more interesting shape than the slow-water eddies that occur "by themselves" along the shallow sides of a river. A large rock will split the water's flow, diverting it in a more intense flow around both sides. But behind (downstream) from the rock, although there is no direct current, there is, nonetheless, water—for water rushes back in from the *jets* on either side to fill the relative emptiness behind the boulder. As this water pours in to fill up this space, it actually reverses direction and flows back upstream toward the rock it has just passed. If the boulder or other obstacle is large enough, the volume of water flowing upstream behind it will be considerable, enough to form a veritable island of calm in the otherwise continuous flow of the current. Such eddies are relatively calm because the water loses much of its speed as it swirls around the boulder and changes direction. The kind of eddy just described is sometimes called a *back eddy* because of the back flow of water within it, but to most kayakers it is known simply as an eddy.

The calm backwater of an eddy is usually separated from the main current by a line of turbulence, the *eddy line.* If the rock or boulder forming the eddy is in the middle of the stream, water flows by on both sides and two distinct eddy lines appear, one on each side. If the rock is near the bank, there will be strong current flow around one side only and only one eddy line—actually the most common case. In certain cases involving very heavy water, an *eddy fence* developes—a line of foaming, boiling water that may

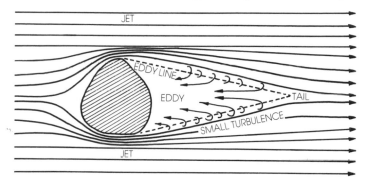

26. A typical rock-formed eddy

actually represent a difference in height between the current and the eddy itself. In most cases, however, your average garden-variety eddy is a friendly spot in the river guarded by nothing more serious than a distinct line of bubbles, small boils, or slight turbulence where the two water flows—downstream in the main current and upstream in the eddy proper—pass or shear by each other. For a clearer picture see Figure 26.

Eddies can be large or small, (large enough to park a dozen kayaks in or too small to even grab with your paddle blade). They can be crystal calm or a chaos of foam, with a stong back-flow of current or no perceptible movement of water in them at all. Surprisingly, an eddy of sorts can be formed by a boulder that is completely submerged in the river (but not too deeply). Such eddies will be difficult for the novice boater to spot, much less to use, but an expert paddler can often turn the slowed-down water flow behind even submerged boulders to his advantage. We will return to eddies and learn how to use them later in this chapter; for now, lest you think I am belaboring a minor subject, just remember that eddies are the single most important new river feature you will encounter as a beginning kayaker. They will be a source of surprise, frustration, and delight, but one way or another you will get to know them quite well.

Other Features

There are other interesting aspects of differential flow in real rivers (the way one part of a river flows at either a different speed or in a different direction than another). Not only is the flow of water faster at the center than at the sides and faster on top than near the bottom, but also it varies with the width of the channel. Remembering that the same amount of water flows by any given point on the bank each second (the flow in "cubic feet per second" or cfs), we can readily see that if the river gets narrower, the water must speed up in order for the same amount to get through each second. If the constriction is a major one—for example, a giant boulder blocking half the stream's width, or a sudden narrowing of canyon walls—then the acceleration of the current will be sudden and dramatic, offering the kayaker thrills or problems, or both. Conversely, if the river opens up into a larger channel, the water's speed will decrease. If the river banks widen out to form a pond or large pool, the current's speed may become so slow as to actually give the impression of stillwater in the middle of a flowing river. These variables are of importance to the kayaker, since hitting a section of fast-moving or slow-moving water unprepared can be as unsettling as skiing from a packed slope into a three-foot wall of deep powder snow. Since no river has perfectly regular, unchanging parallel banks, it means

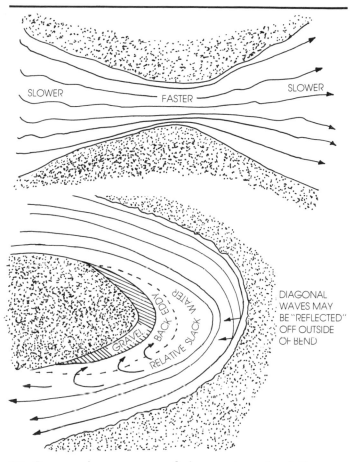

27. Commonly encountered changes in a river's flow.
Top: river narrows. *Bottom:* river bends.

a lot of variety in the course of one run.

The main channel, or fastest flow of water, is not always in the middle of the river, especially where the river turns to the right or left. Water moving in a straight line has a certain momentum that in effect tends to keep it moving that way. When the river channel bends more or less suddenly to the left, the main current tends to push on straight ahead, as it were, until it is deflected to the left by the right bank curving into it. As a result, the deepest, swiftest current at a bend in the river will be to the outside of the bend. The stronger the current, the sharper the bend, the more extreme this effect will be. In some more serious cases, the boater will have to work hard to avoid being drawn, pulled, or even smashed against rocks or cliffs on the outside of a hard bend in the river.

This same phenomenon of current flowing to the outside of a curve will create a larger than normal back eddy at the inside of the turn and somewhat around the corner. The corner of projecting land around which the river is bending casts this *shadow-like* backwater behind it (or downstream) just as a projecting boulder in midstream casts its *eddy shadow* behind it. This calmer water to the inside of a bend can be used to great advantage by the paddler. (By the way, it is this tendency of rivers to flow to the outside of a bend which accentuates typical snakelike *meander* patterns in a river's course, through erosion of land on the outside of a bend and its progressive depositing on the inside.)

But to take advantage of even these elementary river features in your kayak will require at least a few more hours of practice. Not merely, as before, practicing new strokes or movements, but acquiring through practice a certain sensitivity to the movement of living water.

Paddling in Moving Water

You are now definitely ready for your first river run. You can maneuver your kayak with confidence, if not with ease, on flatwater, and you have probably learned some kind of a roll, although undoubtedly it's still a little shaky. Ideally your first river run should be down a gentle friendly river with virtually no rapids. What? Aren't rapids the whole point of this game? Yes, in a way they are; but whereas most beginners with any balance and confidence can "get through" moderate rapids on their first time out, they can't learn much in rapids. And there is so much to learn! Better to go a little slower at first, master some important techniques before you need them, and thus make sure that your first trip down real rapids is terrific—not traumatic.

It goes without saying that it would be best if an experienced kayaker friend led you down your first river. If such a friend or friends are not available, you'll have to use a little extra prudence as a beginner by choosing a very easy river indeed. You won't regret it. But ideally you should learn just a wee bit more before heading downriver. If you're patient enough to spend about an hour paddling back and forth in the current without letting it carry you away downstream, you can learn some important diagonal maneuvers—upstream ferrying and back ferrying, or "setting"—as well as basic eddy turns, before you actually need them downriver.

Most likely, many readers will be too impatient to stay in one section of moving water while the river is calling them downstream. So be it. Learning by doing is a time-honored approach. Just don't go downstream by yourself, and if you have chosen a really gentle, safe river for your first shot, not much can go wrong. You should definitely know how far you're going and where the take-out point is. And you should probably have left a car there, or at least thought about how you are going to get back. Organizing shuttles and a lot of other mundane details that smooth out actual river trips are discussed in Chapter 9, *Practical River Touring,* recommended reading before your first run.

I also want to warn you against an insidious danger: trees. Submerged trees or trees that hang from the bank into the water have a way of trapping boaters who capsize against them. The force of the current "strains" right through the branches and can pin you in a tangle of limbs. Steer clear of anything that remotely resembles a submerged tree! This is an important warning that I'll have occasion to repeat several more times. Far less dangerous are rocks against which a beginner's kayak might broach. Should you wash up sideways on a rock during your first river adventure, just *lean toward the rock*. This will keep you from tipping over. But for a full explanation of why, you must wait till later in this chapter.

The absolute minimum you need to know before heading downstream is how to get reorganized safely when you tip over and find that you can't yet roll up (yes, swimming-pool rolls have a way of vanishing in the river). So before learning any new maneuvers, let's briefly run over the steps of what is loosely called *self-rescue*.

Self-Rescue

When you tipped over in the pool, it was no big deal to get to the side, empty your boat out, and get in again. When you tip in the river it's a little different. First of all, if you have even the shakiest roll, try it—don't just give up and get out of the boat. The habit of trying to roll, and then trying again, is a good one to start acquiring early. But you will go swimming. It's no disgrace; all beginners do. After you've completed your wet exit and have come to the surface with your paddle still in one hand, move immediately to the upstream end of the boat and take hold of the grab loop at that end. A glance should tell you which bank is closer. Hold both paddle and grab loop in the same hand and begin swimming toward the near bank with a modified side stroke, using both feet *and* your free arm.

What is most important here is to stay to the rear of, or upstream, of your kayak. Even with the full complement of flotation bags inside it, your kayak can take in a lot of water; and water, you'll remember, is extremely heavy. Under no circumstance do you want to risk being pinned between your now quite heavy boat and a rock or tree or any other obstacle. Even if the water looks clear of any such hazards, don't take chances. Stay to the rear of your kayak as you swim for shore. Remember, not all boulders break the surface! Your boat is an ornery creature, and it may swing around on you while you try to swim it to shore; one minute you're behind the kayak and the next you find yourself ahead of it. When this happens let go immediately and move to the rear once again before continuing on toward shore! Enough said.

This assumes that the water is not too rough, merely fast-flowing current, so that you can stroke out for the bank right away. Should you find yourself in rougher water, you may have to swim along with your kayak for a while before you can start moving it to shore. Also, in rough water you may lose your grip on the boat and find yourself swimming through on your own. In such situations, where you are not actively swimming toward the bank but rather are being carried downstream by the water, try to swim more or less on your back, keeping your feet in front of you (downstream) and as high in the water as possible. This will minimize the danger of getting a leg caught, for example, between two underwater boulders; and you will also be able to cushion the shock of hitting an obstacle with your feet and legs. Finally—although no beginning kayaker should ever find himself in such a situation—if you are tiring and unable to get your swamped boat ashore, remember that you are more important than your equipment. Let the boat go and get yourself to shore. You'll usually be able to collect your kayak in a calm eddy somewhere downstream, although you may have to hike a bit to find it. If an experienced paddler in the group sees that you are having trouble reaching shore, he may offer you a tow by backing his kayak up to you so that you can grab the rear loop as he paddles toward the bank. This is fine, but don't stop kicking with your legs, as it is hard work towing another boat and paddler. Helpful tows from another beginner, however, are not advised, since they often result in two persons swimming instead of just one. When you have reached shore, it's often easier to remain standing waist-deep in the water while you shove the end of your boat up on the bank and empty it by repeated lifting and lowering of your end. Then take a couple of minutes to catch your breath, and off you go again.

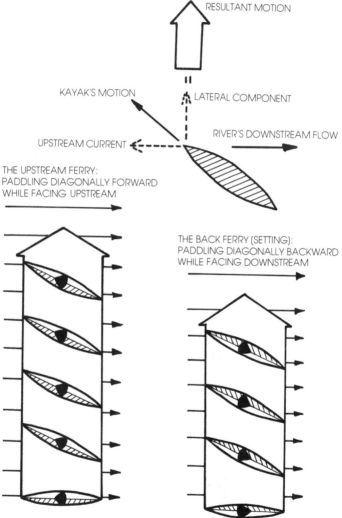

RESULTANT MOTION

LATERAL COMPONENT

KAYAK'S MOTION

UPSTREAM CURRENT

RIVER'S DOWNSTREAM FLOW

THE UPSTREAM FERRY:
PADDLING DIAGONALLY FORWARD
WHILE FACING UPSTREAM

THE BACK FERRY (SETTING):
PADDLING DIAGONALLY BACKWARD
WHILE FACING DOWNSTREAM

28. Ferrying: The river's force cancels out the upstream component of the boat's motion. Only the lateral component is left, causing the kayak to move across the river.

But let's say you're the more patient type, willing to put up with a bit more practice while you get used to moving current without really committing yourself to the river quite yet. You have chosen a broad section of evenly flowing water, with maybe a rock here and there near the sides forming quiet slow eddies. Put your kayak in the water facing upstream and let's learn something new.

Ferrying

Ferrying is the art of crossing the river sideways, without being carried downstream by the current. This skill will be vital later on for avoiding serious obstacles and obstructions in the river's channel. There are two kinds of ferrying: *upstream ferrying* and *back ferrying*. Both use the same principle, and in both the kayaker drives his boat upstream, against the current, but at a diagonal angle. It works like this:

Imagine a kayak moving back upstream and to the right on a diagonal course. In a sense the kayak is moving in two directions at once, straight upstream and straight to the right, but the combination appears as diagonal movement, both upstream and to the right *at the same time* (physicists and engineers refer to the two *components* of the kayak's diagonal motion). But since the river is flowing downstream, its movement cancels out the upstream aspect (or component) of the kayak's motion, leaving only its lateral or sideways motion. What happens is that the kayak maintains its *altitude* in the river, moving neither upstream nor downstream, while it crabs sideways across the current—in this case to the right—as long as the kayaker continues paddling in this diagonal direction (see Figure 28).

In the upstream ferry, you face upstream, point the nose of your kayak in the direction you want to ferry, and paddle with forward strokes. The principle of back ferrying is exactly the same, but the procedure is reversed. In this case, boat and boater are both facing downstream, and you must back paddle, aiming the *stern* of your boat in the direction you want to go. The only variables in either kind of ferrying are the angle at which the kayak is pointed and the force with which you must paddle to achieve a good ferry. The stronger the current, the less of a diagonal angle you will take (since your boat will be swept away sideways in fast water if it is angled too far across the current). You will also have to paddle harder in fast water to keep your place in the river while ferrying laterally across the current. In weaker current, you will be able to point your boat at more of an angle across the current and paddle far more lazily to achieve a good ferry. Now let's try it.

Your boat is already aimed upstream and we want to do a couple of upstream ferries first as it will be easier for you to control your boat's angle while paddling forward. Don't, however, start out from a true eddy behind a rock or jutting bank; instead find a stretch of riverbank where the main current flows smoothly by with no swirls, backwaters, or little surprises. Get in your boat and paddle briskly out, staying almost parallel to shore—that is, pointing almost straight upstream with very, very little angle across the river. Once you have entered the main current a little distance out from the bank, then you can experiment with different bow angles and more or less paddling to see what effect they have on your ferrying. If you've chosen a friendly, even-flowing stretch of river, you should have no trouble in controlling your ferry, and soon you'll be *sliding* back and forth across the current with relatively little effort. Don't paddle any harder than you have to in order to counteract the river's downstream push. Your sideways motion may seem very slow at first, a kind of slow-motion drift back and forth across the river—but that's exactly as it should be. Ferrying across a river seems so effortless and smooth that it is sometimes called *ferry gliding*, a descriptive, almost poetic term that tells us something quite basic about good river-running technique. You don't fight your way across, or through, or down a river; instead you learn to use the river's force to accomplish your own ends. You glide—or at any rate

you will glide once you figure out how. As one kayaking friend says, "You don't have to push the river; it
flows by itself."

As you ferry your way from one side of the river to
the other, notice how the water next to the banks is
calmer, stiller than in the main channel. This is one of
the eddy effects we talked about earlier; though these
places are not sharp or clearly defined eddies, they are
eddylike areas of relatively still water nonetheless.
These are your resting spots where you can sit in your
boat and relax without paddling to keep your place in
the river. As you practice your ferrying, keep your
eyes open for the other kind of eddy—real definite
backwaters behind rocks, which you're going to be
using very shortly.

Now turn your kayak around in the calmer water
near shore to face downstream. It's time to practice
back ferrying (or *setting*, as it is sometimes called). If
you're on the right bank (facing downstream) just turn
your stern to the left, out toward the river, with a good
reverse sweep on the right, and start back paddling out
into the current. It may take a little longer for you to
get the feeling of back ferrying, but it's worth it because this will be one of the best ways to avoid rocks
or other obstacles as you head down the river. Your
boat is facing downstream, as in normal river running,
so you can begin to back ferry in a second. Furthermore, if an obstacle such as a big rock suddenly looms
up in front of you, back ferrying will give you more
time to avoid it, since the maneuver will retard your
forward progress down the river. On the other hand, if
you paddle diagonally forward to one side or the other
to avoid the obstacle, you will be adding to your forward speed and accelerating the moment of crisis by
closing with the obstacle even faster. For all these
reasons back ferrying is definitely a hot tip.

Try back ferrying again a few times until you really
get the hang of it. Remember, to move to the right,
back paddle your stern to the right; to move to the
left, back paddle your stern to the left. The nose of
your kayak will be pointing *away* from the direction

you want to move in. In both kinds of ferrying you will want to become aware of the angle your boat is making with the current, the *ferry angle*. Get into the habit of looking at the surface of the river for ripplelike lines that indicate the exact direction of the current.

After you have begun to get a feeling for both kinds of ferrying, just cut loose and paddle around this one stretch of river in any direction, in any way you can think of. The idea is just to get used to having water moving underneath you. After a while you will develop a sixth sense for what the water is doing and automatically adjust your paddling in response. Try paddling straight toward a tree or other landmark on the bank and notice how the current will drift you below the point you aimed at. Then try again, this time compensating for the drift with a slight upstream aim. With a little practice such course adjustments will become second nature and you will have begun to acquire a kind of subconscious awareness of what the water itself is doing all the time. At first, the beginning kayaker is apt to feel that the boat insulates and separates him from the water. The experienced kayaker feels the water *through* his kayak. Unlike your first practice pond or pool, the surface of a moving river is alive and constantly changing. Your boat, through small movements and reactions to surface currents, will signal you about such changes if only you tune in to it.

The River Roll

Things are going well now. You can ferry and move around comfortably in an easy stretch of river, and you are doubtless getting impatient to see what one of those eddies behind a rock will do to your kayak. But before you get into this new area of technique, which is important enough to merit a whole subchapter of its own, let's practice one last basic skill here in this open flowing water—a river roll. Technically there is nothing different about rolling in moving current than rolling in a swimming pool. Yet psychologically they are worlds apart. If you feel a little ex-cited and somewhat uncertain about trying your fledg-ling roll in the current, don't be surprised—we all felt like that.

Actually, it's only a symbolic act to roll a couple of times in the current right now. But this is very impor-tant symbolism indeed, because your confidence will skyrocket as a result. Don't pick the fastest flowing part of the river for your first experiment; just paddle far enough away from shore that you won't hit bottom when you tip over (test with your paddle to make sure it's deep enough). Then, set up for your favorite and most secure roll—screw roll or the extended-paddle (Pawlata) roll—and over you go. If it works, try a few more. And after a couple of successful rolls near the bank, paddle right out to the center of the river and roll there. (Try it crosswise to the current, tipping over upstream and rolling up on the *downstream side*. If you're curious about why one side is better than the other, read the next section.) There is no better confi-dence builder than a river roll.

Should your roll disappear in the excitement of a river situation, don't be too hard on yourself. It hap-pens all the time, and it just means that a few more hours of rolling practice are in order (in shallow warm water, with a friend to help). Nonetheless, if you can roll in a pool, you ought to be able to roll in the river. It's a confidence game, so go ahead and bluff it through. If you do you can approach the next set of new maneuvers with hardly a concern about tipping over.

Currents and Countercurrents

We have picked, on purpose, a section of river with gentle, even-flowing current for our first expo-sure to moving water. Now you should get ready for stronger currents and more violent effects. Even in this gentle stretch, the few true eddies, formed behind big boulders, will give us a new challenge. But before we paddle into them, we should talk about upstream and downstream lean, and upstream and downstream bracing.

The Downstream Tilt

You will remember that when you were practicing both low and high braces in flatwater, you realized that what was giving you support was the motion of the paddle through the water at a climbing angle. In short, as you pulled or pushed the paddle blade through the water it was tilted up in relation to its movement—just like a water-skier's ski—so that the water it hit pushed it upwards, giving you some support. Now, in strongly moving water, you are going to accomplish the same thing by holding the paddle more or less motionless (but at the correct angle) and letting the water move or push against it, instead of it moving or pushing against the water. Sound complex? In practice it's simple.

The general rule here is that it is always safe to lean or to brace your paddle to the downstream side. Conversely, leaning upstream or leaving your paddle too long underwater on the upstream side will generally result in a capsize. Here's why. Imagine that you're sitting in your kayak pointing across the river, squarely crosswise to the current, but drifting more slowly than the current, so that water is actually passing beneath your boat. One side of you will be di-

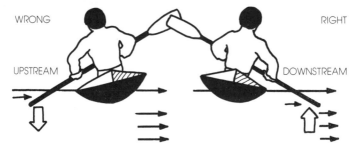

29. Leaning and bracing: the effects of bracing a paddle on the up or downstream side of the boat

rectly downstream, the other directly upstream. Now reach out to the side with your downstream paddle and lay it in the water, power face down, just as though you were about to do a high brace. But notice the action of the moving water on the paddle blade. The water is flowing beneath it, tending to push it out and up. That is, the moving water is only hitting the underneath face of the paddle, so the resulting force is upward. (This is a difficult point to visualize, so be sure to look at Figure 29.)

Now imagine yourself placing the paddle in the same way on the upstream side of the kayak. The moving water will be rushing over the top of the blade, pushing it in toward you, and down, underwater. And since you are holding on to the end of a long lever—your paddle, which is being driven underwater by the force of the current—you will probably tip over upstream as well.

This principle is so important in kayaking that it's really worth a moment's thought to understand clearly. Let's restate it in different terms. If a paddle blade is dipped into the river at an angle, either upstream or downstream, the force of the current hitting it will have a very definite and different effect. If on the upstream side, the current will hit the top of the paddle, sinking it (and you); if on the downstream side, the current will hit the paddle from beneath, raising it and bracing it (and you). In a downstream brace, if the water rushing up against the paddle blade has enough force, you can lean out, seemingly forever, getting just as much support from your motionless paddle as if it were planted firmly on the bank. If the current is gentle, without much force, a passive downstream brace may not be strong enough to hold you up if you really lean on it—but it will still give you some additional support as you lever the paddle in toward the boat (your motion and the river's motion will complement each other). So once again, a downstream brace equals security, an upstream brace disaster.

Naturally this distinction is most important

whenever you get sideways to the river. As long as your boat is aimed either straight downstream or straight up, then there is no real downstream side and you can do an active bracing stroke on either side with no problem. You can even occasionally get away with a dreaded upstream brace (but don't try to make a habit of it), provided you reach out and slap the water very quickly and then get off the brace and get your paddle out of the water. Such a quick upstream "tap" may just keep you upright if you're starting to tip over that way; but if you attempt to actually lean on the paddle upstream, over you'll go.

Downstream lean with your kayak works much like a downstream brace with the paddle. But the term, though widely used, is misleading; it would be more accurate to speak of *tilting* the kayak downstream. Although not as thin and flat as a paddle blade, a kayak is nonetheless somewhat flattened or pancake-shaped in cross-section (this is more true of the new low-volume slalom designs, less true of the more round-sided touring boats). As a result, when tilted sideways to the current, it will react a bit the way your paddle did. If you're sideways to the current and you tilt your boat upstream (by lifting the downstream knee), what happens? As the side seam of your boat (the edge of the boat) dips beneath the surface, moving water will wash over the top deck, exerting a downward push, tending to sink the up-stream edge even further and flip the kayak over.

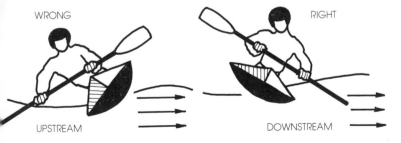

WRONG

RIGHT

UPSTREAM

DOWNSTREAM

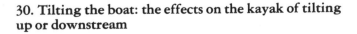

30. Tilting the boat: the effects on the kayak of tilting up or downstream

(This is why you must lean downstream onto an obstacle such as a rock if you broach against it—to avoid flipping upstream.) More or less the same thing happened when we tried to brace with the upstream paddle. To make sure this *doesn't* happen, it's common to tilt the kayak downstream (by raising the upstream knee). This keeps the upstream edge of the boat from accidentally going beneath the surface, say in big waves, and should you start to tip over with your kayak tilted downstream, you can just fall over onto a solid downstream brace and you'll never go over.

If you are already a skier or a climber, you will recognize a parallel between the kayaker's downstream lean and the importance of leaning downhill when skiing or not "hugging" the rock when climbing. Although the reasons are slightly different, the psychology is the same. Leaning downstream occasionally feels as though you are sticking your head into the lion's jaws—but it works. It is an aggressive, stable maneuver that's guaranteed to keep you upright as the water gets rougher. Shrinking back and leaning away from any obstacle in the river (a wave or a rock) always means trouble, especially if you find yourself sideways to the current.

Eddy Turns

Now you are ready to use the downstream brace and downstream lean to master something new: eddies and *eddy turns*. Eddies provide the principal resting spots in a whitewater run and can be used by the kayaker in numerous ways which we'll go into in later chapters. But first you need to learn how to enter and leave eddies without capsizing your kayak—a more likely occurrence than you might imagine. The only reason that eddies are a problem at all is because in the eddy the current's direction is reversed. Water in the eddy flows *upstream* with a few consequent surprises for the unwary kayaker.

In French the name for an eddy is *contre-courrent*, or *countercurrent*, and this term really tells the tale. If

31. The eddy turn, seen from above

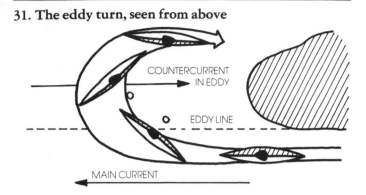

COUNTERCURRENT
IN EDDY

EDDY LINE

MAIN CURRENT

you innocently paddle into an eddy, here's what can happen. As you cross the eddy boundary, the back current within the eddy will grab your boat's nose and swing it around into an upstream turn. Unless you have anticipated this turning action with a preparatory lean of your body, momentum will keep your body moving in a straight line just long enough for you to find yourself thrown to the outside of the turn—and although this is the downstream side in relation to the river, it is really the upstream, or more exactly, the "upcurrent," side as far as the eddy is concerned; your outside edge will dip momentarily beneath the surface and over you'll go. But, of course, this happens only to the unwary. Now let's see how to make a proper eddy turn.

Suppose we are paddling diagonally downstream toward a large obvious eddy behind a rock near the left bank of the river. Our first task is to reach the eddy just behind the rock that forms it (not one or two boat-lengths further downstream where the eddy effect will already be dissipating). We also want to drive or punch through the eddy line with enough speed to carry us well into the eddy; otherwise we might just stall right on the eddy boundary, aimlessly drifting in the surface turbulence which often marks eddy lines. So here we go. With strong forward strokes we bear down on the eddy at about a 45° angle; as our last stroke drives the bow strongly through the eddy boundary, we lean into the coming turn, that

is, to the left. This lean is, of course, not only a tilt of
the body to the left, but also a tilt of the boat (by
raising the right knee). Remember that our eddy is on
the left so that the back water will tend to turn us
"upstream" to the left, and that left—in the topsy-
turvy world of the eddy—will also be downcurrent,
so that we will be leaning in the correct, stable direction. The more experienced kayaker anticipates the
eddy's effect by leaning into the turn a split second
before he really has to. At virtually the same time as
we begin to lean left (the nose of our boat is just driving across the eddy line), we are also reaching forward
on the left side with our paddle, all the way into the
backwater inside the eddy, where we will actually
support ourselves somewhat on a high brace to the
left.

32. The basic position in an eddy turn

If this sounds complicated, it is. The eddy turn is
to kayaking what a parallel christy is to skiing. Without it we won't have a chance in real whitewater. So
let's concentrate a little longer and build up a good
mental picture of this eddy turn. What does it feel
like? As your kayak slices through the eddy line (on
the left) you can feel the backwater of the eddy actually grab the nose and start pushing it left while the
main current continues to push on the stern, accen-
tuating this pivoting. In other words, it's the force of
the countercurrent that is making you turn, and not
your own paddle strokes. Since you have leaned into

the turn, you find yourself in good balance to ride the turning boat all the way around until its nose is pointed square upstream; you have "banked" into the turn like a cyclist or a skier. Once again, like a skier with his pole, you felt not only some support but a definite pivoting action around your paddle which you "planted" in the backwater of the eddy for a brace. The more decisively you perform all these actions—punch into the eddy, lean, and brace—the more dynamic and snappy your turn will be. Depending on the size, shape, and force of the eddy, as well as on your own technique, you can actually whip around into the eddy with a tremendous feeling of acceleration. No doubt about it, a good eddy turn is a real thrill.

But your first eddy turns won't be very good. You will probably not paddle into the eddy line fast enough; and your first attempts at leaning and bracing into the turn will be hesitant and only partly effective. You will avoid tipping, however, if you just commit yourself to some sort of inward lean, however tentative. In fact, our *ultimate* eddy turn will be even more complex, but more effective, because there is a special paddle stroke, called the Duffeck stroke or bow draw, that will really whip and pull you into the eddy. But this preliminary turn is plenty for starters. What you must do now is practice turning into and out of every easy-looking eddy that you see. It will really pay off. Before you can knuckle down to some serious practice, you had better learn how to come out of an eddy as easily as you got in.

Imagine that you're sitting in your kayak in that same eddy, on the river's left bank, that you've just turned into. Now you're facing upstream with the main current flowing by on your left. What you want to do is punch diagonally out of the eddy into the main current and—as you might expect—that current will once again grab your nose and swing you around in a left turn until you're heading downstream once more. It's really *the same thing exactly* as turning into the eddy. The only real difference is that this

33. Coming out of an eddy, seen from above

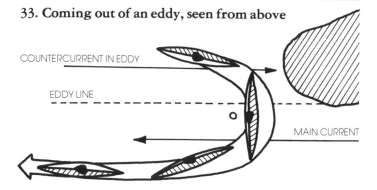

COUNTERCURRENT IN EDDY

EDDY LINE

MAIN CURRENT

time you are moving from the calm water of the eddy back into the action. But since the main current has more force, your high brace to the left will give you even more support. In getting out of an eddy you won't have much space in which to build up any speed before you punch across the eddy line, so it's important to take several really hard, vigorous strokes before you hit the eddy boundary. Back up a stroke or two, if you need to, in order to get this speed. Once again, the sequence is this: Drive diagonally upstream out of the eddy, and as soon as the front of your kayak is well out of the eddy start to tilt the kayak downstream and lean out on a downstream brace. How long do you stay in this tilted, braced position? Until your turn is more or less completed and your boat is well out into the cur-rent. In practice it's obvious. Remember: When turn-ing into or out of an eddy, if you're turning to the left, lean and brace to the left; if you're turning to the right, lean and brace to the right.

After a few successful eddy turns, you will begin to get a feeling for the opposing water, the counter-current, pulling and pushing at the nose of your boat as you cross the eddy boundary. You will begin to adjust the boat's tilt with your knees and hips more as a reaction to this feeling than as a result of intellectual prompting and visual clues. You should try some eddy turns, both in and out, without bracing on your paddle. If your kayak is tilted in the right direction you will both turn and stay up. The paddle brace is a kind of extra security, nice to have if you misjudge the tilt of the boat and a good way of forcing yourself into total commitment on each turn.

If you want to leave the eddy without "peeling off" in a downstream turn, you must try to break through the eddy boundary at a much "steeper" angle—more upstream, more parallel to the shore, less crosswise. This way the main current will not hit your bow broadside and sweep you away in a turn. Instead, you will be in position to continue across the river in an upstream ferry. Actually, it's rather hard for novice kayakers to get out of an eddy and into an upstream ferry without being swept away. It seems that as soon as the nose of the kayak starts to veer off downstream into a turn, all is lost. You just have to accept the fact that a turn has started, brace into it, and enjoy it. The secret of keeping your upstream orientation as you punch out of an eddy is a combination of a very "steep" angle relative to the current and as much speed as you can develop.

What else should you know about eddies? The eddy turn, both in and out, is a very basic technique, and most variations will develop from experience. Like rivers themselves, all eddies are different. Of course, it's also possible to back ferry or *set* into an eddy. This cautious, conservative technique is virtually never seen although it was once, apparently, quite common. Punching into an eddy nose first and whipping around upstream in a well-executed turn is more dynamic, more practical, and more fun. Just as it was hard to paddle your kayak in a straight line at first, eddy turns too will seem very awkward for a while. Keep at it. They get better and better, more and more fun, and, as we shall see in the next chapter, eddy turns are one of the key skills in running real rapids.

The Bow Draw

There is still one more refinement to work on before you can be really satisfied with your eddy turns—the *bow draw stroke*, or as it is sometimes called, the *Duffeck stroke*. By using this stroke rather than merely holding your paddle in the high brace position, you can add a lot of power to the kayak's own tendency to turn, snapping the boat around to catch even the smallest eddies. To get the hang of *draw strokes* in general, and the bow draw in particular, let us momentarily forget our eddy turns and find a calm stretch of river or a large calm eddy in which to practice. In all draw strokes, the kayaker essentially pulls, or "draws," his boat laterally toward the paddle, which he has "planted" in the water well to the side of the kayak. Of course, it feels as though you are drawing the paddle toward the kayak, but if executed quickly and powerfully, the boat too will move, sometimes a considerable amount. A draw stroke straight out to the

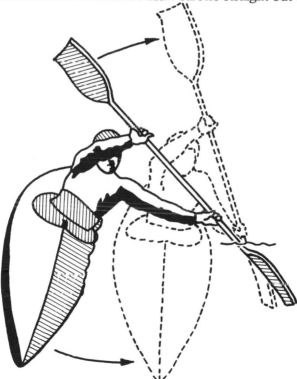

34. The straight or lateral draw stroke

side can be very useful in displacing your kayak laterally to miss a rock or obstacle and a draw stroke toward the front of the boat, a bow draw, will, as promised, greatly improve your eddy turns.

As a first step, try a draw stroke straight out to the side. Reach out into the water, just as for a high brace. In the high brace, you'll remember, we used the paddle much like a lever, pushing or levering up with our top hand in order to create an opposite downward push of the paddle blade into the water, which gave us support. In a draw stroke, however, the roles of the two arms are reversed. The upper hand (left hand if your draw stroke is on the right side of the boat) becomes the fulcrum, and most of the effort is supplied by the lower hand and arm (right, in this case) pulling the paddle shaft strongly toward the boat. The upper hand and arm will, of course, push up against the paddle, but more to fix its position than to apply power. Remember, it's the strong movement of the paddle toward the boat that is actually pulling or drawing the boat to the side. As in a good high brace, the boater must lean out and commit himself fully to the support of the paddle.

The bow draw used in eddy turns differs from the straight sideways draw stroke mainly in the unusual angle at which the paddle blade enters the water. To perform a bow draw on the right, for example, the arm and paddle movement goes like this: Reach forward with your right hand and paddle but at the same time, "open" or "cock" your wrist back to the right so that your right paddle blade rotates from its normal position (power face back) to one with the power face pointing slightly forward. To accommodate this reaching/twisting movement of the right arm and wrist, the left arm has naturally bent, raised, and more or less moved in front of your face, your forehead, or even slightly over your head, so that the whole paddle shaft is now on your right side, slanting down and forward but out a bit from the front of the boat. What a complicated position! you're probably saying to yourself. Yes, it is. The arm/paddle configuration used to

35. The bow draw or Duffeck stroke, showing position of arms

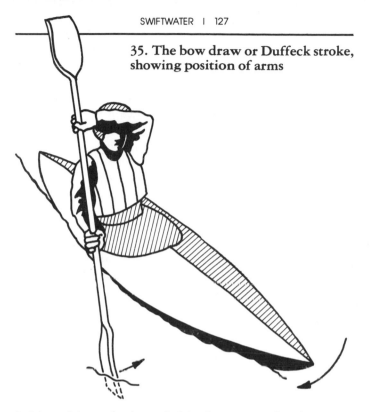

initiate this stroke is probably the most twisted-up position in all of kayaking, but it is highly effective. Take the time now to sit in a chair, holding your paddle in the normal position, and try to move it into the bow-draw configuration. Reread this paragraph and look at Figure 35 just to make sure you've got a feeling for what I've described.

So here we are, paddle blade rotated around and slanted forward. What happens when it enters the water? Nothing at all if you're motionless in stillwater; but if you're moving forward at a good clip, your forward-tilted paddle will enter the water much like a brake, catching and holding a lot of water with its forward-oriented power face. The effect is like planting a ski pole strongly to one side; in this case movement and momentum have been strongly blocked on the right side, so the boat begins to pivot around the paddle toward the right. Your arm position, which a minute ago seemed so awkward, turns out to be very strong for resisting the push of the oncoming water. Furthermore, now that the boat has begun to turn toward the "planted" paddle, you can increase the force of this turn by "drawing" the boat toward the paddle (or the paddle toward the boat). In the case of our right-hand bow draw, you will pull your right hand in toward the nose of the kayak, while to some extent pushing out and forward with your top hand for extra leverage. As the boat has already begun to turn toward the paddle, the power face will no longer be facing almost straight ahead but will instead be facing the side of the kayak, just right for a good draw.

Before you rush out to practice this stroke, and get very tired in consequence, here are a few final considerations, thoughts, and even a warning, about the bow draw or Duffeck stroke. This is a marvelous stroke and, when well-executed, a sure sign of the experienced kayaker. It also takes a good deal of time to master and employ effectively. You definitely won't get it the first time, or even the first day, you try. Fortunately you can make fine turns into and out of eddies without really using the bow draw. A static high brace is sufficient. In fact the only reason to mention the bow draw in this chapter is that logically it belongs with eddies and eddy turns, where it is most often used. (As your bow

36. Using the bow draw in an eddy turn

punches through the eddy line and you reach over into the eddy water, the countercurrent or reverse flow within the eddy will be directed straight against your rotated-forward paddle blade, giving even more power to the bracing, drawing action of the stroke.)

On the other hand, because it is a real hallmark of the experienced kayaker, the bow draw is the most commonly misinterpreted and poorly imitated stroke in all of kayaking. The worst offender is the neophyte boater who, although he is unable to get any effective drawing power from the stroke, cocks his upper elbow and forearm way back *behind* his head while imitating this stroke. Physiologically this is an awkward position

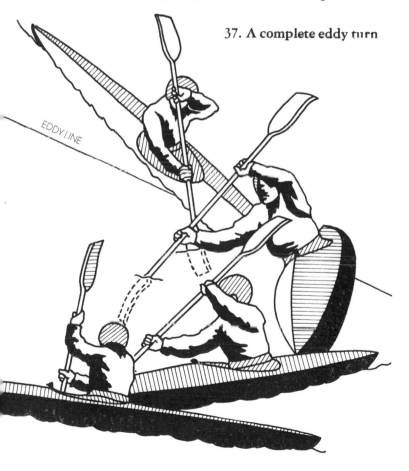

37. A complete eddy turn

EDDY LINE

indeed, and although a momentary surge of forces in the river may sometimes push an experienced paddler's upper hand temporarily behind his head, it's not a position to assume on purpose. Yet because it looks so extreme, almost spectacular, many beginners try to imitate this uncomfortable and ineffective position without actually gaining any force at the business end of the paddle. So beware, it's the action of the draw stroke, not the way it looks, that makes it important. In fact, it's a basic principle of sports physiology that extreme positions—extreme flexion or extreme extension of the limbs—should be avoided. In such positions, one can only react in one direction. And in the particular false interpretation of the Duffeck stroke just described the paddler comes very close to a possible shoulder dislocation—too close for comfort.

By the way, the bow draw's other name, the Duffeck stroke, comes from Milovan Duffeck, a Czech paddler who, although he didn't really invent it, popularized the stroke in international competition. Like the high brace, the bow draw is also considered a *hanging stroke* because the paddler seems to be suspended, at least momentarily, from his paddle.

Now then, enough theory. Before we get into real rapids in the next chapter, that basic eddy turn should become second nature. So practice a bit more before going on: paddle through the eddy line, lean into the turn, and brace. And again. And again.

CHAPTER 5

WHITE WATER

Finally we're ready for the real thing—*whitewater,* going down rivers through real rapids. It should be fairly easy as well as satisfying if you're conversant with most of the techniques discussed in the preceding two chapters. Getting right into whitewater actually requires no more new techniques, no new paddle strokes or maneuvers to learn. Instead it will be a question of adapting what you already know to a new context—rapids. So far, you've practiced kayaking skills in calm or smoothly flowing water rather than in rapids because it's clear that in the excitement of your first rapids you won't be able to concentrate on any specific skills; just getting through will be enough. But now the work is mostly over, and the fun about to begin.

In this chapter, we'll get into a bit more river lore—identifying special shapes and features found only in rapids, and learning how to "read" them from your boat or from the bank. Then we'll talk about your first rapids, maneuvering in whitewater, and finally about how to adapt your eskimo roll to rough water.

River Lore 2

What are rapids, anyway? Rapids, those fierce stretches of foamy-looking whitewater, are formed in several different ways. If the riverbed drops suddenly the current speeds up and becomes increasingly violent; if the river's channel is suddenly constricted, similar conditions result since the same amount of water is being "pushed" through a smaller gap. Rapids also occur where the river's flow is broken or obstructed by obstacles, such as great boulders, in the channel itself. In fact, most rapids result from some combination of these factors. For example, a landslide may partially dam a section of a river, backing up a large volume of water into a small pool above the obstruction. The water level in the pool is raised so much that when the water finally flows over the slide area it drops a greater distance in a narrowed channel, and encounters a lot of boulders along the way which further confuse its flow. A perfect classical rapid has been formed.

The number of rapids you encounter in a given stretch of river—and, to an extent, their fierceness—is greatly determined by the river's gradient: the number of feet per mile that the river drops. A gradient of less than twenty feet per mile usually indicates a moderately easy river, while anything over fifty feet per mile is truly fierce water. But average gradient doesn't tell you anything about the drop of one particular rapid, and the implied ease or difficulty of certain gradients can change drastically with different water levels.

Of course, no two rapids are ever quite the same, and each rapid is caused by a different combination of factors. Broad cascading rapids in desert rivers are vastly different from narrow constricted chutes and drops in high mountain streams. Nonetheless, there are a host of common features typically found in most rapids, and there are also a few typical sorts of rapids. Let's take them one by one.

The Anatomy of Rapids

At the top of most rapids is the *tongue*. The tongue is a large V-shaped patch of smooth slick water, with the point of the V extending downstream. Invariably, this tongue indicates the position of the swiftest, deepest current. In many rapids this is synonymous with the easiest and least obstructed line through, and therefore is often the preferred point of entry into the rapid. The tongue can be recognized not only by its characteristic V shape, but by the fact that it is the last smooth, unruffled water heading into the rapid. This narrowing sheet of smooth water—glassy green in mountain streams or muddy but slick in desert rivers—often extends deeply into the foaming white-water on either side of it. It's not only the most logical entry into a rapid, but the final calm before the storm.

Once into the rapid a variety of features present themselves and a variety of things can happen, but one thing you'll always find are waves, all kinds of waves. *River waves* deserve more than a second thought. In one sense they are the exact opposite of the ocean waves most of us are familiar with. In the ocean, the wave form moves but the water doesn't—that is, as the waves roll in toward the beach, the water at every point merely moves vertically, up and down, now part of a trough, now part of a crest, but not horizontally toward shore. In the river, however, the shape or form of the wave remains stationary, while water passes through it in a steady downstream flow. Thus permanent or *standing waves* are a regular feature in almost all rapids. It's often assumed that subsurface rocks

38. Standing waves in a river

PILLOW   HAYSTACKS, DIMINISHING IN SIZE

ROCKY OBSTRUCTION OR STEEPER GRADIENT

create these waves, but this is only part of the story. Standing waves of the most classical sort are formed wherever a fast jet of water slows down, as a way of dissipating the water's kinetic energy (the faster water, as it were, climbs up on the back of slower water below, forming waves). Waves are also formed when two local currents within the river meet at an angle, for example at a bend in the river where the main current may hit the outside wall hard enough to be deflected back upon itself, causing long angled rollers on the outside of the bend.

In general, though, it's true that most waves in most rapids are formed by rocks. We have already seen that a rock sticking out of the water will form an eddy behind it. Submerged rocks disturb the flow in much the same way, and in a vertical plane as well. Water humps up over the submerged obstacle, falls down into the void created on the other side and is driven back up to create a standing wave *downstream* from the submerged rock. If one wave of any significant size is formed it tends to create a series of other waves tapering off in size behind or downstream of itself, as it in turn becomes an obstacle to the river's flow.

The most regular, and often the most friendly waves, are the *haystacks* commonly found at the bottom of many drops. These haystacks are a succession of watery peaks and valleys, sometimes resembling the giant moguls or bumps found on today's ski slopes, which extend along the line of deepest water and strongest current (usually the center of the river) near the end of a rapid. They often continue on— with diminishing intensity—past the actual rapid into the seemingly flat river beyond, leaving two long, calm eddylike areas of still water on either side. Haystacks often disappear at low water levels, but they are almost as typical a feature at the bottom of rapids as the tongue is at the top. Haystacks are the river's way of dealing with an abrupt slowdown, and usually they indicate an unobstructed channel of relatively deep water. Therefore, even when rather big and awesome (kayakers sometimes disappear from sight between these waves), they don't usually represent a real problem.

Between the top and bottom of any rapid, you can find almost any sort of whitewater phenomenon, but typically you will encounter turbulence, obstacles such as boulders, and certain large standing waves whose troughs—referred to as *holes*—can create special problems for the kayaker.

Have you ever wondered why whitewater is white? Whitewater is *aereated water,* in which numerous air bubbles are caught and trapped in turbulent water that is being whipped around near the surface. It's the air in the water that turns it white. *Turbulence* is a chaotic tumbling of water, as opposed to the smooth flow of the current. Wherever the normal flow of water is broken or diverted or wherever two currents meet or "shear" past each other there will be some turbulence. Eddies, we have already seen, have boundaries, *shear lines* or eddy lines of turbulent water. Waves create lots of surface turbulence, as do rocks, both exposed or submerged. Whether or not turbulent water is of any consequence to the boater depends on how violent and confused its movement becomes. Generally surface turbulence only creates exciting looking whitewater to kayak through, but on occasion boils and whirlpools can form which give the toughest boaters pause. In other words, whitewater as such doesn't spell trouble, but areas of fierce and chaotic spraying foam should be avoided by beginning kayakers (and some who aren't beginners).

Big rocks and boulders within a rapid create some interesting situations. For one thing, they can divide the river into several channels, posing a route-finding problem for the boater. Sometimes you can see on which side of a big boulder the main current passes, and this is the way to go. But certain boulders have an ornery quality that makes them sit squarely in the middle of the main channel. In that case the novice boater not only doesn't know which side to aim for, but he is swept by this main current (at the time it seems like inexorable fate) right up against the rock which is dividing the river and threatens to divide his boat as well. It's reassuring to know that the water bouncing off such obstacles and flowing past on either side creates what is known as a *hydraulic cushion,* a kind of buffer which tends to make collisions with rocks a good deal less jarring than they might be otherwise. In the last chapter you already learned the proper reaction should you hit, or more important, should you broach sideways onto a rock in the river: *Lean downstream onto the obstacle.* This will keep the upstream edge, or gunwale, of your kayak out of the water, prevent you from tipping upstream, and possibly—in the worst of all cases—getting pinned upside-down against a rock. You can hold yourself on the offending rock with your hands and then push your way off, forward or backward, around one side or the other. This is such an important point that you'll be hearing this warning several more times!

Large rocks close together can create a series of small channels, which if they drop nicely are generally referred to as *chutes.* A rapidslike situation which is not actually a drop in the river can be created when numerous rocks block the main channel. Such spots are often referred to as *rock gardens,* and are great places to improve your skill in maneuvering the kayak—under pressure. And finally, large rocks in a rapid (or even some partially submerged ones) should not be viewed only as obstacles to negotiate or as potential troublemakers. They can also provide calm and comfortable eddies in the most horrendous rapids where the boater can rest, catch his breath, and look around without so much as a paddle stroke to maintain his position in the midst of literally tons of cascading, crashing water.

Something Special: Holes

Perhaps the strangest of all whitewater features is the *hole.* Holes are not actually empty spots or deep pits in the river—although many a boater has felt that he was about to be swallowed up and devoured by one. Holes are, in fact, large troughs or depressions formed just in front of or just behind certain big standing waves. As if holes weren't confusing enough to the beginning boater, they also have a bewildering variety of overlapping and loosely defined names: *souse holes, suck holes, stoppers, reversals, keepers,* and so on. Let's stick with a few descriptive names and see what holes are and what they do. But before plunging into our subject (so to speak) I hasten to reassure you that while holes are both common and important features of many rapids, they are *not* something a beginning boater has to deal with right away. They are more typical of moderate to very difficult rapids than they are of easy ones; and the first holes you encounter will doubtless be easy to avoid or to punch through. Yet in the long run, holes may pose problems, hazards, or out-and-out danger, so let's see how they work.

The first step in the formation of a hole is a big standing wave, usually produced by water dropping over a subsurface boulder, ledge, or rock. If this wave isn't big enough to block your progress downriver and a kayak can easily ride up and over it, it is usually called a *roller* and isn't regarded as serious. The first intimation we get of what holes are all about comes when a standing wave gets so big or so steep or both that the force of the current can no longer push a kayak over the top. Your downstream speed starts to push you up the face of the wave, but before you crest over the top, you lose momentum, slow to a stop, and slide backward into the trough at the foot of the wave. At this point it's quite usual for the neophyte to simply tip over from surprise. Such waves are appropriately called *stoppers* and act like a kind of hole, but not quite. Most stoppers will not, in fact, stop a kayak which is strongly paddled right into the wave rather than merely coasting with the current.

What distinguishes a true hole from big waves, rollers, and this kind of stopper is *recirculating water,* or water that's falling back on itself. Water behaves this way when the current pours over a rock or ledge so steeply or abruptly that in its downward fall it does create a kind of empty spot or hole in the river. At the bottom of such a drop, some of the water continues downstream as part of the deep current, and some is pushed back up toward the surface where it joins more surface water in trying to fill up the gap— that is, it tumbles back in on itself. This water falling back into the hole can range anywhere from a little harmless surface froth to something that looks like a big breaker in the ocean, curling back on itself and dumping tons of foamy water back upstream (such monsters are found in the Grand Canyon and on other big western rivers). But the basic pattern is the same: a sharp dip in the river's surface, creating such a steep climb-out on the other side that much of the water doesn't make it out over the next wave top but cascades back (upstream) into the hole. This is almost the same pattern we find in eddy water behind a rock, except that in a hole it takes place in the vertical plane, not the horizontal. Indeed, holes have been called "vertical eddies."

The most important question for the boater (more important for the kayaker than the rafter) is, How much water is getting out of the hole, and how much is being trapped and recirculated? Most holes of any size can be stoppers; that is, unless you're paddling hard they can easily stop your forward motion, sliding you back into the foamy bottom of the hole itself. But some can do more than that. The amount and force of their recirculating water is such that they tend to trap

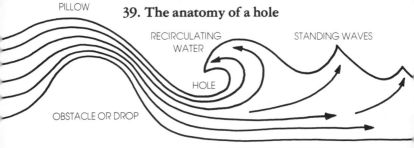

39. The anatomy of a hole

PILLOW

RECIRCULATING WATER

STANDING WAVES

HOLE

OBSTACLE OR DROP

DEEP "THROUGH" CURRENT

and hold you in their trough, whether you're in your boat or not; and escape from such holes requires some difficult maneuvering, desperate swimming, or even rescue from shore. Such heavily recirculating holes are appropriately known as *keepers*.

How do you judge which hole is which? General size and force of falling water are fairly accurate clues. Most smaller holes are easy to punch through and easy to get out of; most truly big holes are not. (A big hole is one where the falling-back water on the downstream side breaks over your head as you meet it bow first— but remember that in the seated position a kayaker rises scarcely more than two and a half feet above the water level.) But the shape of a hole is equally important in determining whether it is a potential keeper or not. A hole formed by a single submerged rock will not spread out very far to each side and is not likely to keep you. One formed by a broad ledge, however, can extend widely across the river, and is more likely to be a keeper. The clue here is how regular the shape of the hole is. A jagged-shaped, irregular hole isn't likely to be a keeper; and its irregular shape (with the downstream wave broken in several sections by differing amounts of foam, turbulence, or clear water) is a good indication that a lot of water is breaking through and continuing downstream. A boat or a kayaker is likely to be "flushed out" of such a hole if push comes to shove. A wide and extremely regular-shaped hole, on the other hand, is a danger sign. If the water falling into a hole forms a fairly smooth unbroken sheet, and the water curling back on itself on the other side forms an even, undifferentiated pattern, then look out; these features indicate that most of the surface water is indeed recirculating back into the hole and not flushing through. Such holes are the true keepers, and because of the action of the water—which in effect reverses direction and falls back on itself—they are often referred to simply as *reversals*.

Some of the very worst reversals you'll ever find in a river are not natural holes created by rocks or ledges in the riverbed, but are man-made. Small dams and weirs are the offenders, and the gravity of the problem is a result of the extremely regular geometry of such man-made barriers. Water pouring over a wier in a smooth drop of no more than a foot can form a reversal in which a hundred percent of the surface water is recirculating—with a lot of force, too—and only the deep current below the reversal continues downstream. Small dams and weirs are found in many nonwilderness streams and rivers, and are a real hazard because they look so innocent. The lucky boater may just shoot through, but if you broach and capsize in the reversal below a weir, you may be there a long time. The only alternatives for a boater caught in such a predicament are to dive deep in order to catch the main current beneath, or slowly to work oneself to one end or the other of the reversal in the hopes of breaking out the side. We'll expand on these alternatives in Chapter 8, but keep them in mind.

And by the way, if this discussion of holes, keepers, and reversals has sounded like a catalogue of horrors, it will be comforting to note that these awkward and challenging whitewater phenomena are only found in difficult and challenging rapids—not in all rapids, and certainly not in those which I hope you will tackle first.

That just about covers most of the common features found in rapids. And knowing what they are, we can now discuss the ranking and classifying of rivers and rapids in terms of the features they contain, the size of these features, and the difficulty or hazard of boating them.

Classification of Rapids

Rapids are commonly classified on a scale from one to six (sometimes written in roman numerals, sometimes in arabic), with Class 1 being the easiest and Class 6 either the limits of boatable water or flat-out impossible, according to different folks' definitions. Other systems (such as the so-called *western*

system, with its 1–through–10 ratings for Grand
Canyon-type rapids) have been developed, but the
one we're going to discuss is nearly universal. It
originated in Europe and was derived from the six-
grade climbing classification. The actual numbers
classify individual rapids but are often applied to a
whole river run, indicating either the most difficult
rapid or the average difficulty (for example, "a Class 3
run" or "a Class 3 run with one Class 4 drop").

Naturally, rating a rapid is a very subjective affair.
It is only meaningful if a number of boaters easily
agree on the same class. And of course, the class of a
rapid can change drastically with different water
levels, so most whitewater guidebooks will specify,
class such-and-such at so many cfs. Generally, rapids
will get tougher the greater the volume of flow, although some technical features do tend to get
"flushed out" and just disappear at very high water.
Big volume is still serious if only for its force and the
problems of stopping, landing, and rescue, so a Class
4 run can become Class 5 at higher water and Class 6
(virtually unrunnable) at flood stage. Rarely, certain
rapids even become more technical (involving more
rock dodging) at low water levels, gaining enough
difficulty to merit a higher classification.

Class 1 is very easy water, scarcely rapids at all.
Indeed, the commonest rapid formation at this level
is called a *riffle,* which is nothing more than a broad,
relatively shallow area (such as a gravel bar) with a lot
of small rocks on the bottom causing equally small,
choppy waves to be scattered about over the whole
surface. The greatest problem encountered is to
avoid scraping the bottom of your kayak. Class 1
water does not have very fast current, but it can contain small regular waves and distinct eddies. A Class 1
rapid would be neither very narrow, nor obstructed
with rocks, and there would be no doubt about the
best line to take through it. Naturally, Class 1 rapids
don't drop very much and a first-time beginner would
probably feel quite comfortable in one.

Class 2 rapids are still easy, but something more than just riffles. They drop more, can have faster current or a narrower channel, and even rocks and obstacles in the water, though these would be pretty easy to avoid. Waves are big enough to give one a real up-and-down feeling going over them, and eddies are sharp enough so that a boater will flip at the boundary line unless he can do a proper eddy turn. There may even be a couple of channels, but the right way to go is obvious. In short, Class 2 rapids should be very comfortable water for someone who has mastered the few basic boating skills. Beginning boaters probably won't tip over in Class 2 rapids; although they may feel excited, they won't feel threatened.

Class 3 rapids are moderately difficult (trivial for the expert, a little too much for beginners, and a good solid challenge for most intermediate boaters). In Class 3 rapids, for the first time, the kayaker encounters waves and holes that can stop him cold, or at the very least get him completely wet as his boat crashes through them. There are rocks here that absolutely have to be avoided and decisions to be made about which line or which channel in the river to take. In Class 3 water, too, confidence and suppleness become important for the first time, since a timid, stiff boater will flip right over when the first large wave hits him. In large western rivers, Class 3 often means nothing more than bigger waves—much bigger— than Class 2 waves but still regular and easy to get over. In the narrower rockier rivers of the East and Southeast, as well as in the mountain streams of the Far West and Northwest, Class 3 rapids often occur in a *pool-drop-pool configuration.* That is to say, although the drop may be a bit fierce, containing a couple of big rollers or a hole or two to avoid, it is also short, starting and ending in backed-up pools of relatively calm water where the boater can relax and get it all together again. In short, Class 3 is what we think of as real rapids, neither technically difficult nor dangerous, but still somehow quite serious. This is the sort of rapid you will be proud to get through if you're a beginner, and will still find very interesting even if you've been boating for a few seasons. To kayak Class 3 rapids reasonably you should have a strong eddy turn, a good downstream brace, a fair roll, and lots of paddling practice behind you.

Class 4 rapids are hard—so hard, in fact, that someone who comfortably boats Class 4 water can be considered quite an advanced kayaker (but remember, there is a difference between just squeaking through and feeling at home in a given rapid). Whereas a Class 3 rapid can usually be taken as a straight shot, Class 4 almost always demands some serious maneuvering in the midst of a lot of whitewater. Class 4 rapids have a steeper overall gradient and contain bigger individual drops, bigger and more irregular waves, and of course bigger holes that must either be avoided or correctly negotiated. A Class 4 rapid can be an unhealthy place to swim through; and should you go for a swim, you probably won't get any help from fellow boaters, at least until the actual Class 4 stretch is past, so you should have a solid eskimo roll. These rapids are serious enough that you won't want to run them "blind." Either previous experience or a good view from the top of a rapid is necessary, otherwise most prudent boaters would land and scout a Class 4 drop from the shore. If the rapid is short (of the pool-drop-pool variety) a Class 4 rapid will be significantly tougher than Class 3; but if a rapid is very long and continuous, this quality alone can raise the classification one notch. For example, a quarter mile of continuous Class 3 rapids without any calm water and few or no eddies to rest in could well be classified as Class 4, since it would demand a lot more from the boater than a short Class 3.

Class 5, as you can imagine, is very tough indeed. It is not only more difficult technically, it's dangerous —that is, if you are not equal to the paddling. For this reason, class 5 must be considered the province of experts only. Although it's hard to characterize Class 5 water precisely, any or all of the following might be encountered: horrendous holes; keepers and reversals; boiling, unstable eddies; big boulders and obstructed channels that require difficult maneuvering and precise timing to get through; powerful and irregular currents; a steep gradient with big violent drops; and big, irregular waves. In addition to a full range of paddling skills, it's pretty clear that the Class 5 paddler must have a bomb-proof roll and equal parts of experience and self-confidence. Class 5 drops usually must be carefully scouted from the bank and can be as physically fatiguing as they are technically demanding. It's interesting to note that the majority of active kayakers in this country have never run a Class 5 rapid, and most of them have no intention of ever doing so. Those boaters who are active at this level of difficulty usually boat such water more for the challenge than the fun of it. Even for experts, Class 5 represents the limit of reasonable boating. If you don't belong in Class 5 water but try it anyway, you will be asking for a broken kayak, serious injury, or worse.

Class 6, after all we've said, must seem virtually impossible. Some paddlers and whitewater guidebooks define it as just that. Others, bolder and perhaps more modern, say, No, Class 6 isn't impossible, but in fact represents the limits of the possible. Everyone agrees that a Class 6 rapid would be passable only under the best conditions (ideal water levels) by highly committed, expert paddlers, and even then only with considerable danger to their boats and themselves. Since this chapter, and indeed this whole book, is addressed more to beginning and average whitewater boaters than to hotshots, we won't spend much time talking about this extreme limit of difficulty except to make one point: not all rivers and not all rapids are runnable. This is not a totally obvious point. The beginner might be tempted to assume that no matter how fierce a given rapid looks, it could still be run by an expert kayaker far more skilled than himself. Not so. There are always limits (although it's true that these limits are pushed back little by little, generation by generation). To become an expert boater—kayaker or rafter—you must develop judgment as well as technique. It's good judgment when you tell yourself, Don't run this rapid now, you're not ready; you'd better portage your boat around it. It's also good judgment to say sometimes, This drop is unrunnable, period. Many rapids and falls are. And whitewater boating, although a high-risk sport, is also a rational one because boaters in general have recognized and respected their own limits. In short, there are rapids beyond Class 6, rapids that no one would try to descend. Knowing this is good for our egos, and it makes rivers in general just a little more mysterious, a little more wonderful.

Let's close this section on whitewater river lore with two encouraging thoughts. First, there are more than enough easy to moderate river runs (Class 1 to Class 3) in most parts of the country for even the most cautious, prudent or just plain timid beginners to kayak to their hearts' content. And we're only talking of whitewater. The number of streams and lakes available for flatwater canoeing and kayaking seems infinite. Second, our classification of rapids is only a technical one, having to do with difficulty and to some extent with danger. The esthetics of a river run completely escape such classification. In no part of the country is it necessary to boat the limit of difficulty to experience beautiful river valleys, canyons, and scenery. The esthetics of a run are highly personal, but many sportspeople, attracted to whitewater by its challenge and excitement, are shocked to find out how much they enjoy the calm-water stretches between rapids, just because it's here that they have time to take in the river's beauty. Rivers are like that.

Running Rapids

Now that you know what to expect in whitewater, let's work on adapting basic boating skills to this new dimension. Running rapids is what this whole book, and this whole sport, are all about. Learning how to run rapids in a fiberglass kayak isn't something you can do in an instant. You must first go through a whitewater apprenticeship, a period of consolidation as you become a solid intermediate whitewater boater. Finally, if you work long and hard enough, you can get really good—good enough to feel at home in even the fiercest rivers.

You've done your homework; the preparation phase of this apprenticeship is over; and you can almost hear the first rapids calling. So that's what we'll cover next—what to expect and what to do in your very first whitewater run. Then we'll go on to an ancillary skill, reading the river from your boat and from shore, and we'll end this chapter with a section on maneuvering in whitewater.

First Rapids

Perhaps no other boating experience will ever be quite as deliciously, spine-tinglingly exciting as your first run down real rapids. One of the ongoing charms of whitewater sport is the way a river, even the same stretch of river, is always changing, always different, always new. But still nothing will ever be quite as new as your very first rapid. Without wishing to spoil any of this novelty, I'd like to prepare you for some of the things that may happen, tune you up for your first true whitewater experience so that it will be a positive one. After all, it's better to enjoy all the novelty and excitement from the seat of your kayak, high and dry, than while swimming through the rapids with a succession of rollers breaking over your head. (I must confess, though, that I had to swim through my very first rapid, "Old Scarey" on the South Fork of the American River in California, and in fact didn't get through that particular rapid without crashing until my third try.)

Hopefully, your first downriver jaunt through rapids will be in the company of one or two experienced friends. This will spare you a lot of trouble in trying to "read" the water and pick the best line—or even having to get out of your boat to scout a rapid before you know what rapids are all about. (Reading water will be covered later in this chapter.) In addition to having a good guide or two, try to pick a well-known and rather easy river run, no harder than Class 2. Actually, if you feel both aggressive and confident with the skills learned so far even a couple of Class 3 drops probably won't spoil your trip, although they're very likely to get you wet. But for heaven's sake, don't choose a long and sustained intermediate run for your first whitewater paddling. Not only will you regret it, but your more experienced friends may get very tired of towing you and your gear to shore. Disorganized overambitious first trips have a way of turning into epics, real survival situations.

But not us. We've picked a comfortable Class 2 run, we are *not* alone, and we're ready to go. Often there's a certain delay at the *put-in* (boater's lingo for the beginning of a run), while one or two people shuttle a car or other transportation around to the *take-out* spot. (Several good strategies for shuttles are described in Chapter 9, *Practical River Touring.*) But this is a great time for a beginner, who may well be feeling a little excited and keyed up, to put his boat in the water and warm up (and loosen up as well) with a little paddling. Even if there is no waiting around and the group is about ready to push off, a short warm-up will certainly help. In the slack water near shore try a few bracing strokes to either side: lean over onto your paddle and lever back up with the classical high brace. Then holding your paddle in the air, rock the boat back and forth with your hips and knees, trying to stay loose below the waist, moving the boat, and moving *with* the boat, without actually moving your torso. Now perhaps try a few quick forward and backward strokes and a couple of turns, spinning the kayak around in place. Finally, ferry back and forth across the current just to get the feel of moving water again. You'll discover that a few minutes of such a paddling warm-up before heading downriver will really pay off. You'll feel much more relaxed and more confident.

Of course, the ultimate confidence builder before setting out is to quickly and smartly whip off a couple of rolls. However, in the excitement of your first big day on the river, rolls have a way of disappearing, especially if they were shaky to start with. So don't try one unless you feel quite confident in it. If you do, find a quiet pool of slack water or an eddy, check the depth with your paddle to make sure you have enough clearance, set up in rolling position and . . . over you go.

Now you're heading downstream, maybe pulling off an eddy turn or two, possibly coasting over some sparkling, choppy riffles, and waiting for that first real rapid to come into view. There is a myth about rapids roaring and about always being able to hear them long before you see them. It's true that many rapids do indeed roar; but the loud sound is often due to magnifying echoes off canyon walls. In many cases you may not hear the rapid until you're almost upon it. If you do hear it, the adrenalin will start pumping for sure.

The best bet for a beginner is to follow someone else through the first few rapids. You will doubtless start right in the tongue and take a straight shot through, riding over every last haystack until they disappear in the river below the rapid. If you are in a larger group, several of the more experienced boaters may want to run the rapid first, if only to find the easiest line for you to follow. The usual procedure is for the rest of the group—you included—to "park" in one or more eddies above the drop and wait for them to get through, as mid-rapids collisions can be both embarassing and wet. It's well to check with the leader or leaders in such a case to find out if they are actually going to take the easiest line through, or if they're looking for extra thrills in the form of side waves or even a small hole to play in. As a beginner you want to be pretty sure you're taking the easiest line.

Finally it's your turn. Probably following another boater but feeling very much alone for all that, you find yourself sliding down the glassy water of the tongue toward the confusion of foaming waves below. What now? The best advice at this point is to paddle, whether you need to or not. This is because the most common beginner's mistake in rapids is to freeze up, stiff and static, motionless and rigid in your boat, and this is just what you don't want. If you just paddle strongly ahead into the waves, you will be far more likely to stay loose and make a dynamic, not static, passage through the rapid. Furthermore, your alternating forward strokes on each side of the boat will tend to work like mini-braces, supporting you and correcting any slight imbalance or tilt to either side even though you are not consciously bracing at all. Finally, if you just keep paddling forward, you are much less likely to be stopped by any big wave or incipient hole you encounter. Should you see an extrabig wave or large foamy trough loom up in front of your kayak, dig in with a couple of powerful strokes and paddle your way right through it. That's it. Keep going . . . and now you're through. Your first rapid, and really, it wasn't as hard as you'd expected. . . .

As your first run continues through various rapids, you will doubtless relax more and more; and your confidence will increase with each rapid that you get through without crashing. Of course, if the run you've chosen is too hard, the opposite will happen, and by the time you reach the take-out, having swum most of the way, you may never want to see a kayak again. Unfortunately, this is a pretty common occurrence, so be conservative in your choice of a run, and don't let it happen to you.

The first few rapids, even riffles, that you go through may well pass by like a blur. But as you calm down and become accustomed to your new whitewater environment, you will grow more aware of what is happening between boat and water. You'll discover that even the most regular looking waves, as in the haystacks at the bottom of many rapids, aren't truly regular. They will invariably hit your boat from different angles, now from this side, now from that, even if you're trying to cross them all head on. Here, too, you'll discover what a good friend your boat can be—provided, that is, that you can stay loose and supple at the waist and hips. First one side, then the other side of your kayak will be lifted and/or twisted by the impact of different waves, but once you pass a particular wave the boat will settle back to its original alignment, and that's that. In other words, you don't have to correct or compensate for each unruly movement of the kayak. And you don't want to lose your balance as a result of all this rocking and tilting down at the water line. So by relaxing at the hips and waist you can more or less detach your upper body from the kayak, letting your body "float" quietly above the kayak, which occasionally behaves like a bucking bronco beneath you. This advice isn't absolute: there will be many situations in kayaking where you'll want to brace yourself solidly into your boat. But the beginner's most common mistake is to stiffen up and not give the boat its "head." (Those readers who are also downhill skiers will see the analogy between riding a kayak over waves and an expert skier riding over big moguls or bumps by relaxing his legs so the upper body can travel in a smooth line, unaffected by the roughness of the terrain below.)

The very same kayak which was so difficult to paddle in a straight line when you first tried it out in flatwater will track quite well in the faster, more powerful jets and currents of a rapid. Realize that your kayak can get through worse water than you might believe possible, almost on its own, and let it go.

Finally, a word about fear. You may experience no fear whatever on your first run through rapids, but many beginners do. Feeling fear doesn't mean you're unsuited for whitewater; it just means that you're normal. Even the superexpert has his threshold of fear, however high; and this fear coupled with well-developed judgment tells him when it's time to portage around unrunnable drops. But for the beginner, fear is harder to deal with. How much anxiety is okay? What to do about it? And how much fear is *too* much—a sign that this sport isn't for you? Before trying to answer these almost unanswerable questions, consider why they're so important. In the middle of a rapid, the whitewater kayaker is essentially alone. It's true that we go boating in groups, that other boaters can pick up lost gear, can help a swimmer to shore, and can sometimes perform daring rescues when someone's in real trouble. But still the kayaker is alone. It's you and your boat and the water, and this in itself can be frightening. Then, too, there are powerful forces about: literally tons of raging churning water. And in the back of every boater's mind is the knowledge that this is a dangerous sport, that one can be badly hurt or even drown running rapids. Such things have happened and continue to happen every year. True, serious accidents are rare and fatalities rarer still, and both can usually be attributed to obvious oversights or extraordinary bad luck. But an awareness that they can happen quite naturally adds fuel to any possible anxiety or fear the new boater may feel.

A certain amount of fear is not only natural, it's healthy. But because kayakers essentially go through rapids by themselves they must be capable of dealing with this fear, putting it in perspective, keeping it within reasonable bounds—and most important, not being paralyzed or incapacitated by it! So if your first rapid scared you, you simply have to figure out *for yourself* if it was too much or if you can keep this natural fear under control. Because if you can, there are some fine strategies to build up technique and confidence and overcome your fear altogether. If, on the other hand, your first whitewater adventure turned out to be the most awful, frightening thing you've ever done, far better to realize it, admit it, and from now on enjoy your whitewater comfortably from a raft.

For those who were scared but not too much, for those who know themselves to be timid or nervous but still got a real thrill from shooting the first rapids, here's what to do. First, ignore the ultrafast progress of other beginners you may know who are either very brave, very skilled, or have a background in similar water sports (such as surfing, or flatwater canoeing) which permits them to do things in a kayak you wouldn't dare. Second, spend more time than you normally would in the practice pool or pond and in easy nonwhitewater stretches of the river, practicing and perfecting the basics: paddle strokes, eddy turns, braces, ferrying, and above all rolls. If you accomplish a roll in flatwater and then repeat it literally hundreds of times, day after day, it will ultimately become a semiautomatic reaction to tipping over, and you'll find yourself rolling up in whitewater whether you believe you can or not. There is no confidence builder like a strong eskimo roll, and it's safe to say that without it you'll never boat any but the easiest rivers, and nervously at that. In short, build up your kayaking technique to a level of proficiency well above what you would normally need as a beginner for easy river runs, and your confidence in rapids will soar.

Next, avoid challenging situations at first. Make up your mind to spend a lot of time boating very easy stretches of water, letting confidence and technique grow slowly, bit by bit. Thus, having "survived" a particular Class 2 rapid, don't follow the urging of impatient friends and go with them to a harder Class 3 run next weekend. Instead find someone who will repeat the run you've already made with you; maybe do it several times more till you've really got it mastered. It's terribly important to let the people you're kayaking with know exactly where you are in terms of technique and confidence (or lack of it), and to find companions who are patient, helpful, and supportive while you are working on building up your skill and reducing your apprehension.

Finally, try to be mentally prepared for river situations. Something you're not expecting will shake you up a lot more than an eventuality you've pictured to yourself. For example, on your first run through rapids you're going to get wet. Waves will hit you, splashing in your face, maybe hard enough that you'll have to shake the water out of your eyes before you can see where you are going again. If you're ready, this will seem normal. The other thing most beginners are never ready for is tipping over in whitewater. If you're lucky, you'll remain upright through every rapid on your first trip, but at least one crash is usual. What surprises and frightens some beginners when they do crash is the confusion and turbulence they encounter underwater. When you fall in rapids you feel as if you're being pushed, pulled, and pummeled by the water all at once. Unless you grip you paddle hard and tuck quickly into rolling position, the paddle itself may be pulled out of your hands. In any case, turbulent water is nothing like the calm stillwater of the practice pond, where you are able to do wet exits and, later on, rolls with no problem. Being underwater in a rapid can feel as though you're being churned in a giant washing machine, especially if you're not prepared for it. Under such circumstances, it's no disgrace if your newly learned roll disappears altogether, or if you even forget to try it in your haste to get out of your boat. (Rolling in tough whitewater is a special trick which we'll cover at the end of this chapter.) If you're expecting all this, however, it's no big deal. If it hits you unprepared, you may feel that you've been pounced on by a gang of trolls and beaten with cudgels.

Perhaps the above advice isn't for you. If you're confident and aggressive, and only feel more excited with each new rapid, well and good. This is your sport and still more excitement lies ahead. But try to be patient and understanding with those who are a little more timid, a little more hesitant than yourself. One of our concerns here is with women. Young boys are usually taught not to admit they're afraid, even when they are. As young men learning to kayak, they will very likely bluff it through, and after a few whitewater runs, their technique will improve and their fear all but vanish. Not so with many women. Women's reactions to fear and stress—in our society anyway—

are more honest than men's. But admitting that you're scared isn't the same thing as saying that whitewater kayaking isn't for you. Take your time, find your own pace, and build up your confidence slowly. Above all, don't let yourself be bullied into trying ever harder rapids by a husband, boyfriend or other male companion who makes the mistake of assuming that you're just as macho as he is. Women make superb whitewater kayakers, and can accomplish with technique and finesse what many men can only do with brute force. But every year too many women are scared out of the sport because they get hustled into it too fast and too hard. Don't let this happen to you or to a lady you're fond of. Men who are honest enough to admit that rapids scare them had better follow this advice too.

Fear is a nebulous yet terribly important aspect of whitewater boating. It's opposite is confidence—not rashness, but the assurance gained through knowledge and technique. But enough about fear. Hopefully, you've enjoyed your first run through rapids; to make sure that succeeding ones go even better, you'll need still more knowledge, still more technique. Now you must learn to read the river and maneuver in whitewater.

Reading the River

Reading water is an art, and like any art it takes time to master. Experience and patient observation will teach you far more than I can outline in a few pages. But there are some general patterns that can help you make sense out of your first experiences.

Most of the time you will be reading the river from your kayak. Since the kayaker is essentially sitting in the water, his view of things is somewhat limited (both rafters and canoeists sit higher off the water); and instead of seeing the whole shape of a river feature as one does from above or from the bank, the kayaker learns to recognize some sign or indication of the upcoming river feature, a kind of river shorthand.

But before looking ahead you should become sensitive to the movement of surface water all around you. This is easy to see and can tell you a lot about the currents beneath. There are usually a lot of lines, ripples, mini-waves, wind ruffles, and so forth on the surface; a river is far from an undifferentiated mass of flowing water. Look for the tiny line of bubbles and swirls that marks even the gentlest eddy line. As you cross a relatively still pool in the river, look for patches of moving surface water—a kind of river within the river—that tell you where some current is flowing through the pool. You're not after hard information at this point; rather, you want to build up a sensitivity to and an awareness of patterns of moving water. You can do this even when you're not kayaking at all. Just by watching the flow in a tiny brook, for example, a stream far too small to kayak in, you can build up your awareness of moving water and spot typical patterns which repeat themselves on a larger scale in big rivers. Even a rain gutter rushing by outside your house can exhibit micro-eddies, standing waves, and reversals—all in miniature. Thus, the very first step in learning to read water is to pay attention to water, all moving water, whenever and wherever you find it.

Next, focus on the river, but not on rapids. Earlier you learned to spot eddies by the rocks that cause them. Now look more carefully at the surface of the river ahead of you to spot evidence of submerged rocks. Rocks just below the surface produce a humping-up or *pillow* of water on top of themselves and a shallow depression in the water just downstream. If the overall surface of the river is somewhat rippled or choppy, then a smooth or glassy patch can be a telltale sign of a large flat rock just beneath the surface—the kind of rock you always scrape over at first, even though it's the only rock in the whole river! Conversely, if the river's surface is relatively smooth, a small patch of foamy water would signal the presence of a rock just in front of it.

Your ability to read water becomes more crucial

as you approach the top of a rapid. Ideally, the novice will have a more experienced companion leading the way, but everyone, novice included, will want the best possible view of things before launching into the drop. To get such a view it's common to start back paddling as you approach the drop. Not only does this give you a lot more time to see what's down there, but also you can easily back ferry right or left to line up in the middle of the tongue. If the current near the head of the rapid is too swift for you to maintain your place by back paddling while you look things over, it's often best to *eddy out* in the last feasible eddy before the drop and look things over from there. Of course, if the rapid seems challenging or problematical and you can't see a good line through it from your boat, you will want to land and scout it from shore—but that's another story.

The first function of river reading is to help you avoid obstacles; the second is to pick the right route. The latter comes into play, for example, when there are several tongues, or chutes, leading into a rapid. In general (but not always) you will want to follow the main current—the strongest and deepest—and you must be able to determine which is which. Size and length of the tongue, size and regularity of any standing waves you can see below it, even the color of the water can give you a clue as to where the deepest channel lies. There is no hard and fast rule for distinguishing the main channel but as a beginner you should make a guess and compare it with the (hopefully correct) decision of the more experienced boater who is leading you down.

Often the obvious line or main current through the rapid is split by a big boulder partway down. Again, in this situation you will want to look ahead and identify the main channel of the split—where most of the water is going—and follow it. If you select the wrong channel, the force of the main current may keep you from reaching it, and if you do nothing you may well broach against the rock itself. Look for the wider channel, higher standing waves, more foam, or any other indications of greater volume on one side. With time such judgments tend to become almost automatic; meanwhile, it's a lot better to have an experienced kayaker in the lead, reading the water and making such decisions. To make sure that the boaters following him get the message, the leader will want to use a very simple set of *prearranged* signals. These are usually and most easily made with the paddle: holding the paddle up at a 45° angle to the left means go left, same thing on the right, and pointing the paddle straight up overhead can mean stay in the center or take it straight. Some boaters agree that if the leader holds the paddle horizontally overhead with both arms extended it means: problems ahead, stop, eddy out, and wait. Whatever signals you use, they should be simple and few.

Scouting a rapid from the bank is another story altogether. In the first place, getting out of your boat to look means you're already concerned about the difficulty. Add to that an optical effect which makes whitewater look even fiercer from above (the same way a cliff looks steeper from the top), and you can see the problem. Although you may indeed spot the best route through from up there, you may also scare yourself to the point where you tip over from sheer nervousness. However, forewarned is forearmed, so you should mentally adjust for the fact that everything looks a little harder from the bank (especially if you're standing high above the water).

Most of the features already discussed are equally or more obvious from the bank, but one thing is particularly easy to spot from above: white versus blue water (or green, or brown as the case may be). Large patches of blue water in the middle of an otherwise white rapid usually indicate eddies—often not clearcut, typical back eddies but *partial eddies,* sometimes caused by mostly submerged rocks. Eddies within a rapid can have a double significance. They may work well as temporary resting spots, places to stop as you descend the rapids; but, more likely for an unwary beginner, an unseen eddy in the middle of a rapid can reach out and snag your boat when you least expect it. Your bow may inadvertently cross a shear line between currents (an eddy line) and be held by the counter current while the stern swings around. Suddenly you'll find yourself finishing the rapids backward. Should this happen, don't panic; it's usually not worth the struggle to try to turn back around and, believe it or not, your kayak will work just as well backward as forward. On the other hand, the better you understand the water, and the more potential traps, detours, and obstacles you can spot when you scout a passage from the shore, the smoother your run will be. Likewise, if you've gotten on a hard river run—despite all urging to the contrary—and in your attempt to scout a tough rapid you can't see any reasonable line through, then for heaven's sake, don't just get back in your kayak and resign yourself to a bad trip! Portage instead. As your boating skills develop, so will your ability to read water, and soon you will be spotting obvious lines where before you saw only a chaos of foam.

Maneuvering in Whitewater

In your first rapids you were content to line up at the top and then go straight. If a more experienced kayaker told you that halfway down you should paddle to the left, you would look at him in disbelief. Yet after a few whitewater runs, you can now clearly see the necessity for maneuvering within the rapid itself: realigning yourself, avoiding obstacles, moving right or left, slowing down and speeding up, and finally rolling.

We've already seen that you can be inadvertently turned sideways or backwards in the middle of a rapid. Learn to avoid this with a hard reverse sweep/ low brace to the rear quadrant whenever you feel your nose start to veer off of its direct line. Such corrective braces are especially useful for staying lined up as you crest over a series of big haystacks at the bottom of a rapid. Here you want to wait until your boat is just coming over a wave, poised on the very top, before applying the paddle to the top of the wave, right behind you. Since the nose and stern of the kayak are momentarily in the air at this point, your corrective stroke will get the maximum result, whereas if you try to turn when buried in the trough between two waves you'll just be wasting your strength. (Like the skier who turns at the crest of the bump or mogul, you want to pivot your boat back in line at the moment of least resistance.)

But, of course, sometimes you will get twisted out of line with the rapids and find yourself going sideways. To learn to handle this situation (and because

40. Drifting sideways through a rapid on a downstream brace

it's fun), pick an easy series of low and regular waves and practice taking them sideways on purpose. The trick here is to use the security of a downstream brace, reaching over the crest of every wave to brace the paddle in the downstream water on the other side. Floating along motionless with your paddle held in a high brace position on the downstream side would probably work fine, but some unexpected little variation in a wave form could conceivably sink your paddle if you lean on it too long, so it's better to keep reaching downstream over the crest of each new wave for a brace. This is the way you will handle far bigger waves and even holes later on. You can try this sideways approach on progressively bigger waves, but once you get used to being sideways in a rapid you are ready for some real maneuvering.

Timidity and hesitation are the real problems in whitewater. On first encountering a situation that involves moving sideways in a rapid—say, for example, that at the top it's easiest to stay on the right side, but at the bottom one must move left to avoid a hole— the neophyte will usually turn the boat's nose a few degrees and take a few ineffective paddle strokes with neither the hope or the conviction of getting where he wants to go. You simply have to believe it's going to work . . . and go for it.

To move laterally in a river you have several choices: you can use a draw stroke, which may move you sideways a foot or two, no more; you can back ferry; you can turn sideways to the current and stroke out for shore; or you can turn completely around to face upstream and do an upstream ferry. In whitewater, your choices may be more restricted. A draw stroke works fine to pull your nose just to the right, or left, of a sudden obstacle, such as a small rock, that looms up before you. But this stroke must be applied quickly and strongly, and it generally takes some time before beginners can use it effectively in whitewater. But a draw stroke or two is not sufficient to move you and your boat to another part of the rapid. Back ferrying is great where it works, because it slows you down and gives you more time to get where you want to go. But in rapids the foamy, aerated nature of the water and it's uneven unsteady surface make holding a precise ferry angle and executing a good back ferry difficult—except in riffles and gentle regular Class 2 water. An upstream ferry is even more problematic, since you must turn all the way around, and in many rapids you'll have neither the strength nor the control to do this. So by far the best solution in the majority of cases is to turn your boat sideways and paddle like hell. Beginners are hesitant to do this because the sideways position looks like trouble in turbulent water. However, after running several easy rapids sideways on purpose, you'll no longer feel timid about this.

A good rule of thumb for your maneuvering strategy in rapids might be this: If the main problem is large waves, holes, or hydraulics (heavy current effects) then forward speed will help you punch

through. If the main problem is rocks and similar obstacles (for example, a rock garden), then back paddling and back ferrying will be more helpful in avoiding collisions. And, finally, since it's easier to slow
down and speed up than to move laterally in a rapid,
try to pick the right line at the start and stick to it.

Aside from the rare stopper or souse hole that a
beginner may encounter in easy rapids, rocks are the
commonest source of crashes and spills—plus the
complicated countercurrents, shear lines, unexpected
eddies, and foaming hydraulic cushions that go with
them. You've already learned to lean onto any rock
on which you have the misfortune to broach. It's a
good rule always to lean onto, or brace into, *any* obstacle you encounter in your downstream path—a
sudden wave, an awkward curling eddy fence, a jet of
water pouring sideways off a boulder—you'll probably remain upright if you do. But sooner or later you
will tip over in the middle of a good fierce rapid, right
where you least wanted to. What then?

As river rolls are harder than rolls in a swimming
pool, likewise, rolls in rapids, in turbulent water, or in
big waves, are that much harder than rolls in
smoothly flowing current. To have a chance of succeeding you must be quite determined, and you must
practice in rapids. No, not in the thick of the action,
but in safe, deep water near the end of a series of nice
regular haystacks at the very bottom of a rapid (with
an inviting pool of calm water just below, in case).
Most folks have a preferred rolling side, the right side
for most of us. So having picked your spot, paddle
from a side eddy out into the last waves so that you
are crosswise to the current with your *right side*
downstream. Now, put your paddle in rolling position and capsize to the left, upstream, and roll back
up on the right side, downstream. This is the easy way
to roll; as you come up on the downstream side, the
current will add power to your sweep and help the
bracing action during the final recovery phase. At
first it's best to stack all the cards in your favor. If it
works (and it will) try several more rolls, possibly

venturing further upstream into bigger haystacks to get more of the feeling of a whitewater roll.

All well and good. But in real life when you're descending real rapids you can't be assured of always falling toward the easy side, of always rolling up downstream. If you're lined up with the current when you crash, there won't be any downstream or upstream side, so you shouldn't have any special problems—or any help—from the current. But should you get sideways and tip so that you find yourself trying to roll up on the upstream side, you'll surely have trouble. If the current is strong, it will doubtless sink your paddle right at the end of the roll since you will be in an upstream brace position—a classical no-no. What do you do? Be patient, try again. Remember that the powerful inverted sweep at the start of a roll has the effect of turning your boat, just as a normal upright sweep stroke would. So after one, or at most two tries, you will no longer be coming up on the upstream side . . . and your roll will work.

In no special order of importance, here are some thoughts and suggestions about getting your roll to work in whitewater. In rapids, for the first time really, it is imperative that you assume the protective tucked-forward position when you tip over. You know there are hidden rocks about, and you don't want to take a chance of being hit in the face. The top of your helmet can take a terrific blow safely. (My own helmet has numerous scratches on it from just such rocky encounters.) Second, stay calm and patient underwater. The two most common reasons for missing a roll in whitewater are: failure to set up properly (being in too much of a hurry to roll up) and trying to lift one's head out of the water too soon in a panicky reflex to get air (again, too much of a hurry). The cure for both is the same. Stay underwater a little longer; force yourself to be calm and collected; set up for the roll carefully, scrunching your body up close to the surface of the water, and feel with your paddle (perhaps slapping it) on the surface to make sure it's at the right angle before you start. And then, when everything's just right—pow! a strong vigorous roll. It'll work. If you've tipped in the middle of big waves, you can become quickly aware of the up and down movement of the water around you and time your sweep to coincide with an "up"—this will lend force to your roll. The hardest river rolls are in foamy, bubbling, aerated water where you can neither feel nor grip the surface with your paddle blade for a good sweep. These rolls will defeat you at first and, in fact, no matter how good your roll becomes, there will always be some spot somewhere that will defeat you and send you swimming. Yes, even experts and champions do swim, but not often. Still, your goal, like theirs, must be: Never swim!

To really make your whitewater rolls work, you need determination and lots of it. If your first attempt doesn't work, don't get out of your kayak. Each time a roll fails at least you get a breath of air; so don't worry about that. Just force yourself back into rolling position, reorganize your paddle, think a moment about what you might have done wrong, and then try again. And again. If you're trying a screw roll, then after a couple of failures I would suggest sliding the paddle shaft forward to get an extended grip—the extra leverage should do the trick. Yet no technique will help as much as the simple determination to *make that roll.* It may sound easy to keep trying to roll while you're reading this book at home, warm and dry, but it is another matter altogether to keep trying when you feel as though someone is trying to beat you up and drown you at the same time, upside-down in cold, turbulent water. But a determined effort is worth it, and it will work. One friend of mine jokingly refers to an eskimo roll in real rapids as a combat roll, as if to underscore its seriousness. There are few things quite as satisfying as righting yourself after an upset in heavy water. Your first unplanned roll in whitewater will not only be a kind of moral victory; it will also be your passport to new worlds of advanced boating. Without a strong river roll you can't go far.

Indeed, everything we've covered in this chapter

has been only an introduction to the world of white-water, the realm of rapids. Where do we go from here? How does one become a really good kayaker? In truth, only time and the river can turn you into a whitewater expert. But to sharpen your skills and speed you on your way, we'll go into a few more steps, techniques and tips, and a little more river lore in the next chapter, *Wildwater.*

CHAPTER 6
WILDWATER

Having learned to paddle, learned to roll, learned to boat easy and even moderate rapids with confidence, where do we go from here? Probably by now you've had the opportunity to observe a couple of expert kayakers or at least quite good ones, in action. Unlike yourself and other beginners, they're not content just to get through the rapids. In the middle of what must seem to you like horrendous water, they can stop, look around, dart back and forth, almost dance on the water, accomplishing more with one or two relaxed paddle strokes than you can with a furious sustained burst of paddling. These expert boaters have really come to terms with the whitewater environment. They are in their element and you can see it by the relaxed exuberant way they play in the rapids.

Playing is the key to this chapter on wildwater. As we pointed out in the Introduction, wildwater is less a precise term than a good image to describe the more advanced aspects of whitewater boating (although the term wildwater has traditionally been used to designate downriver races). "Playing," on the other hand, does have a very specific meaning for kayakers, as we'll see, and playing in rapids is the very best way to break into the world of advanced whitewater kayaking. In addition to playing in rapids, this chapter will cover specific features found in harder rapids and techniques for handling them, and finally will touch briefly on "heavy hydraulics," kayakers' slang for the very biggest water and the limits of the kayaker's art.

The advice in this chapter, however, will be less specific and far more condensed than that given up to now. In kayaking, as in many other sports, the first steps are simple, precise, and easy to express—it only takes a few days to go from no skills at all to the level of a competent beginner or even an aspiring intermediate kayaker. But then the pace slows and the path is no longer so obvious. There are many ways to become a strong kayaker, but all of them take time. There are no short cuts. Becoming an advanced kayaker, much less an expert, takes patience, repetition, good models to copy, and above all many rapids and many days on the river. It's possible only to sketch out the general approach to getting hot, not to guide you step by step. On the other hand, the thrill of discovery will be constantly with you. And, truly, in advanced kayaking getting there is at least half the fun.

Playing in Whitewater

To the kayaker, playing has a very specific meaning. In one sense it's almost the opposite of "running" rapids, because the boater at play in whitewater tends to remain in one place, working his kayak in opposition to the current, counteracting the river's force instead of allowing it to sweep him away downstream. We can best define playing, then, as that whole range of whitewater maneuvers in which the boater is not actively trying to get through the rapids. And by the way, rubber rafts cannot play in rapids; this exhilarating sport-within-a-sport is really only possible in kayaks or decked whitewater canoes.

Typically, kayakers do most of their playing in the large, well-formed waves found near the bottom of a drop, although truly skilled boaters can play in every part of a rapid. Typically, too, the kayak will mostly be kept facing upstream when playing, although virtually every other configuration is possible, even standing on end, as we shall soon see.

To the less experienced kayaker the very term play often appears to be a misnomer. What the better kayakers seem to be doing at the foot of these rapids looks a lot more like work than play; and indeed it will take a while before your first attempts at playing have anything at all playful about them. It also looks rather precarious at first, and it's certain that you need a good roll if you're going to get anywhere. But remember that playing in rapids is not only the fastest and easiest, but probably the safest way to develop and test your whitewater technique. If you can play in Class 2 water then you can comfortably boat Class 3; if you can play in Class 3 then you can safely handle Class 4, and so on. Now, how do you get started?

Getting Started

Before we can start playing, we want to be sure we're in the right spot and then take a look around to see exactly what the water is doing. You are already familiar with haystacks, the regular standing waves below many rapids. Haystacks, of course, lie in the main channel or deepest part of the river, and long slackwater eddies are usually found on either side. The next time you encounter this configuration, don't just ride over all the haystacks, one after another. Instead, as soon as you can, turn and paddle for one of these large side eddies; catch it with a good eddy turn, and then, when you are sitting comfortably in the slack water, bow upstream, take a good look at the waves out to your side. Each wave has an upstream and a downstream face, and it's the *upstream face* that particularly interests us. Here the cur-

**41. Ready to surf: the boater facing
upstream beside a set of regular waves.**

rent forces water uphill toward the crest of the wave.
If we can manage to put our boat in the right position
on the upstream face of a wave, we can balance out
two opposing forces: gravity will be pulling us down
the wave (upstream) while the current pushes us back
up (downstream). And caught, poised between these
two forces, we can do some mighty nice things with
the kayak.

Generally your first introduction to playing will
involve nothing more than sitting motionless in your
kayak, parked in the slackwater eddy, and watching
more experienced friends paddle bravely out to
"surf" on the upstream sides of standing waves. Pay
attention to what they're doing and build up a clear
mental picture of it. Even if you don't dare try it in
big waves, you can repeat the pattern in easier waves
on an easier stretch of river.

Before you learn to surf, or ride waves, it's a good
idea to practice some exciting high-speed ferrying
back and forth across the line of haystacks or standing
waves. The ferrying we've done so far (back ferrying
or upstream ferrying) has depended on maintaining
the correct angle to the current and paddling hard
enough to cancel out the river's speed. Now you're
going to attempt to slide across the line of waves with
hardly a paddle stroke, truly *ferry gliding*. To do so,
still facing upstream, paddle forward and out of that
slackwater eddy, but not at such a crosswise angle that
you'll be swept away by the main flow in a downstream turn. This is nothing new, you've done it every
time you've come out of an eddy. But you probably

haven't yet paddled out of a side eddy into such big waves. As before, when you enter the main current you will want to raise the upstream edge of your kayak (assume a downstream lean) and reach your paddle downstream in the high brace position. What happens? Without paddling, you should feel yourself move rapidly sideways across the haystacks to the other side. This is because every time your kayak happens to get on the upstream face of one of the waves, it will start to slide down it. This upstream movement gives you the forward speed necessary for a good ferry. If you managed this ferrying maneuver right square on the upstream face of one good wave, you would probably have shot all the way across on the face of this one wave—but chances are you didn't. You were probably swept downstream somewhat as you moved sideways, and it was the upstream faces of several waves in succession that gave you the needed "push" to get across. With a little more practice you'll be able to drive out of the slackwater eddy right into a good ferrying position on the upstream side of whatever wave you've chosen, and then— watch out! The speed with which the wave shoots you sideways will really surprise you. It's powerful and sudden, but if you have the correct (downstream) lean and tilt, then you can just ride on your downstream brace, and no matter what hits you or how much foam flies in your face you won't crash.

Naturally once you've passed across the line of haystacks and hit the other slackwater eddy, you must rapidly reverse your lean and tilt—but you should be familiar with this necessity after all our practice with eddy turns. Try to recognize the eddy water by feel as much or more than by sight. Some new force grabs the bow of your boat, the ride is over, and *voilà,* you respond with the proper tilt of your hips to coast safely in to a stop. Suppose you're crossing the current to your right. You will be leaning right as you ferry across facing upstream, and then in the new eddy you'll switch to a leftward lean. That response should be nearly automatic by now.

Surfing Waves

After you get the hang of high-speed ferrying across bigger waves, you'll be ready to get into true river *surfing*. Surfing in a river bears the same relation to ocean surfing as river waves do to ocean waves; that is, it's almost the converse. In the ocean, both the wave form and the surfer move through space (surfers often speak of a "long ride"). But in the river, both the wave form and the kayak surfing it appear to be motionless; it's the water beneath which is in constant, often violent motion. To surf a standing wave in the river, the kayaker must put his boat into some kind of equilibrium between competing, opposing forces—between the tug of gravity pulling down the upstream face of the wave and the force of the current pushing you backwards up the wave and trying to sweep you on downstream. (In this case the kayaker is facing upstream.) It's not easy at first to find such equilibrium. You will lose it time and again, and be swept away downstream. But it's fun trying, and even more fun when you get it. Once you do get it, the feeling is anything but static—so much water is rushing by underneath, that it is just as if you really were moving at a good clip. Quite a thrill!

To begin surfing your kayak, you'll need a good stretch of river with at least one big, smooth, well-formed wave. You'll need to have other boaters around who can already surf pretty well so you can watch and imitate, since figuring out the nuances and timing yourself is almost impossible. And, finally, you'll need some conviction. The truth is that most beginning-to-intermediate kayakers can't catch waves because, subconsciously at least, they don't *want* to. They don't really want to be out there in that foaming trough in front of the wave, not sure which side to brace on, expecting at any second to tip over, and worst of all not really confident in their roll. So it's far better to wait a while, sit tight in those eddies and watch the better boaters play. Soak it all in and form a clear image of what surfing is all about until you're

42. Surfing the crest of a well-formed wave

sure you want to do it. Then go for those waves with everything you've got!

The trick in catching and "holding" a wave is to get to the right spot—not on the edge where the wave is ill-formed, flatter, and more turbulent as it blends into the side eddy, but squarely on the front or uphill face of the wave—nose down in the trough, stern up on the crest. The typical beginner's mistake in trying to get there is to misjudge the force of the current and get swept too far downstream. As a result you wind up on the backside of your chosen wave, paddling uphill to get over the top to the spot where you want to be. It's a struggle you usually can't win; you just tire yourself out and never do catch that wave. Far better in such a situation to relax, drift backward, and stop yourself with a couple of strokes just in time to catch the upstream side of the *next* wave below you. In fact, the best approach for would-be surfers is to paddle out well above the wave you intend to catch and then let yourself drift backward slowly, paddling or ferrying as needed to get to the spot you want. Eventually you'll be able to paddle right out into place with more confidence, precision, and power.

So now that you've caught your wave, what can you do with it? You will find that the first challenge is just to stay there. The water of any given wave is alive, changing, veering and shifting its flow somewhat from one second to the next; and you, the kayaker, must compensate for this. If the nose of your boat gets pushed off to the side, one way or the other, then you will suddenly have a downstream side and you'll want to tilt the kayak slightly to that side. But not too much, for then the current will have more bottom surface on your kayak to push against and you will be swept away to that side. To counteract this tendency, you'll want to use your paddle as a "rudder," holding it in the classic low brace/reverse sweep position, rear blade vertical and close to the stern, on the *opposite* side from the way the water is trying to push you. This is actually, to a slight degree, the upstream side, but the ruddering action will not flip you as an upstream brace would because you are only at a slight angle to the current (and trying to correct back into line). Furthermore, you can maintain a compensating downstream tilt of the kayak with your knees and hips.

Your kayak will also be sensitive to weight shift while surfing. By leaning way back in the cockpit, you can take pressure off the nose, making it much easier to move from side to side—either to get it back in line or move it to one side to start a long drift across the wave. On the other hand, by leaning forward, you can bury the nose all the more deeply in the trough at the foot of the wave, either to hold your position better, or to try for an end-over (as we'll see later).

From this point, you're on your own. There's no limit to what you can do with waves once you've learned to surf them: cruising back and forth, spinning around in place, surfing them backwards or even sideways, feeling and responding to the ever-changing push and pull of the current, balancing and rebalancing dynamic and constantly changing forces. Obviously, it will take time and the first time you try to surf a wave you must be prepared for frustration, dis-appointment and a few crashes. Just roll up and try again. Watch your friends and any better boaters that you meet on the river to see how they catch and surf waves. From experience, they will pick the best shaped waves, and of course really skilled boaters all

43. Surfing in a deep, troughlike wave

have their own personal style. When you see a move that looks interesting, try to copy it.

Playing in Holes

After making progress with easier waves, you will graduate to bigger, steeper ones, and ultimately you can try to play, not in waves, but in holes. Holes, you remember, are usually deep troughs or depressions in the river where the downstream water tends to fall back in on itself (or, in big holes, to crash back in on itself). Holes can be really mean; they can stop your boat, or capture and recirculate you, and the biggest, meanest holes must be avoided at all costs—even by experts. But at the safer end of the spectrum, holes can be a lot of fun if you're ready for them. Make sure your kayak is ready too, by using *ethafoam pillars* to reinforce its decks (this calls for split flotation bags). Otherwise it's easy to pop side seams. In any case, when you feel ready to stick your boat into a hole on purpose, take a good look first from a side eddy and try to figure out whether most of the water is flushing through. Don't pick a keeper to play in.

To get used to holes, enter from the side, facing upstream. But as your nose starts to drop sideways into the trough, reach out downstream with a good high brace and try to stick your paddle squarely through the foamy back cushion of tumbling water and into the deeper downstream current beneath.

44. In a small hole: the boater is crosswise to the river, stabilized on a downstream brace.

You'll get great support from this brace, and your boat will probably swing around to lie sideways in the hole. What now? The first time you try it the sensation will be overwhelming: noise, foam, water crashing everywhere. As you sense the river flowing by around you at head level or higher, you'll understand, perhaps for the first time, why such spots are called holes. Stay as calm as you can, keep the upstream edge of your kayak well-raised, and feel the amazing amount of support you receive from that downstream high brace. And then try to figure out how you're going to get out of there. Of course, the first time you try to get into a hole on purpose, your exit will probably be upside-down in your boat, having overdone some movement or just panicked because of the newness of the situation. So before going any further we had better discuss a couple of special techniques: rolling in holes and sculling.

It's the water, not the roll, that is different in a hole. If you tip upside-down, assume your rolling position, and reach for the surface with your active paddle blade. You may be surprised to find that there is no surface—at least, none you can feel. Often you will encounter only a bubbly, aerated froth, and if your instinct tells you that your sweep stroke won't work very well, it's right. With little to bite on, your paddle will probably dive and you'll blow the roll. If the water feels like this it's often best to just wait, compose your spirit as best you can, and hang out under the boat until things feel different. Then—pow, up you come. This works because your kayak is such a large pointed shape that it will probably be pushed or pulled out of the hole before long (more easily than a swimming kayaker, at any rate). It may seem like forever but it will probably only be a few seconds; stay in your boat until it feels right to roll.

There are a couple of other things you can do. If you're feeling insecure, enter the hole so that you are bracing downstream on the side on which you normally roll. This will facilitate things greatly should you crash. If the water is frothy and aerated but not violent and turbulent, you can extend the paddle a little, sliding your back hand down the shaft until it meets the blade. This will give you slightly more leverage. However, when the water is violent and turbulent (far more likely, in and around a hole), you generally want to avoid any kind of extended-paddle roll, since it will add to the leverage on you too, increasing the risk of a dislocated shoulder. Sometimes, too, if the hole has a steep back wave, you can do a half-roll back up before you have gone completely over by just sticking your paddle out into this steep downstream wave and letting the force of the current lift you back up.

Finally, by the time you get interested in playing in holes, you should be working seriously on your offside roll. Everyone rolls better on one side than the other (usually on the right side if you paddle a right-control paddle), and it's often best to try a roll on that side first. But if you fail, coming only partway up and then crashing back, your paddle will be set up perfectly for a roll on the other side. Try it. For a good boater, failure to roll usually means that you're trying to come up on the upstream side in heavy water. Thus, even if your off-side roll is weak you will be helped by the downstream current if you try it in this situation.

Sculling is a special paddle stroke which many kayakers learn but never use except to show off in a swimming pool or calm eddy. In truth, sculling is not very useful in the river except perhaps when you're

stuck in a hole, leaning on a high brace that's beginning to collapse. As with all the other strokes we've
encountered so far, you'll want to learn and practice
this one in calm water first. Remember the sweep
stroke, in which your paddle describes a wide arc out
from the bow and back toward the stern. To scull, just
do the center part of this sweep stroke, then reverse
the angle of the paddle and sweep it forward (but not
all the way, of course); then reverse the angle again
back to what it was, and sweep backward, then forward
once more, and so forth. In short, make a continuous
back-and-forth sweeping motion on one side of your
kayak. The key is the action of the wrist, which cocks
the paddle blade up at a climbing angle each time you
change the stroke's direction. From above it would
look like you were stirring the water in a lazy figure-
eight pattern. And what does this accomplish? It's a
kind of continuous self-renewing brace. You'll remember that in all bracing strokes, support from the

45. Sculling

water is gained by a combination of correct (climbing) paddle-blade angle and movement—either the paddle's movement through the water or the water's movement against the paddle. In sculling, we continually change paddle angle and direction of movement so that the bracing effect doesn't run out, as it would otherwise. With a little practice, you can lean out on your sculling paddle more and more. Ultimately you will be able to do what is sometimes called *deep sculling*, where the boater virtually lies on his side in the water, but continues to scull and doesn't tip all the way over because the force of the sculling keeps him up. Clearly, this sort of sculling can be useful if you get sideways in a hole and find that your static high brace into the rushing downstream water is not giving you all the support you need. A skilled kayaker playing in a rough hole may get knocked over so that his head is actually in the water and yet save himself from going completely over by a few strong sculling strokes.

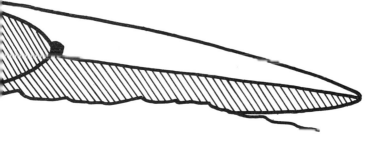

Coming back now to the problem of getting out of a hole once you've gotten in, let's look at several options. Often if the back wave of a hole isn't too high you can just reach over it with your paddle to get a good purchase in the downstream water on the other side, and this sort of extra-high brace will just pull you up and over and out of the hole. Otherwise you'll want to work your way out one side or the other—forward or backward (in relation to your own position crosswise to the river). If forward, out the far end, then use a kind of sculling stroke, stressing the forward component and using the back-stroke only as an ongoing brace and recovery, and at the same time shift your weight forward. Eventually your kayak's nose will bite into the side wall of the hole and you'll be able to pull yourself out. In reverse it's just the same: use an unbalanced sculling stroke, and lean back.

You'll discover that, as with waves, no two holes are alike, and by watching more experienced boaters, you'll constantly learn new things you can do with them. Since even easy holes are more violent and less forgiving than standing waves, you'll find that nervousness and even outright fear may be the strongest obstacles to playing in them. But take your time, be careful and conservative about which holes you try to ride, and it will increase your boating skill a hundred percent.

There is one more really classical playing maneuver that we should mention: The nosestand, or tailstand, or ender, or end-over, or simply—as it's commonly called—the *endo*. An endo involves burying the nose (or sometimes the stern) of your boat so deeply in a standing wave or hole that it is grabbed by the deep current and sucked further down, standing the kayak almost perfectly vertical in the river, and then is spit back out—sometimes throwing boat and boater into the air. Endos have the same justification as rollercoaster rides—they're a real thrill. Most result in a capsized boat, but since they are only attempted by kayakers to whom rolling up is no longer a big deal, this is not a special problem. Of course, even rank be-

**46. In a turbulent hole: the boater sculling
on his downstream side in order to stay up.**

ginners can do unintentional endos when they lose
their line and their kayak plows into a wave where it
doesn't belong.

In a true endo, the kayaker will lean forward once
his boat is in an upright position, causing the boat to
keep going, falling over itself, truly end over end.
Sometimes while in a vertical position the kayaker can
reach out and snag a side wave with his paddle, causing
the boat to rotate 180 degrees and come back down
rightside-up. This is often called a *pirouette.* However,
even for experts, endos often seem more like a "river
happening" than a consciously executed maneuver.
Waves or holes that can produce a good endo are
relatively few and far between. And the good spots
become well known, like Endo Rapids in the
Westwater Canyon of the Colorado, or Nosestand
Rapids on the North Fork of the American River
in California.

If you find yourself in a good spot for a nosestand,
get in position facing upstream and with a few strong
paddle strokes drive your boat into the trough of the
wave or the bottom of the hole as hard as you can,
leaning forward to bury the nose even further. It will
either happen or it won't, but when it does . . . what a
surprise!

So much for our short introduction to playing in

47. A nosestand or "endo"

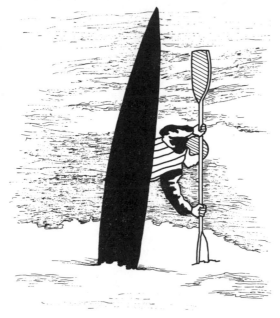

whitewater. This kind of play is more than just fun; for most kayakers it is also the simplest, fastest way to improve their basic skills, to get really hot. There is another way, however, which this book will neglect. But it deserves mention and the omission of this important subject also deserves an explanation. I'm talking about racing.

A Word on Competition

Whitewater racing—which is really two disciplines, slalom and downriver, in kayaks as well as single- and double-place decked canoes—is surely one of the most exciting forms of competitive sport. There is no doubt whatever that if you have the opportunity to participate in any whitewater competitions (and most do have novice and intermediate classes) your boating technique will improve greatly as a result. In a slalom race, one must pass between pairs of striped poles suspended on overhead lines above the water to form successive *gates*, which in turn define a certain path down the river. A downriver race is much longer, and contestants paddle from start to finish at full speed, nonstop, choosing their own line. Naturally a slalom race will do more for your technique, since each boater is obliged to turn and maneuver in a specific spot (there are even reverse gates that must be negotiated stern first and upstream gates that must be entered from below). And slalom courses are always set up early, permitting several days of practice before the actual race. Even if you have no real competitive urge, the discipline of following a slalom course will add precision to your paddling.

However, whitewater competitions are expensive to stage and quite complex to run properly. As a result only a few are held in any given area each year. Some clubs or racing enthusiasts keep sets of gates suspended above a certain stretch of river for ongoing training and practice. If possible ask permission, get some advice, and use them to improve your skill. But most kayakers don't get the same opportunity to race that they do just to run rivers. This is the first reason that whitewater racing is not stressed in this book. The second is that the many refinements of racing techniques are so varied and complex that, properly speaking, they deserve a whole book of their own. Whitewater racing is too exciting and exacting a discipline and, yes, even an art form, to justify compressing a lot of advice into a few pages.

One good friend, Roger Paris, a nationally known and respected whitewater instructor, coach, and former world champion, goes so far as to insist that the best way for rank beginners to make progress is by paddling through slalom gates on stillwater, from the very first day. And he may be right. The problem is that most beginners don't have gates set up in their practice pond, and even if they did few would have an experienced competitor to guide them through any such gates. Bad habits can be formed just as easily in gates as in an open river.

But if you have the opportunity to participate in

any whitewater slalom events, don't pass it up. Competing can do as much or more for you as any amount of playing. Watch the best racers and copy them, and if you can get some good coaching, great! But competitive paddling is not the only road, and for many noncompetitive personalities it is not the best road to becoming an expert kayaker. The river is always the best teacher. And for most of us, most of the time, playing in whitewater is the best and most enjoyable way to tune in to all it can teach us.

Difficult Rapids

There seems to be no limit to the difficulty of the rivers that expert kayakers can and do run. One generation's impossible run becomes a commonplace weekend outing five years later. But every boater senses his or her own limits, limits of comfort, limits of safety, limits of competence. Good judgment dictates that you become aware of your own limits, and respect them.

On the other hand, limits can always be pushed back, by working (or playing) at it with the help of a certain amount of daring. There are few things as satisfying as successfully running a rapid far harder than anything you have done before. How far you should go in an effort to find and overcome new whitewater challenges is largely a matter of personality. Some kayakers aren't happy unless they're constantly stimulated by harder water, while others very quickly find the kind of rapids they like best and are content to stay right there, boating for pleasure, not for challenge. There is no one way, no *right way* to kayak, or to run whitewater in any craft. You may have no ambitions to boat Class 4 or harder water, yet it's good to know something about it. But whatever your ambitions, don't neglect playing, as the resultant increase in boating skill will pay off handsomely.

Two main sources of difficulty are found in harder rapids: obstacles and obstructions requiring decisive mandatory maneuvering just to get through, and so-called *heavy hydraulics*, the powerful and treacherous effects of high-volume currents. Of course, the two can occur together for a kind of ultimate challenge.

The Indirect Line

In tough situations, the kayaker doesn't necessarily want to take the most direct line through the rapid. Up to now we have talked about entering down the tongue and trying to follow the line of deepest water and swiftest current. But in tough rapids or at high water, this line is also where you will surely find the meanest, biggest, deepest holes. And once embarked in the strongest current flow, it may become almost impossible to turn out of it should the need arise. There are also cases where the main channel sweeps right up onto giant rocks, splitting around them and creating further turmoil, holes, turbulence, and the like downstream. In such situations, clearly, the wary boater would prefer an *indirect line*.

Sometimes the kayaker avoids the direct line by merely picking a side channel and following it through —in kayaker's jargon, *running it on the right,* or left, as the case may be—but more often the indirect line involves *eddy hopping*. Eddy hopping simply means that instead of descending the rapid in a single straight shot, you pick your way down, slowly and carefully, from one eddy to the next. How does this help? Well, for one thing, you will sometimes have to change channels—moving laterally to get to another section of the river—and if you catch a good eddy below a rock just at the point where you have to begin crossing the river, then you can punch out of the eddy facing upstream and do an upstream ferry across the current to reach your new line. This is a real advantage because you can paddle forward more strongly and maintain a better ferry angle even in strong current than you could by back ferrying or just paddling sideways while the current swept you along.

Blossom Bar, a marvelous Class 4 rapid on the Rogue River in southern Oregon, forces the kayaker to use this technique. The central and right-hand chutes are virtually impossible at the top, and only the far left-hand chute is possible. After the first small drop, however, this good passage closes out in a chaotic jumble of rocks (often with the wreckage of smashed Rogue River dories strewn across them), and the boater has to move at least thirty feet to the right to the next open chute of water. Just by paddling diagonally downstream, you could never reach it in time. Instead, a large eddy below and to the right of the first drop offers a temporary resting spot out of which you can easily reach the correct line with an upstream ferry, peeling off into the chute and threading your way on down the exciting but more obvious whitewater below.

Eddy hopping is also a very useful means of scouting a rapid *on the run*. While it's generally true that you don't want to run a drop unless you can see a clear route all the way to the bottom, there are many situations in which skilled boaters can break this rule. The idea is that as long as you can see at least one side eddy that you can safely reach, you can go for it, and once there look for the next reachable eddy and so forth, all the way down the rapid. This is a great strategy when the river sweeps down and around a long bend—when most of it is out of sight, yet it doesn't seem that threatening, and scouting from the bank would take a long, long time. The only reasonable alternative is to proceed cautiously from eddy to eddy.

Naturally this alternative is not open to beginners or to boaters who lack confidence in their eddy turns and ferrying skills. And even good boaters must remember to spot eddies on the side of the river from which they could land, scout further, and even portage if necessary. It would do you no good to be parked safely in an eddy above an unrunnable waterfall if you were in the middle of the river unable to get to shore. When a whole party is using the eddy-to-eddy strategy, it's best for each boater in turn to wait in their own eddy until the one ahead has been vacated, since some whitewater eddies get awfully crowded with just two kayaks in them. And finally, like every technique we've mentioned so far, eddy hopping must be practiced in safe easy rapids, long before you need it in earnest to negotiate a serious passage. Take a familiar stretch of whitewater and, as a game, set yourself the challenge of catching every single eddy in it. It will be embarrassing how many you miss at first, but with time you'll get them all.

Eddy hopping, in another sense, is also a means of moving back upstream—sometimes even in the middle of pretty fierce whitewater. You can ferry sideways out of the "head" or top of one eddy to catch the very end or "tail" of another eddy further upstream; then move up in its backwater and ferry out again to a still higher one. Tricky, but so much easier than fighting the current like a salmon. Remember, in a direct contest of strength you will eventually tire and the river will win.

Big Water

This brings us to the most one-sided contest of all—*heavy hydraulics*. This colorful expression is usually reserved not for big waves (although on western desert rivers waves can be gigantic) but for powerful current effects, reversals, whirlpools, boiling and unstable eddies, giant holes, and so forth, which occur with some frequency on the biggest rivers, and even on much smaller rivers at high water and flood stages. For most boaters, the best advice regarding these ultrapowerful hydraulic phenomena is simply to avoid them. Yes, there are holes so big that no expert, no champion would even think of going near them. But on some western rivers such as the Colorado and its tributaries, heavy hydraulics are so much a part of the scene that boaters are forced to find ways of dealing with them, even though the best lines in such rapids will avoid the worst water.

There are several approaches for boating heavy water; and although it's clear that this subject goes beyond the reasonable limits of boating instruction, total ignorance is even worse. This kind of kayaking is the province of experts, and as a result two basic approaches to heavy water have developed since there are really two distinct classes of expert paddlers: racers and purely recreational paddlers. Speed is what racing is all about, and good racers don't merely strive for speed; they integrate and use it as a basic part of their paddling technique. Also, because of the discipline of slalom gates, they have a good instinct for line, and have developed the ability to follow a given line once they've decided on it. As a result, experts of this class will seldom drift into big rapids; they prefer a lot of forward speed and will attempt to *paddle* their way around or, failing that, through any ugly waves, holes, or rip currents.

The other school of very gifted but non-racing oriented paddlers will more often attempt to *brace* their way over or through the same class of difficulties. These paddlers will often drift into big rapids sideways, feeling that in this position they are ready to scoot forward or backward out of the way of a big hole that may loom up, and at the same time are in the stablest position to ride on a strong downstream brace. Perhaps the best exposition of this "soft" approach was written by the almost legendary Walt Blackadar, an Idaho doctor and big-water enthusiast. The article appeared in the Winter 1971 issue of the *American Whitewater Journal*, and makes interesting and controversial reading. Naturally, the partisans of any given style of paddling always tend to exaggerate its merits, but, in fact, there's more than one way to skin a cat, or run a rapid. Most paddlers approaching the level and status of expert will probably have synthesized a personal style of their own, including or rejecting the many lessons they've learned from other, still better paddlers. In big water, if it works, it's okay.

The classical big-water nightmare is getting caught and kept in a large, powerful recirculating hole. There is, by definition, no easy way out. What can you do? Initially you try to stay upright, using a high downstream brace—perhaps extending the paddle somewhat to try to reach real downstream water on the other side of all that foam—and then you attempt to paddle, brace, or pull your way out of there. If you tip, however, it's pretty important not to get out of your kayak, since many holes can hold a body much longer than they can keep the larger form of a kayak. So try to roll, and if you don't make it keep trying—a dozen times if you have to. Do everything possible to figure out which is the downstream side and try your roll on that side. If you can't roll back up at all, you may be able to "grab" green water by sticking your paddle straight down where water flows past, or out of, the very bottom of the hole. This can pull you out, but be sure to hang onto your paddle tightly.

Finally, if you are forced to get out of your boat, hold on to the kayak if you can; it may pull you out of the hole, and besides it's more likely to smash you if it's being tossed about by itself. As in any keeper you can attempt to dive as deep as possible to hit the non-recirculating deep current and get swept out of there. But do *not*, no matter what advice you've read, take off your life jacket; if the water's that big, you'll need it to stay afloat once you get out of the hole.

But this is a relatively somber note on which to end this discussion of more advanced rapids. Difficult rapids need not, and should not, be a horror show. In a way, it depends on you, the paddler. If you're ready for the next increase in difficulty, then it will neither shake your confidence nor hurt you. It's only when you skip several steps and jump too far ahead of your present boating skills that you are courting disaster. Think of difficult rapids (Class 4 and harder) not as an ordeal but as an ordeal but as a reward, a treat that you come to naturally after a patient and adequate whitewater apprenticeship.

They say the first steps are the hardest; and already you've been through a lot. You've learned to paddle, roll, read water, and run rapids. Well done! Whitewater boating is an open-ended sport, and with patience you can become as good a paddler as you want. But for those who haven't been seduced by our sporty little kayaks, in the next chapter we're going to introduce several boating alternatives: various sorts of inflatables and rafts.

CHAPTER 7

BOATING ALTERNATIVES: INFLATABLES

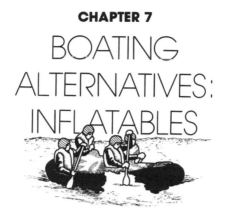

It's about time we looked at another side of white-water sport. Rafting, the basic alternative to kayaking, may be somewhat less sporty and definitely less individualistic in that it allows passengers a free ride, but it still has its share of thrills. Rafting demands skill, strength, and judgment, and it's a permanent and honored part of the river-running scene. If you decide to row a raft, you will in no way become a second-class citizen among whitewater boaters. Indeed, rafts and rafters are quite in demand, since even the most fanatical kayakers recognize their superiority for carrying gear on extended trips and appreciate the extra margin of convenience and safety that results from including rafts in the party.

In this chapter we will look not only at rubberized rafts but at a couple of other boating alternatives as well: the small one- and two-man inflatable kayaks, and a curious (not truly inflatable) one-man craft known as the *Sportyak.* These small craft require less skill and practice to handle than fiberglass kayaks and are far more stable, at the expense of maneuverability and playfulness. They do bring the boater into closer contact with whitewater than a large raft would, but at a considerable sacrifice of carrying capacity.

The rubberized raft, bulbous and ugly, yet marvelously stable and functional, still remains our basic boating alternative. First introduced as army-surplus items after World War II, these pontoonlike rafts have literally opened up river running, especially in the West, for thousands of people who might never otherwise have had a whitewater experience. But the day of the army-surplus raft is long gone. Rafts and rafting equipment are now quite sophisticated, and even the best inflatable rafts need a good deal of special outfitting before they are ready for serious whitewater. But before we get into the two basic aspects of rafting—outfitting the boat and whitewater rowing—let's briefly review some of the attractions of rafting to see if it's really for you.

First and foremost, if you're looking toward whitewater river running as a family sport, and if family includes preteenage children, then by all means become a rafter. You can give your family a wild yet really safe ride in a raft. If you love rivers yet hate water (not at all uncommon), then take up rafting. If you are drawn toward river touring and whitewater more out of a desire to explore exciting new country than from a longing for physical action, then take up rafting. And, finally, if you feel yourself to be more of a group-oriented person than an individualistic performer, then consider rafting. The group ambience aboard an inflatable raft is cheerful and relaxing—and very supportive when the boating gets rough. The loneliness of the kayaker ought to be as proverbial as that of the long-distance runner.

But remember, the rafter boats through the same water, with all the same features, as his kayaking companions. So all the earlier sections on river lore, nomenclature, and river features, as well as many of the basic boating strategies discussed in the preceding kayak-oriented chapters apply directly to whitewater rafting. In the rest of this chapter let's assume the similarities and only talk about the differences, in both equipment and technique.

Outfitting a Raft

Choosing and buying your rubber raft ought to be a simple exercise in comparative shopping once you've eliminated the extreme ends of the spectrum. At one end are the brightly colored but tragically inadequate *poly-vinyl minirafts*. These are scarcely more than swimming pool toys which nonetheless get launched with regularity on whitewater rivers and are responsible for a lot of wet and traumatic experiences, and for a lot of people giving up the sport before they really begin. Never mind if they seem able to float four people, these flimsy little rafts are virtually uncontrollable in serious water (the impractical plastic oarlocks are telltale evidence of this). Such rafts are never sold by reputable whitewater outfitters and turn up instead at general sporting goods outlets. Avoid them at all costs; not only are they impossible to row effectively in whitewater, but the light plastic material will rip and disintegrate at the very first meeting with a midriver rock.

Serious, practical whitewater rafts are made of heavy rubberized fabric that can take a lot of beating. But beware of overkill. At the other end of the spectrum are boats that are too big, too rugged, too bulky and awkward for any sensible amateur river runner. The amateur, for-pleasure-only distinction is important because commercial outfitters on the larger western rivers have really gone to the extreme limits of size and maneuverability in their quest for a rig that will take yet a few more paying customers safely through dangerous big rapids. In this category we place rafts with spare pontoon float chambers lashed to each side for greater stability (at the expense of maneuverability) and such fanciful contraptions as the famous *G-rig*—three ordinary rubber rafts, lashed side by side to form a giant flexing platform that can mush its way through the biggest holes. Such hybrid monsters as the G-rig, (named after Georgie White, a pioneer woman outfitter and river guide in the Grand Canyon) may well be valid solutions for transporting lots of people through big water, but in most instances they merely negate the sense of sport and involvement that should always be part of a whitewater experience.

Another craft, far more traditional and classic, which is likewise outside the normal realm of amateur pleasure boating is the *sweep-rigged raft*. Sweeps are giant flat-bladed oars rigged not to either side, but fore and aft. Sweeps were used to control rafts on the Mississippi in Mark Twain's day, and are still used with great effect to steer big, heavy rafts down the Salmon and other rivers. But their overwhelming disadvantage for amateur river runners is the great size and strength of the frames needed to support the huge sweep oars—not at all the kind of rig you can put on a car-top carrying rack. A far more noble craft is the double-ended wooden dory, which has a large place in the whitewater history of the American West. But the problem of transporting so bulky a boat makes the dory equally inappropriate for amateur river runners.

Choosing your Craft

So now that we know what we don't want, let's look at the range of practical rafts for most whitewater. Army-surplus rigs are no longer available, so about the only way you will be able to save any money in outfitting a raft is to look for a second-hand one. This is a fine idea, but be sure to doublecheck everything, especially the tubes for worn, frayed spots. If you start off with new equipment, there's no way you will get away with spending less than $500 to $600 for a rig that will carry, say, four people and their gear. And as a matter of fact it's quite easy to spend well over $1,000. There are fewer manufacturers of whitewater rafts

48. A simple whitewater raft

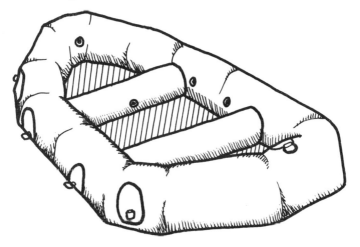

than there are of kayaks, so in a way your choice will be simpler. Near the top of the list, in both price and quality are the Avon boats. These inflatables are really the Cadillacs of whitewater rafting. They are produced in England, so perhaps the expense of importing them keeps their price so high. In any case, serious river runners rave about them. Avon makes several boats specifically for heavy-duty use (the Adventurer, the Professional Mark II, and the Spirit, from $1,300 up), and a number of smaller dinghy-type craft, which are quite serviceable in small rivers.

A fine series of whitewater rafts are made in Japan for Campways, and these are a good deal more affordable. These boats are all named after Indian tribes (the Paiute, Hopi, Miwok II, Shoshone II, and Havasu II) and are really dependable, tough boats seen on whitewater all over the country. Prices start at $600 for the tiny 11–foot Paiute, and go up to about $1,500 for the massive 17–foot Havasu II. Rogue Inflatables, an Oregon company, manufactures two models (approximately 15 and 18 feet long) with a lot of innovative construction features and multiple reinforcements in their distinctive bright orange tubes, for around $1,300 and $1,500.

But don't despair at these prices. Some real bargain rafts are available which are very serviceable white-water craft without, however, all the quality features of the top models. Northwest River Supplies, for example, offers a big, solid 16-foot raft for about $300 and a great little 11-footer for around $200. And there are a number of other quite acceptable rafts in this price range.

Which brings us to specifics. How should you choose? And what size raft do you need? Most non-commercial whitewater rafts range from 11 feet (tiny) to 18 or 20 feet (spacious) in length; your choice will be largely determined by how many people you plan to boat with, and to some extent by the size of the rivers you plan to run. Big water, big raft. And vice versa. In any case, try to avoid buying a raft that's bigger than you really need. The bigger the raft, the harder it is to row and control and the more likely it is to get stuck in tight chutes and the like. It's also a big expense, so try to get some specific advice from someone who already rows in whitewater and can suggest a rig that's just right for your situation. For example, a 13– or 14–foot raft is a good family-sized boat.

The Rest of the Rig

You'll need more than just a good raft (and the pump and patching kit that should come with it). A rowing frame and oars will complete your outfit. (The other alternative, a paddle raft, is discussed in the next section.)

Rowing frames are needed because big rubberized rafts are simply too squishy to be rowed as is. They would bend, deform, and generally mush around, even if one could attach an adequate pair of oarlocks to them. A rowing frame is a kind of box-like framework that is lashed to the raft, generally right in the center between the two cross tubes. It serves the double purpose of making the raft itself more rigid and of supporting a pair of oarlocks. Rowing frames are made either of metal or wood, but the state of the art is doubtless a contoured frame of aluminum tubing that wraps neatly over the side of the raft, forming a cargo-carrying framework inside the boat, and incorporating a smoothly inclined rowing seat, so that the rower can apply power with his legs as well as with his arms and back. Several outfits manufacture such frames (they tend to cost at least $200) and if you become a real dyed-in-the-wool whitewater rafter, you will probably wind up buying one. On the other hand, one of the few ways to save money in outfitting a raft is to make your own rowing frame out of 2×8 timber. A wooden rowing frame (bolted together and painted

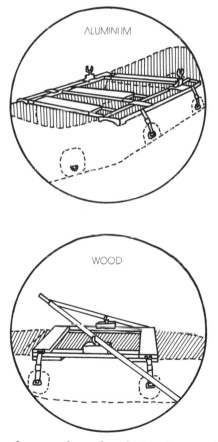

49. Rowing frames of wood and aluminum tubing

to resist the constant wetness) is simple, sturdy, serviceable, and cheap. A good way to start.

All rowing frames are lashed to D-rings on the outside of the raft's tubes. One-inch or wider nylon webbing is probably the best material for this (fantastically strong and it can't damage the tubes). Obviously, you must take care that nothing angular or sharp is caught between frame and raft where it could abrade the tubes, and that the frame itself has no sharp protruding parts.

Naturally, *oarlocks* are incorporated into all rowing frames, but they're not all alike. Three main types of oarlocks are found on whitewater rafts, and there are experienced boaters who will swear by each type. One is a U-shaped, pivoting oarlock that holds the oar by means of a metal pin that passes through the oar and bridges the top of the open U. This kind is mechanically complicated and hard to repair. For sheer simplicity the post-type oarlock is hard to beat. It's a simple metal pin, upright and stationary. A metal strap attached to the oar shaft just hooks around this post. Skillful oarsmen, however, tend to prefer the third type, a pivoting ring (sometimes open on top), through

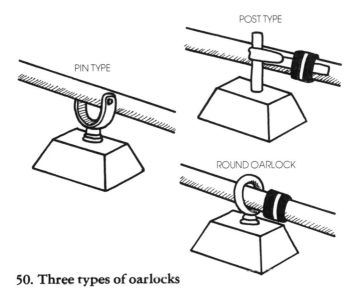

50. Three types of oarlocks

which the shaft of the oar is inserted up to a clamped-on stopper. The advantage here is that one can change the blade angle by rolling the wrist (*feathering* the oars) and also pull the oars inboard if needed to pass an obstacle. This permits the experienced rower to do more with his oars, but could be confusing for a neophyte. All three oarlocks are shown in Figure 50.

And finally, the oars themselves. Good long, strong wooden oars (generally, of ash) are almost works of art and at the very least examples of good craftsmanship. They can also be bloody expensive, the best ones selling for over $100 a pair. On the other hand, if you're a beginner you may well break a few oars your first season, so don't buy the very best. Different sized rafts require different lengths of oars. For small boats 7– to 8–foot oars will do. Bigger rafts call for up to 10–foot oars. But the individual boatman's preference and the type of river may dictate longer or shorter oars. And every raft should carry at least one spare oar.

Since buying and outfitting a raft can be so expensive it's a good idea to tag along on a few raft trips before you even think about buying your own. This is something a rafter can do that a kayaker cannot. And, if at all possible, try to spend some time rowing a raft of the sort you are planning to buy before you actually make your purchase. Rowing is hard work, so most rafters are only too glad when someone offers to spell them at the oars. To prepare you for this moment, let's see what can be done with a pair of oars.

Whitewater Rowing Technique

What happens once you get your raft into the river? Your first impression will be one of size, weight (or more precisely, inertia) and consequent sluggishness. Don't worry, in some ways a fair-sized rubber raft is much easier to handle in actual rapids than in open flatwater.

Nor is basic technique for whitewater rafting very

complicated. The basic theory of controlling a raft—of rowing—is quite simple. The art, the subtlety of it is a matter of experience, of reading the river and timing one's strokes so that currents and countercurrents do most of the work. The difference between a beginning oarsperson and an experienced rafter is *not* one of rowing technique, but rather of judgment and timing—being able to figure out in advance what the water will do to the raft. Still, your first impression that the raft is an enormous, slow-moving object is somewhat correct; because of its size and inertia, it takes a few good hard strokes of the oars before anything happens. Because of this "delayed response," looking ahead, planning ahead, and getting the raft moving in time are all of prime importance.

Most people, even if they've never been in a row boat, have a kind of intuitive picture of how rowing works. In a traditional rowboat (of the Sunday-morning-outing-in-the-park variety), the rower sits with his back to the bow of the boat, reaches forward with both hands to place the oar blades in the water behind him, and then *pulls back* to obtain a forward stroke. It sounds and looks topsy-turvy. Why face away from the direction of movement, anyway? Wouldn't it be nicer to look where you're going? The answer is that a backward, pulling stroke, which uses the motion of the whole body, is stronger and more efficient than a forward, pushing stroke of the oars.

But it should be obvious that in whitewater facing backward simply won't do! In a complex obstructed rapid you just have to be able to see where you're going. The solution is a technique that was first invented and used by a pioneer Utah boatman, Nat Galloway.

You enter the rapid with the boater at the oars facing forward, downstream, (Many rubber rafts are symmetrical and round-ended, making it a moot point whether the craft is traveling bow or stern first. But in the early wooden skiffs used by Galloway and his companions, this procedure meant entering the rapids stern first, with the pointed bow aimed back upstream.) In this position, your most powerful stroke is backward, upstream, resisting the current. Not only does this backward pull of the oars slow down your raft, and thus give you more time to cope with what's coming; but you can also from this position do a very effective back ferry. Back ferrying in a raft works the same as back ferrying in a kayak (see Chapter 4). By angling the rear of the boat to one side or the other and pulling backward against the current in that direction, you can move the raft laterally across the river in the same direction in which its rear (stern) is pointing.

Suppose, for example, that a large rock looms ahead which you want to pass on the right. With a *turning stroke*—pulling on the left oar while pushing on the right so that the two oars oppose each other—spin the boat until its front is pointing diagonally left, its rear diagonally right. Then pull straight back. The current will cancel out part of your work (the upstream component) and only the lateral component of your rowing will take effect: the raft will move rightward across the current. When you've moved right far enough to avoid the offending rock, an opposite turning stroke of the oars will straighten out the raft and you're off with the current until the next maneuver. Basically, this one maneuver, the back ferry, is damn near all you can do to steer a raft in whitewater. But that doesn't mean it's ineffective. On the contrary. With the leverage provided by long oars and a good rowing frame, a strong and determined boatman can really move even an overloaded raft, back and forth, zig-zagging through a tricky rapid.

Here are a few important variations on the theme of lateral movement in rapids. Because of their sleek, streamlined design and high power-to-weight ratio, kayaks usually ferry at a rather "steep" angle—that is, not turned very much across the current. Not so with big rafts. Because it's hard to really get them moving, you will generally have to start ferrying earlier and at a "flatter," or more crosswise, angle. In big water, the sort found on western desert rivers such as the Colorado and the Green, the current is often so overwhelmingly strong that the only effective ferrying angle is 90 degrees, or completely sideways to the current. At the more moderate angle of a normal diagonal ferry, a good part of your effort would be wasted, since the upstream component of your stroke would be completely overwhelmed by the infinitely greater force of the current. But at 90 degrees to the current, all your stroking force will take effect and you'll get there faster. This is only true in really big water, and the normal diagonal ferry is indeed useful if the force of the current is not so great as to completely negate the upstream component of your rowing.

There are also big-water situations where you really do need as much downstream speed as possible. For example, a fast-moving tongue with a rock at the bottom may require that you break through the diagonal waves alongside the tongue. If these waves are large you may need all the momentum you can muster to punch through them. A normal back ferry might slow you so much that you couldn't break through to the side, and you would be slid along the diagonal wave back into the tongue. In some situations you have to push for forward speed from the very moment you enter the tongue, and perhaps all the way through the rapid. This is particularly true in snarly water (with unusually strong eddies and hydraulics) where you must ensure that the raft keeps moving at the same speed as the current. When a raft goes slower than the current it can become particularly vulnerable; it may even stall on the face of a wave and slide back into a trough or a hole. In really giant water, loss of forward speed can easily result in flipping the boat.

But these situations are exceptions rather than the rule. Your basic technique is to pick a good line and back ferry around obstacles or to change channels. And when all is said and done, the very best rafters and first-time beginners will all be using the same few maneuvers, the same strokes. The difference—and it is enormous—lies in the timing, precision, and the anticipation of these strokes. Last-minute course changes in a large raft just don't work. It takes a lot of effort to get that big hunk of nylon and rubber moving across the current. For this very reason, some rafters learn to read whitewater better and faster than do kayakers. A partially hidden eddy or a sideways-curling wave can be used to slow or turn the raft, or actually to slide it sideways, but only if spotted early enough.

Because of their inherently limited maneuverability and the problems of changing course in midrapid, rafters will tend to do more scouting from the bank before serious drops than will kayakers. The rafter cannot sneak down a difficult drop by hopping from one safe eddy to the next as a skilled kayaker can, so the initial choice of lines is critical. When you can't see your whole line through the rapid, it always pays to beach your raft and scout from the bank.

Having chosen your line, it's vital to enter the tongue of the rapid at just the right point. Many rafters work out the problem of precise entry into the rapid by turning their boat sideways, broadside to the current, as they drift slowly toward the head of a drop. In this position they can row forward or back (toward one bank or the other) until they reach the point from which they want to start their descent. Then, on the very brink of the tongue, a couple of snappy unbalanced turning strokes will spin the raft 90 degrees so that you are lined up facing the rapid as you slide over the edge at precisely the spot you've chosen. Why is it important to line up with the current as you drop into a rapid? It's not just a question of visibility, but rather that big waves and holes, when run at anything other than a head-on angle, are potential turnovers.

Armed with this very elementary theory about how to negotiate rapids in a raft, you will obviously need some time and a good number of whitewater runs to become really competent at the oars. But you will also have one great advantage: rubber rafts are very forgiving. They tend to bounce off rocks you aren't quick enough to avoid, and typically they mush through and squish out of awesome holes whether you do anything or not.

A recent trip down the Westwater Canyon of the Colorado illustrates this point. A good friend of mine had just bought a used raft and was making his very first trip in whitewater. Now, the Westwater Canyon is a well-known and moderately difficult stretch of boating with a number of hard, technical Class 4 rapids. There were about a dozen kayakers on this particular trip, and quite a few of the weaker ones had a lot of trouble with some of the drops. They flipped, couldn't roll, came out of their boats and had to swim, *even though they had all been kayaking for several seasons.* But while our first-time rafter did make a lot of mistakes, he sailed through all the tough spots high and dry. In a sense his boat had run the river for him. By contrast, it would have been a dangerous, unpleasant mistake to have taken an inexperienced kayaker down the Westwater at that water level. So there you are: rafts do, in fact, make an apprenticeship on the river a good deal easier than you might think. Far easier than getting into whitewater via kayaking.

This is not to suggest that you take off down the first whitewater run you can find without having practiced rowing. On the contrary, if you can stand to spend a couple of hours rowing your raft around on an easy flat stretch of river, you will be far more confident when you first hit whitewater. Unfortunately, rowing a good-sized raft on flatwater (just for practice, with no beautiful scenery to watch) is terrible drudgery, so you won't be able to practice for long. Concentrate on getting the hang of turning strokes—a combination movement in which the two oars work in opposition, one arm pulling, the other arm pushing. Some people instinctively know how to turn a rowboat or raft; others get terribly flustered when they try to figure out which paddle to push, which one to pull. It's simple. By working the oars in opposition with a push-pull motion, you will swing around or turn toward the side on which you are pulling the oar. For example, pushing the right oar while pulling the left one will swing you around to face your left. Take the trouble to work out this turning motion until it's automatic and you no longer have to think about what to do.

That's it for the basics, but there are a number of tricks that will help you out in special whitewater situations. Sooner or later, for example, you will encounter tight rocky channels or passages through which your raft will barely fit. This occurs most often at low water levels or in boulder-strewn mountain rivers. The trick here is to protect your oars from being caught, held back, and snapped by rocks on either side. As soon as you have lined up for the slot, ship your oars by pulling the handles in and back, so the blades are resting on the forward tubes, well inboard from the sides of the raft. If you forget to do this you will soon be using your spare oar.

A broken oar is a great bother, although not necessarily a disaster, provided you remembered to carry a spare or spares. But it's well worth learning to avoid classical oar-crunching situations. Another common one occurs if your raft should be swung sideways by the river, say in the haystacks near the bottom of a rapid. In this position, broadside to the flow of current, one oar will be downstream, one upstream, and in heavy water this can set you up for trouble. Just as the kayaker's paddle is supported on the downstream side and driven beneath the surface on the upstream side (see Chapter 4), your upstream oar can be pushed violently beneath the surface by a strong current if you get it in too deep. It can be pulled out of your grasp, twisted about, and broken or lost (depending on your oarlocks). But the downstream oar can be a still worse problem. In shallow water, you can easily stick the downstream oar so deep into the water that it touches the bottom, and in this case the raft will be pushed right into that oar by the current. The oar will snap and your rowing frame might even be bent or damaged. Also, if an oar that is unpinned hits a rock or the bottom and comes back at you, it may take a few teeth with it. Altogether, it's not healthy to let your raft get broadside to the current—even if you don't *hang* an oar, you can still flip.

This brings us to *high siding.* Although it's true that you're much less likely to be flipped over in a raft than in a kayak, the biggest waves *can* flip even the very biggest rafts. The worst offenders are sideways curling waves, which can lift one side of the raft, threatening to flip it around its long axis (much easier than flipping it front to back). In this situation (or any other where you feel that your raft is close to being flipped over) the passengers must move quickly to whichever side or end of the boat is being lifted up in the air—hence the term "high siding." Applying movable ballast in this way is usually enough to keep the raft from going over. But it does take a little forethought and must be seriously explained to the raft's passengers, since people's instinctive reaction is to do the exact opposite. When a giant wave rears up over the boat, the natural inclination is to shrink back and, if anything, to move away from the threatened side of the raft. This makes a capsize all the more likely. Remember, the passengers must move *toward* the wave that's threatening to overturn the raft and hang on to the very edge of the raft until the danger is past. For this reason, too, experienced boatmen always have their passengers (if there are only a couple) ride in the bow, to weigh down the front of the raft as it's lifted up by each new wave.

The procedure to follow if you get stuck on a rock is similar to high siding. Many "collisions" with midstream rocks are merely friendly nudges; the raft hits and bounces off to one side or another, the whitewater equivalent of bumper cars at an amusement park. But if you see that you are actually going to be driven against a rock and held there, passengers and boatman alike should move toward the rock (or the downstream side) rather than shrink away from it. If you don't do this, the outside or upstream tubes of the raft may be pushed beneath the surface and the raft completely swamped and then wrapped around the offending rock below the water. This would be a major disaster. But if everyone moves close to the rock, the raft is more likely to stay afloat, and you are more likely to be able to push, bounce, or pry it off the rock and back into the current.

Naturally, these are not the only ways you might get into trouble in a raft. But your raft is far more likely to keep you out of trouble than the reverse. In fact, you will discover that your trusty rubberized boat is able to make it through tough sections seemingly on its own, even where you feel quite at a loss to control and direct it.

And now, before leaving the subject of inflatable rafts, let's say something about *paddle rafts,* which we have shamefully neglected so far. As the name implies, paddle rafts are not rowed by one person but are paddled with single-bladed canoe-type paddles by all hands on board. Passengers become crew, everyone participates, and a good time is had by all. And any common whitewater raft minus its rowing frame makes a perfect paddle raft.

The concept is appealing but there are, alas, a few drawbacks. First, to obtain any control at all you need a full complement of paddlers; hence you have little or no room for cargo and baggage. But enthusiastic paddlers alone don't guarantee much control over the raft in whitewater. The traditional arrangement is for half of the paddlers to sit on each side (straddling the tubes and pulling in their legs whenever a rock comes too close), while one person, sitting in the rear with a somewhat larger paddle, acts as the steersman. The steersman not only uses his paddle somewhat like a sweep oar to maintain directional control, but also has the difficult job of trying to coordinate everyone else's efforts. And this is the rub. It's almost impossible to obtain any coordination among four, six, or eight paddlers unless they paddle a raft together all the time. But this is seldom the case. The best to be hoped for is that everyone can dig in and paddle forward or backward on command. The steersman is constantly shouting: "Left side forward! Right side back!" and so forth. Because they are so much fun, paddle rafts are promoted by commercial outfitters on moderate rivers, where a semicontrolled raft is not in real danger. But for good reason, most serious whitewater rafters stick with a pair of oars. In actual practice you just cannot duplicate the control afforded by a solid rowing frame and a good pair of oars, certainly not with an enthusiastic but ill-coordinated crew of paddlers.

51. A paddle raft

Mini-Inflatables

If you are more attracted by paddling than rowing and yet you feel that kayaking is not your thing, you still have some very interesting options among the mini-inflatables. Mini-inflatables are small one- and two-person inflatable kayaks (although a unique, not-truly-inflatable craft called the Sportyak is also going to sneak into this section). Most inflatable kayaks are open boats, not decked-over like a rigid kayak, so that the paddler sits *in* them, not *inside* them. They are also unsinkable, quite easy to paddle, and hard to tip over. Finally, they're fun and rather cheap. They must have some disadvantages, you are probably thinking, and indeed they do. But they are splendid boats, and if they didn't exist many people might never experience a true whitewater adventure.

As with the fiberglass kayak, the paddler in an inflatable kayak has a very intimate relationship with the water—one of the most important criteria for being a participant, not merely a passenger, in whitewater boating. You are definitely on your own in one of these boats. And unlike some of the larger rubber rafts, these small craft give one a sense of scale that is continuously impressive. Big waves both look and feel just as big or bigger than they really are.

On the negative side, inflatable kayaks are just not very sporty. You can go *through* a great range of rapids rather easily, but you can't do much *with* these rapids. That is to say, you can't surf waves or play in holes, most of the time you can't even make very good eddy turns, and often you can hardly steer your boat at all. But you can get through, with hardly any special skill, although you may feel like a bit of flotsam bobbing along over the waves, bouncing off rocks, and ultimately spinning out of control into a quiet pool at the bottom of the drop. This, of course, is the real reason why the more ambitious whitewater boaters always wind up paddling fiberglass kayaks rather than inflatable ones; the inflatable kayak's range of movement and control is too limited. The inflatables are definitely for running rivers, not for playing with them.

There are two other disadvantages to inflatable kayaks. They are very sluggish to paddle in flatwater; they don't knife cleanly through the water as a hard-hulled kayak does. And a paddler in an inflatable always gets very wet. In rapids, he will usually be sitting in at least six inches of water that's sloshed into the bottom of the boat. For this reason, people paddling inflatable kayaks on longer trips generally wear wet suits.

Just what do these craft look like and how do they work? Inflatable kayaks are a good deal shorter than traditional 4–meter fiberglass kayaks. They look like compressed front-yard wading pools, with pointed ends. They are made of rubberized cloth, and unlike most rafts, which are gray in color, most inflatable kayaks—who knows why?—are some shade of orange. Their appearance is functional but definitely not sleek, and for this reason, coupled with the relentless way they bob up and down big waves, they are commonly known as *rubber duckies*. The commonest are Tahitis, Pyrawas, and Sea Eagles. Two-man inflatables are also available. They are slightly longer, harder to paddle, and less fun. Amazingly, prices for one-man rubber kayaks are around $100; when you consider the cost of buying and outfitting a

52. An inflatable kayak, top and side views

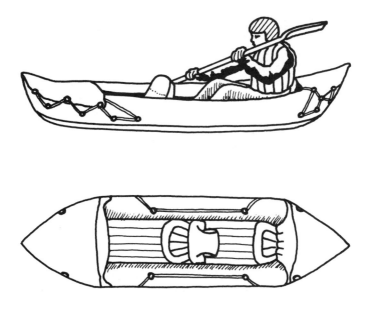

raft, this is a real bargain. The only ill-designed thing about these craft are the flimsy paddles that are usually sold with them. If you're planning to do a lot of whitewater in one of these inflatables, you should look around for a stronger paddle, perhaps a standard kayak paddle in a short size.

As to paddling an inflatable kayak, there's a lot less to it than with a regular kayak. You sit in the bottom of the boat, legs extended, and just paddle. While in theory you could use almost all the kayak strokes described earlier (except of course the eskimo roll), in practice all one uses is forward and backward strokes, with an occasional sweep or brace. Nonetheless, if you're going to try any amount of whitewater in one of these rubber duckies I strongly recommend reading all four earlier chapters on kayak technique. Paddling an inflatable is much easier—and less traumatic, since they almost never tip over—but many of the same paddling principles and all of the river lore apply.

Very occasionally you will see a rare type of inflatable kayak, a true decked-over kayak of normal 4–meter length with cockpit, bracing system and all, only made of inflatable rubberized tubes. These are true hybrids, neither fish nor fowl, seemingly offering all the disadvantages and none of the advantages of either the inflatable or rigid kayak. Since they cost just as much as a fiberglass kayak, and are just as tippy but don't work as well, it's best to ignore them.

(A far more interesting cousin to the modern fiberglass kayak is the original foldboat, a canvas-covered boat with a collapsible wooden frame. These boats, often simply called "Kleppers" after the German company that pioneered their manufacture, are not really serious whitewater craft, since anything harder than Class 3 rapids is out of the question. They are, however, great boats for moderate river touring, especially for true expeditions in remote wilderness settings. They hold a lot of gear, far more than any fiberglass kayak, and the one-place foldboat—there are one- and two-place models—can even be rolled, although not with ease. Foldboats are a rare and anachronistic sight on most whitewater stretches, but they still have a respected place among river-running craft.)

Another rare boat worth a second look is the Sportyak, a strange bathtub-like contraption that is extremely riverworthy. It's been around for some time but has never become really popular with river runners, perhaps because of its ugly-duckling appearance, which contrasts strikingly with the sleek and graceful kayak. The Sportyak is small, about 7 feet long and scarcely more than 3 feet wide, and is made of an extremely tough, rigid plastic. Inside the shell are several hollow compartments for buoyancy and just enough room for one boater. But although the Sportyak is so small, it is rowed not paddled, with the boater facing downriver in the time-honored Nat

53. The Sportyak

Galloway tradition. Six– or 7–foot oars (relatively long for such a small craft) give the boater an amazing amount of directional control, but it's still not the boat you would choose for playing in standing waves. The Sportyak is unsinkable and nearly impossible to tip over, and as a result, offers an exciting but rather carefree and safe mode of running rapids. A couple of river outfitters are now taking their clients down western rivers in Sportyaks to provide a greater sense of participation and adventure, and it's our guess that we'll see a lot more of these curious boats in the future. Even the Grand Canyon has been run in Sportyaks. They cost around $125 ($165 for the slightly larger 8–foot model) and a special waterproof cargo compartment as well as fore and aft spray shields are available.

All these boating alternatives—rafts, paddle rafts, mini-inflatables and Sportyaks— offer certain advantages. The most important is that none of them demand a long, hard apprenticeship before you can begin running rapids. But it would be wrong to view them as means to an instant wildwater experience. Rafting techniques are not as complex as kayaking techniques, and rafting likewise seems to demand less personal commitment than kayaking. In rafting one's sense of risk is diminished, but nonetheless, don't be lulled into a false sense of security. No matter what craft you choose, no matter what style of boating, whitewater is still whitewater, rapids are for real, and a wild river is always a serious place. So serious in fact that we turn next to an important and sobering subject—safety.

Tired from too much traveling
Starting under sullen skies
Days passing by too fast
Paddling past creeks, deer, heron
Moonscape canyon walls converging
Upsidedown in unfriendly water
Safe in sudden eddies
Silent on sandy beaches
Watching waves by moonlight
Smiling for no reason
Afterwards, missing new friends

PART TWO
THE WHITEWATER
SCENE

CHAPTER 8

SAFETY

In whitewater, safety is first and foremost a state of mind. As in most environmental adventure sports—rock climbing, ski mountaineering, scuba diving—experience, judgment, and a calm but alert spirit are far more important than any special safety equipment in keeping one out of trouble or in dealing with trouble should it occur.

Insurance companies consider kayaking a high-risk sport, and they are correct. The kayaker, however, takes a slightly different view, distinguishing between potential danger, which abounds but can be avoided, and unavoidable risk. The level of unavoidable hazard can be kept very low indeed by learning what the real dangers are, how to avoid them, and how to deal with them. In fact, whitewater boating would probably be much less attractive if it were completely safe. As in mountaineering, potential danger elevates the whole enterprise to another level of seriousness and commitment. You can relax and even play in the river, but you cannot be irresponsible and get away with it. Of course, facing up to possible danger (and, in large measure, cancelling it out through a combination of judgment and technique) adds another dimension of personal satisfaction to the sport.

To get to this point, you must learn as much as you can about the hazards of whitewater boating, as well as how to react should the worst happen. You should be ready to rescue other boaters in trouble and to administer emergency medical treatment (even more than first aid) if needed. To this end, our safety chapter is divided into three sections: safety principles and common dangers; river rescue; and typical first aid situations.

Safety Principles and Common Dangers

Some of the basic principles of safe boating are so obvious that it almost hurts to repeat them. The first and most obvious point is, Don't boat alone. (I wouldn't even mention this if I hadn't encountered a shocking number of solitary kayakers last season.) Running rapids by yourself is sheer folly. In mountaineering, despite the greater risk, a certain glamor and mystique is associated with solo ascents; this is not so in kayaking. Whenever you run a drop in your kayak, you do so by yourself, fundamentally alone, even if there are other boaters at the top and bottom of the rapids. You have no rope and no helping hand for aid or comfort. For this reason, whitewater boaters do not consider it more difficult or more daring to run rivers alone—just stupid! A party of three is a fine solution for a small trip, although two kayakers boating together would be neither unusual nor unsafe. Of course, for bigger more serious trips, larger groups are in order. There really is safety in numbers.

This brings up the whole question of leadership, mutual responsibility, and the interaction among members of the same boating group, especially kayakers. Whitewater river running is a free thing, magnificently so; and kayakers themselves tend to be free spirits, escaping from social regulation rather than recreating it anew on the river. Experienced kayakers, therefore, tend to boat together in a very loose and unstructured way. They have no designated leader, and they make no rules. At first glance, it looks like anarchy. And yet, in a party of experienced kayakers there is a strong sense of river etiquette and an informal but real group dynamic at work all the time.

The overriding principle of river etiquette is, Don't interfere with other boaters when they're actively involved in some stretch of water. For example, you don't just move blindly out onto a wave if someone else is already surfing it, or you wait until there's room in an eddy before ferrying over to it. Likewise, boaters starting down a drop will adjust their line to avoid someone playing at the bottom; and kayakers waiting to play in waves at the bottom of a rapid will tend to wait until the drop is clear of boaters coming down from above. These are simple matters of common sense and courtesy, but they make boating in larger groups a pleasure, not a pain.

The informal and usually unexpressed organization of a group of experienced kayakers comes down to one simple idea: each boater is mentally concerned about the welfare and whereabouts of his companions all the time. Thus, even though the group may be strung out along a stretch of river, with various kayakers out of sight of each other, everyone knows who's ahead and who's behind. It's just a matter of paying attention. In a similar way, whoever happens to be in front will behave like a leader without actually being designated as such, trying to pick a good line for the boaters following him, warning them of any unexpected hazards or problems, and waiting below a hard spot if he senses that it may cause problems for some of the other boaters. Then, too, whoever happens to be last will act as a "sweep," checking to see that no one is left behind, for example, with boat trouble. Neither role is official, designated, or permanent. And the whole thing works well because each boater senses and accepts his share of responsibility for the welfare of the group.

The picture changes, however, if there are a number of beginners or inexperienced boaters in the group. They will have enough trouble just getting through the rapids themselves, and may need a bit of help to do so. In such a group it's common to designate a leader and another experienced boater to come last and sweep the river. It's also a good idea to have several of the more experienced kayakers waiting at the bottom of a drop before the beginners start down, either to assist in recovering lost equipment or to help tow a swimming beginner to shore if needed. And if there are enough experienced boaters in the group, a fine idea is to have the beginning or weaker kayakers follow them down the rapids, one on one; it's both a confidence builder and a way to show the weaker boaters the best line. The psychological and moral support that whitewater boaters can give each other is really amazing and is itself a significant factor in safe boating.

The remaining general safety principles are so simple that they sound like a preflight checklist. First, obtain some advance knowledge of the river you are about to run. Either read a good guidebook, talk to boaters who have done the run at similar water levels, or—best of all—include in your group at least one person who's done the run before. Don't just blindly put in on an unknown stretch of river. And remember that there is an important judgment to be made here: when you find out about your proposed river run, you must decide whether or not it is actually within your personal range of whitewater skills. If not, put it off for a while.

Always leave some word of where you're going and how long you expect your trip to take. Not with just anyone, but with someone who knows what river running is all about, and who can respond appropriately if you don't return on schedule. Next, be sure your equipment is adequate and in good repair. Don't take off on a whitewater run with a leaky, unpatched kayak, inadequate or no flotation, or a cracked paddle shaft. In addition to checking for functional equipment, make sure there are no loose cords, life-vest ties or other paraphernalia in which you could become entangled, and which might possibly trap you in the cockpit of your boat. Rafters, of course, will have their own equipment checklist which is usually a matter of watertightness and of tying everything down.

Finally, once on the river, don't run blind drops without some form of scouting. A *blind drop* is one where you can't see a clear route through to the end (where the river bends around a corner, for example). If you get in the habit of just paddling straight into such situations, you will naturally make it most of the time, but sooner or later you will encounter some very nasty surprises. Either rely on the knowledge of someone who has run this particular drop, land and scout around the blind spot from the bank or use the eddy-hopping technique, descending carefully from safe eddy to safe eddy (never leaving one until you have spotted another which you can definitely make and from which you can land if necessary). This last option requires a pretty competent level of skill on the part of all members of the group.

So much for our checklist of basic safety procedures. There is nothing hard or objectionable about any of them. You must also be keenly aware of several major dangers in the river—potential problems which cause most accidents and most deaths, situations where the proverbial ounce of prevention is worth a pound of cure. A really enterprising writer who only wanted to frighten his readers could doubtless think up dozens of river dangers. But actually there are only a couple of killers—entrapment and hypothermia.

Entrapment means being caught and held underwater, in your kayak or out. If this happens, you have very little time indeed to free yourself, perhaps from an overwhelming force, and if you don't free your-

self, drowning is likely. There are several possible
situations in which entrapment can occur, but the
most insidious by far is against submerged tree
branches. No, trees don't grow in rivers, but they're
there, just the same. The ones to watch out for are
large dead snags, carried away at flood stage and
deposited almost at random in many rivers; also
look out for trees and shrubs growing right beside
the water, which sometimes bend over, dragging
branches through the water, or become partially
submerged when the river rises above its normal
banks in spring flood. Kayakers sometimes refer to
these hazards as *strainers*, and this term holds the key
to why they are so terribly dangerous. When flowing
water hits a submerged rock, it bounces back off and
then flows to either side, forming a hydraulic cushion
which not only protects you from head-on collisions
but also tends to push you off the offending rock.
Not so with submerged branches. The current flows
directly through them, tending to pin any object—
such as an overturned kayak—against the tangle of
branches that caught it in the first place. Thus, if you
capsize against a submerged tree, you will be held
against it by the full force of the current straining
through. Add to this the fact that such submerged
branches are seldom neat and clean, but are often
horrible, spiky, confused tangles—just the thing to
snatch and entangle your life vest or spray skirt, or at
the very least prevent you from sweeping your paddle in an effective roll—and you will see why experienced kayakers take every possible precaution to
avoid paddling into, or even near, submerged trees.
Treat them like poison! If you see a few branches
protruding above the water, change your line to
give them a wide berth, and stay equally far away
from overgrown banks, especially at high water.
It's not a question of the difficulty of the river. A
submerged tree in a gentle Class 2 riffle can be a
death trap. Stay away!

The other entrapment situations tend to involve
rocks. Broaching sideways onto a rock in fast water is

a nasty one. In this case *lean downstream, onto the obstacle*, and then try to push yourself off either forward or backward. Shying away from the rock you're about to hit and leaning upstream is, of course, a sure invitation to tip. But if this should happen, you're probably still all right, even if your kayak is strongly pinned against the rock—provided that it doesn't wrap. *Wrapping* means that the kayak is bent sideways by the force of the current and is quite literally wrapped around the rock—with every likelihood of trapping your legs so that you can't get out of the boat. This is a certain drowning situation if you're upside-down, and a real nightmare if you're still upright against the rock, as you could go over at any second and in any case will probably need outside help to get free. Fortunately, this grim scenario isn't very likely in a fiberglass kayak. These boats broach on rocks all the time without wrapping, since they are quite rigid and would probably break apart before they did wrap. Wrapping is, however, extremely likely in a plastic kayak that's not adequately reinforced and stiffened by ethafoam pillars. So if you own a Hollowform River Chaser, do not under any circumstances take out the stiffening pillars; you might even consider putting *more* reinforcement around the sides of the cockpit.

The final possibility of entrapment occurs when swimming with your kayak (if you couldn't roll up and had to bail out). The danger here is that your foot might get wedged and stuck between two boulders. To avoid any possibility of this, attempt to keep your feet high in the water, either lifted in front of you if you're still being washed through a rapid, or kicking near the surface if you're swimming your boat ashore. However, you learned long ago to swim behind, that is, upstream from the kayak, so there should be no chance of being pinned between it and a rock.

The other real killer that the whitewater boater must be aware of is *hypothermia*. Hypothermia is the modern, accurate, and rather fancy expression for what used to be called "exposure." It means lack of heat, and it's lethal. But the real reason that it's such a common danger is that so few people take the possibility of hypothermia seriously.

Although one thinks of hypothermia more in connection with ill-prepared hikers caught out in severe weather, a moment's reflection will convince you that kayakers are in a perfect situation to lose body heat as a result of long hours of exertion in a cold, wet environment. Many of the finest whitewater runs are on mountain streams (because these provide a steeper gradient and hence more rapids), and naturally their water is quite cold. Even the desert rivers of the sunbaked Southwest, once known for their warm water, are now icy cold, because they are almost all dam-controlled, and only the coldest water, from the very bottom of their backed-up lakes, is released to flow downstream. Thus in the Grand Canyon today, though the air temperature may be 100 degrees, the water is still cold enough to give an unprotected swimmer convulsions. Altogether, cold water is a fact of life for the kayaker. So is being wet, if only from the spray of big waves and the consequent steady heat loss from evaporation.

Because they ride more in the water than above it, kayakers are more susceptible than rafters to heat loss and possible hypothermia. Yet no kayaker need fear this condition if he or she is aware of it and takes a few precautions. It's a matter of being adequately dressed, and extra clothes—whether a wet-suit tunic or top, a wool sweater, or a paddling jacket—weigh so little that there's really no reason not to take some along on every river trip! You don't have to wear them until things cool off, but take care to start dressing for cold *before*, not after, you get chilled. The medical symptoms, consequences, and treatment of hypothermia are discussed further on, under "Emergency Medical Treatment," but the crucial point is that you must recognize hypothermia as a serious whitewater hazard and act accordingly. Only boaters who don't take it seriously are in danger from hypothermia. Clever beginners tend to overdress anyway, because of the likelihood of swimming rather than rolling; and experts have learned by trial and error just how cold they'll get, and how to keep warm. It's generally the overconfident intermediate kayaker who is most likely to make an error in judgment, leave the wet suit at home because it's "too much trouble," and get seriously chilled or worse. Respect the effects of cold water, and you'll be all right.

River Rescue

When we speak of *river rescue* we mean helping to get another boater and/or his equipment safely out of the water. The simplest case might be picking up a lost paddle floating beneath a rapid; the toughest might involve life-and-death decisions in trying to extricate a trapped boater from a desperate situation.

"You never go down twice to the same river," said the pre-Socratic philosopher Heraclitus. And in the same sense, no two rescue situations will ever be the same. There's no way to give you a basic procedure to follow in all cases. Instead, here are a few likely situations to start you thinking about river rescues, a few items of equipment you'll find useful in rescue situations, and a couple of warnings about not-so-obvious mistakes that have proven fatal in the past.

Kayakers soon discover that it's quite an awkward business to recover someone else's equipment and still maintain control over their own boats. To recover a paddle floating in the water, grab it up and hold it tightly next to your own paddle, blade to blade and shaft to shaft. In this way you can keep on paddling, albeit a bit crudely. If you try to balance the recovered paddle on the front deck of your own kayak, it will either fall off again or else totally prevent you from paddling.

Recovering a loose kayak floating by itself is more of a problem. There's really no efficient way to do it. About all you can do is push it with the bow of your own boat, eventually nosing it into an eddy much as a good sheep dog noses and herds a stray lamb back into the fold. Aiding a kayaker swimming in the water with his equipment is far easier. Back your own kayak up to the swimmer so he can hang onto the rear grab loop while he continues to kick, and then paddle strongly in an upstream ferry for the nearest bank. Often it's not really worth giving a swimming kayaker a tow—for example, if there's a nice calm pool just below, or if the water is so rough that you may get into trouble yourself. Exercise some judgment before rushing in to help.

This is, of course, the light-hearted side of river rescue: just helping out and reducing the inconvenience of an awkward situation, not at all a life-and-death situation. Sometimes you know in advance that some of the weaker boaters of your party are going to have trouble with a certain drop, and you can take steps to expedite the inevitable mopping up and reorganization afterward. This may only take the form of stationing a couple of experienced kayakers in convenient eddies at the bottom of the rapid, ready to help. Or, if there are one or two rafts in the party, it's often ideal to have them run the drop before any of the nervous beginners, since drifting people and equipment can easily be stashed on board a large raft. Sometimes inexperienced and insecure kayakers may not be ready for one or two of the hardest rapids on a given run though they can handle everything else with confidence and enjoyment. In such cases the whole hassle of helping a swimming boater and rescuing his equipment can be avoided if a more experienced kayaker volunteers to take the beginner's boat down the scary drop. It requires a short walk back to get the extra boat, but can save a lot of time and grief.

River rescue involving inflatable rafts is at once easier and more difficult. Easier because there are usually more people around to help, and more difficult because a raft in trouble or up-side down is such a bulky awkward object. There are several typical situations. The one that sounds worst but is relatively the safest is when a raft flips completely over, throwing passengers, boatman, and whatever gear isn't tied down into the water. Actually, everything should be tied on, so it's really only a question of taking care of the people and the raft. If you wind up under the raft itself, get the hell out of there—dive and swim to the outside. If you're still in rough water, you can hold onto the rear of the raft (avoid the front or downstream side, since you could get crunched between it and a rock), and in some cases you can even climb on top of the flipped-over raft. As soon as you have reached some sort of calmer water, the next task is to get the raft back upright. If it isn't too enormous, or too heavily loaded, this is a relatively simple job, provided you have tied one or two lines across the bottom of the boat (laterally, from side to side). Several people climb up on one tube and, hauling back on these lines (or line), can actually raise the other side and flip the raft back over rightside-up. Like many "river emergencies," a capsized raft is easily dealt with if you've thought about what to do in advance. (Fortunately, too, rafts don't flip very often.)

More awkward is the case of a raft that has wrapped and stuck on a midriver rock. The first step here is to shift the weight (people) to the side of the boat next to the rock in order to avoid swamping the outside or upstream tube and wrapping the raft around the rock below the water line, which would infinitely compound the problem. The next step is up to the imagination of the rafters: bouncing, pushing, lifting, or partially deflating the raft, off-loading some of the gear (either onto the rock or onto another boat), waiting for the water level to change, or hauling from shore on an attached rope—all have been tried, and may or may not work, depending on the circumstances. A rule of thumb for such cases is first make sure that everyone is safe, and then, as you attempt to free the gear, try not to make the situation any worse.

The use of a line or rope in a river-rescue situation is one tactic that's capable of doing as much harm as good. To the mountain climber, being tied to a rope is an automatic expression of security. In moving water this is emphatically not the case. And sad to say, quite a number of climbers have perished in attempted river crossings as a direct result of being tied to a rope. The very belay which would have saved them in a fall from a cliff drowned them in swift water.

The fatal error in moving water is that of tying the rope around one's waist. In this position, if one falls over backwards and the rope is taut, one's body acts like a "deadman" anchor and is driven deeper by the force of the current. However, if the rope is held in the hand or looped high around the shoulders, one's body will tend to plane *up* in moving water even if it's swept away downstream.

But as long as you are aware of such danger, a line or rope is awfully useful on the river. Let's see how it should and shouldn't be used. In trying to pull a wrapped or broached boat off a rock, a rope can be very handy provided you have an easy way of attaching it to the boat. It's often nearly impossible to reach a stranded boat, and even when you do, you will seldom have much time to fiddle around with typing knots. But kayaks have grab loops at both ends and most rafts are festooned with lines and D-rings, so if you carry a couple of carabiners (climbers' oval snap links of aluminum), you can easily clip your lines directly to a stuck boat and, from the right angle, possibly pull it off. In setting up such an operation it's important to realize that in a direct confrontation with the river's force you will usually lose. The current is too powerful and water itself too heavy for anyone to succeed by directly opposing the force which is pinning a boat to a rock. Pull and push from the side, and try to arrange things so that the water's force helps you, however little. And, finally, though it's usually impossible to lasso an unreachable boat stuck out in midstream, there are occasional absurd circumstances in which there's nothing else to be tried.

The most critical rescue situations are those in which you must try to save a trapped boater. Hopefully you'll never have to make the effort, and such situations, fortunately, are rare. Still, when they do occur you have very little time in which to do anything, so it's very important to have thought about this possibility beforehand so that you'll have a general idea of how to respond. The situation we are most concerned with is that of the kayaker who is trapped in his boat. This could be the result of broaching and then wrapping around a rock; or of being caught sideways between two rocks so that the force of the water pouring between them bends the kayak enough to pin the boater's legs inside; or even from being jammed too far forward in the kayak after a sudden frontal collision with a rock. Or he may have run into a partially submerged tree and capsized, only to be trapped by the branches and pinned against them by the force of the water straining through. In all but the last case, the boater is trapped by some weakness in his kayak, especially the front deck being squashed down over the legs or a sideways bending at the cockpit. In the equipment discussion you learned that plastic kayaks are more susceptible to such buckling than fiberglass ones and must be heavily reinforced with internal foam pillars to be considered safe. But even a fiberglass kayak can bend and wrap under certain circumstances.

If your boat should ever broach on a rock and you feel that your legs are perhaps being trapped by the kayak's buckling, try to lean downstream onto the obstacle, cling to it if you can, but *don't* for an instant lean upstream. If you do, you'll flip, and your friends will have only seconds to reach you. Should you ever be trapped underwater, you might as well put all your energy into one desperate attempt to pull free. Do it immediately before the pounding of the water and lack of oxygen exhaust you, and hopefully with the proverbial strength born of desperation, you'll break free.

If a companion appears to be trapped, start acting right away; don't stop to doublecheck whether or not he's really in trouble. In the best situations, you can get to a trapped boater either by paddling or by

swimming. When you reach him your first priority is
to hold his head above water while other efforts are
being made to free his boat, or to free him from the
boat. If you can't reach a trapped boater who is still
above water, then by all means throw him a line
which has a loop in the end for him to put an arm
through or to put around his shoulders. But be careful about the direction the rope is pulling. It should
help to keep him upright, but if you don't take into
account the direction of both pull and current, a rope
can easily have the opposite effect.

Finally, if a boater is trapped underwater and it's
taken you a long time to get to him, don't give up!
Once you have freed the body and brought it to the
surface, you can start giving artificial respiration right
there in the water (it's been done). Get the body out
of the river as fast as possible, continue the artificial
respiration, and use heart massage if needed. Too
many people have been brought back, literally from
death's doorstep, for any layman to make the decision
that someone has been underwater too long and not
attempt resuscitation.

Naturally, kayakers aren't the only boaters who
can be trapped in the river. It's possible for any
swimming boater to be trapped by rocks or caught
and recirculated in a big hole. Especially in a bad reversal, a rope from shore might be the best, or only,
way of helping a trapped boater out. For all these reasons I always carry at least 50 feet of light perlon line
(5 or 7 mm), a couple of carabiners, and a couple of
nylon webbing loops, even on short, easy afternoon
kayak trips . . . just in case.

This short rope is also handy if you need to *line*
your boat down an unrunnable stretch of river. Lining
is sometimes easier, sometimes harder than portag-
ing, depending on the terrain and the water. To line a
kayak, attach your rope to the rear grab loop and put
your spray deck in place on the kayak to seal it as
much as possible; then let the kayak out much like a
dog on a leash. Lining a raft is more like having an
elephant on a leash. Make sure you have a long,

strong rope and plenty of manpower.

The whole subject of rescue, and especially of entrapment, can get a little grim. Nonetheless, thinking about the worst eventualities well in advance will not only help you to respond in an emergency, it will also decrease the chances of ever having such an emergency. Awareness of danger is the first step in avoiding danger, or at least greatly reducing it. And thinking about how hard it is to rescue someone in a swiftly moving river will surely give you more respect for the river itself—not as an enemy to be overcome, but as a challenging playground where carelessness can have a heavy cost.

Emergency Medical Treatment

The finest whitewater runs are surely those that take us farthest from the beaten path, away from towns, houses, and roads. But wilderness boating, like any other wilderness sport, throws us back on our own resources, especially if one member of the party gets hurt. This is not just a question of knowing how to administer first aid. First aid is commonly defined as immediate assistance rendered to an injured person until a doctor arrives or until the victim is transported to a doctor or hospital. But on a long, multiday river trip, we must realize that the doctor simply isn't going to come, and getting to one may take a few more days. So the wilderness boater must be prepared to go beyond the limits of normal first aid if someone is hurt or sick.

The place to begin is the traditional Red Cross first aid courses—first basic, then advanced. But if possible, don't stop there. In many areas, *EMT (emergency medical technician)* courses are available. These are rather intensive courses given by a physician, and they take one a good deal beyond the material covered by the Red Cross first aid courses. Finally, there is *CPR (cardiopulmonary resuscitation)* training. These courses are not for specialists, but are designed for lay people and are given by the American Heart Association in most major cities. It would be ideal if at least one member of every whitewater boating group had taken a CPR course, since the total procedure it covers, including cardiac or heart massage, is exactly what you need in case of a drowning. Granted, good judgment can almost entirely eliminate the likelihood of anyone ever drowning on a whitewater trip, but isn't it still better to be prepared for the one-in-a-million eventuality?

Basic reading for medical emergencies is the *Red Cross First Aid Handbook*. But much better is a book on emergency medical treatment written especially for mountain climbers (so far there are none written especially for river tourers) called *Medicine for Mountaineering*, edited by James Wilkerson, and available at most climbing and backpacking shops. Naturally, the whitewater boater can totally ignore the sections on frostbite and specific high-altitude problems such as pulmonary edema; but this book is definitely the best source of information for the layman about emergency medical procedures in the field. I won't attempt to compete with it in the remainder of this chapter, and will assume that everyone is capable of putting together a reasonable first aid kit to be carried on longer river trips. But we should briefly look at the three most serious medical emergencies specific to whitewater boating: hypothermia, dislocated shoulder (a serious problem for kayakers), and drowning.

Hypothermia is a Greek word meaning "too little heat." It is the extreme and dangerous cooling of the body's inner core. When you start feeling cold, and for some time thereafter, the body is able to maintain a stable and normal core temperature by a slight alteration of both circulation and metabolism. But eventually, if you continue to lose heat faster than your body can produce it, your core temperature will begin to go down. Past a certain point the process becomes irreversible: the heart begins to "fibrillate," or beat in an aimless erratic way, and death follows.

The initial symptoms of hypothermia (as opposed to just feeling chilled) are poor coordination, slow movements, thickness of speech, intense shivering, muscle tensing, a general feeling of fatigue, and deep cold or numbness. The basic treatment is to stop any further heat loss by using more clothing and insulation, and to warm the victim up fast. In a river situation this means getting the victim ashore (more than likely he's been swimming in very cold water), and then using hot drinks, a fire, or body heat from others in the party to warm him. Or a hot bath, if there's a house nearby. Note that it does no good just to put the victim in a sleeping bag—which is merely insulation, not a heat source—since the patient is unable to provide enough heat himself.

In advanced cases—where the victim's core temperature is below 90° F—there will be a blueness or puffiness of the skin, a decrease in shivering followed by a rigidity of muscles, dilation of the pupils, and a slow, weak, or irregular pulse. Obviously, a victim at this stage would have no chance of surviving in the river, but if the onset of hypothermia goes unnoticed, a wet, cold boater could continue to lose heat and reach this critical state even after being helped to shore. At this point the application of external heat (such as a fire, or the warmth of other bodies, or even a hot bath) is no longer sufficient, since it is the inner core temperature which is dangerously low. You must force hot fluids if the victim is conscious, hot enemas if he's unconscious. And at the same time, give yourself hell for ever allowing such a situation to develop. Prevention, not treatment, is the answer to hypothermia. And lest you think that the danger is far-fetched, I personally know one kayaker who went into severe hypothermia after a particularly harrowing swim in the Grand Canyon in the middle of summer! Hypothermia is not just a problem for folks who want to kayak in midwinter in Maine.

A dislocated shoulder is to the kayaker what an injured knee is to a skier—the most common of all injuries, and one that puts you completely out of action. Even though there's no ski patrol on the river, the paddler is probably the luckier of the two, because in most cases a dislocated shoulder can be easily and quickly treated. Kayakers are particularly prone to anterior dislocations of the shoulder (the humerus pops forward out of its socket) because of one particular maneuver, the bow draw, or Duffeck stroke. In this stroke, the upper arm is in an abducted and externally rotated position (bent up and back, in layman's terms), and can easily be pushed to the very limit of its range of movement. What then? A little extra force and the arm is levered right out of the shoulder socket. You're always using the paddle as a lever to exert force, and it's easy to forget how much force this lever can exert on you. The potential stress on a kayaker's shoulder is so great that anyone who has a history of recurrent shoulder dislocations should check with a doctor before taking up the sport.

To guard against a possible dislocation, avoid needlessly exaggerating your arm position in a bow draw. Cocking your upper arm back over your head every time you come into an eddy won't really improve your technique, and it's a bad habit to get into because in rough water—watch out! When your upper arm does get bent back over your head, however, you can more or less protect it by keeping your lower arm well bent and that elbow in at your side. This will seem confusing if you no longer have a clear mental picture of the bow draw; consult Chapter 4 to refresh the image.)

There won't be any doubt if a dislocation occurs; the pain alone will let you know. Once the injured kayaker has gotten himself and his boat ashore—perhaps with a good deal of help—the idea is to *reduce* the dislocation as quickly as possible. Typically, after only twenty minutes the muscle spasms around the dislocated joint become so intense that there's no way to overcome them, and in such cases the reduction often has to be performed surgically. So it's best to get right to it as fast as possible. There's almost no way you can hurt the victim, and you can do a world of good.

The procedure works like this: Ideally the victim should be lying prone on some sort of a shelf, with the affected shoulder protruding slightly and the arm hanging freely down. Naturally, you won't find any operating-room tables beside a whitewater stream, but the deck of a kayak makes a fine platform if you can prop it up high enough off the ground. Be inventive. With the victim in place, one person should hold or steady his chest (so he won't be pulled right off) and another should apply slow, steady, even downward traction on the dislocated arm. This traction, or steady pulling force, can be applied in several ways, but in all cases it is best done with the victim's arm fully flexed at the elbow to take strain off the brachio-radialis muscle. The wrist can be held or tied up at shoulder level; then, using a bandanna or other sling looped over the victim's elbow, apply traction either by direct downward pulling or by tying weights to the elbow sling. The idea is to fatigue the contracted muscles which are now effectively holding the end of the bone out of its normal place. This reduction is easier with women, who tend to have less developed muscles, toughest of all with highly muscular athletes. It may take some time—five or ten minutes is not unusual—to overcome the resistance of these muscles and pop the arm back in place. Just be patient and remember that this is a slow, steady pulling maneuver, not a sudden jerk. If you and the victim are alone, you won't be able to attempt the reduction with the victim lying prone. Instead, rig up some kind of sling that effectively holds and immobilizes the victim's torso against a tree trunk, and then apply the same steady traction straight out from the body. Once the dislocation is reduced, immobilize the arm in a sling and figure out what to do next. The victim won't feel like paddling, and he definitely shouldn't.

The last situation a whitewater boater has to be prepared to deal with is a drowning—or more accu-

54. One method of reducing a dislocated shoulder

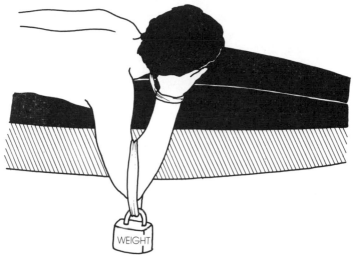

WEIGHT

rately, "near drowning," since "drowning" is normally used for the irreversible end result—an unconscious, nonbreathing victim who has spent a lot of time underwater. The basic response is to give mouth-to-mouth resuscitation fast—even in the water, while you're trying to get the body ashore—and to supplement this with cardiac massage if there's no discernible pulse. The full CPR treatment. Every first aid textbook has a long and detailed section on mouth-to-mouth resuscitation (and does a better job than I could). But you should review this procedure, which most outdoors people are already familiar with, and make sure you've got it down cold before you do much river touring. You're crazy if you don't.

The idea that nonprofessionals should attempt a cardiac resuscitation as well as mouth-to-mouth in an emergency is rather a new one, but a lot of lives have already been saved as a result of the CPR training courses. Cardiopulmonary resuscitation is a tricky procedure to learn, and it should only be presented and taught by certified instructors. If you just start thumping down on a victim's chest without knowing what you're doing, you'll probably break a few ribs, but you won't bring him back. So do seek out and attend a CPR training program. If you haven't had one, better just stick with mouth-to-mouth respiration, which has an excellent chance of reviving victims if they haven't been without oxygen longer than five minutes. In very cold water a victim may have a good chance even if he's been underwater much longer, because of a phenomenon known as the "mammalian diving reflex," which in essence shuts down the body's metabolic systems, greatly reducing the need for oxygen and increasing the chance of survival.

How long should you keep trying to resuscitate a victim? Longer, anyway, than seems reasonable. A lot of "drowning victims" have opened their eyes after half an hour or more of resuscitation efforts. If you're successful it will be one of the best moments of your life, but in the excitement don't forget all the other first aid basics, such as treating for shock, which should be almost second nature if you're really prepared for long remote trips.

It's almost a shame to end a chapter on safety with a section on first aid, because when you need to render first aid, your boating trip has definitely become unsafe. Remember that whitewater safety is first and foremost a state of mind—a complex and subtle state of mind compounded of strong informed judgment and an intelligent concern for other members of your party. When every member of a whitewater party shares this state of mind, then we really have safe boating.

CHAPTER 9

PRACTICAL RIVER TOURING

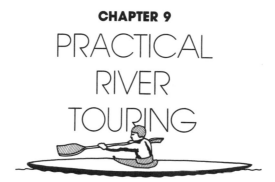

Under the topic of "practical river touring" falls a host of important tips, tactics, and strategies for running and enjoying wild rivers that don't deal directly with getting your boat down rapids. Not whitewater skills, but such things as planning trips, organizing transportation, repairing boats, river camping, and the like. These are extras, but vital extras nonetheless, without which you might never even reach the river, much less enjoy it. For convenience, we'll break this somewhat nebulous subject in half, first discussing essentials that come before and after even short, one-day trips, and then turning to longer, multiday river trips.

Before and After the Run

Like the one-day ski tour, a short river run is a delightful exercise in controlled irresponsibility and unfettered fun. You're there to go boating, period. There's no bulky baggage to deal with, so the boats (kayaks and rafts) are light and responsive. No com-

plicated planning, or figuring out menus, or food buying, and you don't have to wonder if everything is
really waterproof. The short one-day run is white
water sport par excellence. But the day begins long
before you see the river.

Transporting Boats

Even the lightest kayaks are long and awkward
objects, and a raft complete with oars, spare oars, and
a rowing frame can be a monster, even if it's deflated.
So our first task, getting ourselves and our gear to the
put-in, is not entirely without problems. Whitewater
boaters usually rely on some kind of car-roof racks to
transport all their paraphernalia. But a word of warning to kayakers: don't just throw your boats up on an
old ski rack and lash them on. You can easily damage
fiberglass kayaks on a roof rack if you're not careful.

The thing *not* to do is to put your kayak on an
ordinary roof rack rightside-up, and then tie it down
tightly. This will buckle and fold the bottom of the
boat, may weaken or pop the kayak's side seams, and
will eventually ruin it. The only roof racks on which
you can safely lay a kayak rightside-up are specially
designed canoe and kayak racks which have curved,
cradlelike supports (saddles) for the rounded bottom
of the boat. The best are the Yakima boat racks ($35
to $45), but they have one problem: you can only
carry two boats (or three on the larger van model),
because they take up so much room in this flat position. This is not very convenient if you must shuttle
boats for an entire group.

A simpler, cheaper system is to buy a set of four
"Quick-N-Easy" roof brackets for under $20, and
make your own roof rack out of two-by-fours. These
are heavy-duty cast-aluminum brackets that clamp
strongly onto the rain gutter of your car. This set-up
permits great flexibility in stacking boats on the
wooden cross members, which are bolted to the
brackets. If you want to lay your kayak flat on this (or
any other) rack, turn it upside-down. It's a lot

stronger this way, but this method of transport is still recommended only for short trips. Kayaks are far stronger if they're stood up on their sides. In this position, also, you can easily stack four, five, or six kayaks across the top of an average car rack (and, if need be, make a second layer on top of the first). Perhaps the best and most efficient kayak racks are homemade modifications of the two-by-four idea, designed to always carry the kayaks on their sides. The simplest of these has a short length of galvanized pipe sticking up out of the center of each wooden cross piece, so that even one kayak can be tied against it. (Normally you need three or four kayaks side by side to prop each other up securely.) And you can also make deluxe racks where each kayak is supported in a nylon webbing sling. (See Figure 55 for several types of carrying racks.)

55. Two types of cartop kayak racks

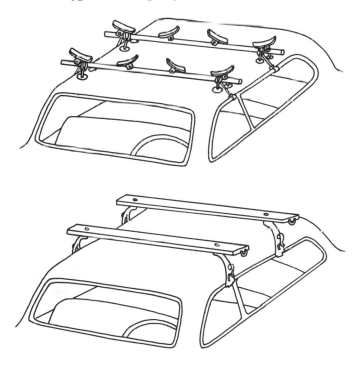

Whatever system you use, remember to tie your boats down securely. Just using lines or rubberized bungee cords going from side to side is insufficient. You should have at least a nose rope connecting the forward grab loops to the car's front bumper, and preferably a tail rope as well. Kayaks are slippery objects and don't want to stay on a car roof at 55 mph. Rafts don't need special racks, but they are heavy, so tie them on well.

Shuttles

The logistics of setting up a river run involve more than lashing boats onto a car. Now we have to face the shuttle. *Shuttling* means organizing return transportation from the take-out point as well as getting all boaters and equipment to the put-in. It usually commits you to having at least two cars in the party, it involves a lot of unavoidable extra driving, and is generally a pain.

Depending, of course, on road connections and access to the river, a typical shuttle might go something like this: Everyone drives to the put-in point and unloads all the boating gear. People change into whatever they'll be wearing on the river, and put dry clothes in one of the cars that will be left at the other end. Then, while most of the boaters are getting their equipment ready (blowing up rafts and flotation bags, carrying boats to the water, and so on), two members of the group drive two cars around to the take-out point. This may be only a few miles away by river but is usually more by road. They then leave one car (the one with dry clothes, beer, and material for tying down kayaks on the roof) at the take-out, and drive back together to the put-in. At the end of the run there are two possibilities. Either you tie all the boats on top of the car you've left there (hence the disadvantage of Yakima-type roof racks, with only enough room for two boats) and everyone squeezes merrily in for the drive back to the put-in where the other car or cars are waiting. Or else a couple of boaters drive back around to get all the cars and bring them back while everyone else waits with the boats at the take-out.

Clearly, there's no easy way of doing it. And, indeed, shuttling is the stupidest, most boring part of whitewater boating. No matter how you organize it, you wind up doing a lot of waiting around when you would rather be in the river or on your way home. It's probably a tribute to the fascination and excitement of whitewater boating that people put up with the bother of shuttling at all.

There are a couple of variations on this theme, but no easy way out. If the shuttle is fairly short and you're in good shape, you can substitute a bicycle for one of the cars, reducing your dependence on the dreaded machine. In this case, you might want to drive down to the take-out and cycle back to the start, since a long bicycle ride to fetch the car after an exhausting river run could be a little too much. Then, too, one boater can always hitchhike back around to get the car. We wouldn't advise trying this just anywhere, since many people are averse to picking up mysterious dripping-wet strangers clad in sinister-looking, black wet suits. But in certain areas with consistent and friendly traffic, hitchhiking can be a reasonable alternative to the usual shuttle. Finally, in certain very popular river-running areas there are people or organizations that will shuttle your vehicle around to the take-out point for a fee. Don't laugh; it can really be worth it. For example, on the Rogue River (which is a beautiful multiday wild river run) the shuttle back and forth takes virtually a whole day—a day you could spend on the river.

So after an early start, a long drive from the city, and a well-organized shuttle, here you are: ready to peel out into the current for a good whitewater run. All the time it takes to set this up may prove to be an advantage, since many of the best short runs, west and east, are dam-controlled, and it takes time for the daily water release from upstream dams to work its way down the river. If you had been ready at 9 a.m.

the river might have been unrunnable. Now, after shuttling cars, it's 11 a.m. and the water is up—good boating.

And here's one last hint to help you get into the water and on your way. If you still have a long walk or a stretch of awkward or brushy terrain to cross before reaching the river, you and a companion can carry your boats down to the water together. Just pick up a couple of strong branches and slide them through the grab loops at the stern and bow, forming handles that won't hurt your hands as the rope would. Then, with one person in front and the other behind, you can easily carry two kayaks at a time down to the water with paddles, helmets, and the rest of your gear stuffed into the cockpits. This is far easier and more comfortable than the usual method of carrying your own kayak over your shoulder. If you're rafting, just hope that you don't have far to carry your rig; even small ones are brutally heavy.

Repairing Boats

Almost everything that might happen on a short river trip has been covered now, except for the possibility of damaging your boat. Unfortunately, this isn't a rare occurrence, but a rather common one. Fortunately, it's usually not too serious. Rocks are usually the culprits that tear up boats, cracking, puncturing, or ripping them. Occasionally, though, when eddies get a little too crowded, a careless boater in a sharp-nosed slalom kayak can broadside another boat, putting a neat hole in it. To avoid damaging other boats, as well as to prevent cracking the kayak's nose on rocks, many boaters split a tennis ball and tape it over the pointed nose of their kayaks as a kind of bumper. And this brings us to the whitewater boater's universal repair kit—gray tape.

Gray tape, or to be more precise, *duct tape* must surely be one of the wonders of the twentieth century; sometimes one gets the impression that almost

everything is held together with gray tape somewhere. Ski patrolmen call it "avalanche tape," film
production crews call it "gaffer's tape," river runners
often refer to is as "boat tape," but whatever it's called
it's invaluable. You can buy duct tape at any hardware
store in two-inch-wide rolls and you should always
carry some on the river. With it you can patch a broken kayak, repair a broken paddle shaft, seal up a rip
in your spray skirt, even patch a leaky flotation bag. If
it's convenient, just toss a whole roll of tape into
someone's dry storage bag. If space is a problem, you
can take a considerable hunk of tape with you by un-
rolling a long strip and then rolling it up around the
very center of your kayak paddle where it won't get
in the way.

Gray tape can be used temporarily to seal up
some leaks in rubberized rafts, but it's primarily a
kayakers' and canoeists' remedy. To patch a raft that
has sprung a leak or has been torn on a jagged rock,
you have to beach the raft, dry out the damaged area,
and go through a procedure very much like patching
the inner tube of a bicycle tire, only on a grander
scale. It's a time-consuming but easy task, and all raft
manufacturers supply patching kits. On the other
hand, rafts tend to bounce off rocks which would
punch holes in kayaks, so patching on the river is a
relatively infrequent occurence.

To patch a rip in a fiberglass kayak on the river,
again you must land and dry out the surface of the
boat—otherwise even gray tape won't stick. But
don't start to worry every time you notice water
sloshing around in the bottom of your kayak. All
kayaks leak a little, mostly through the spray skirt.
Just keep a large natural sponge in your cockpit stuffed under the seat, and use it to "bail" periodically. If
you have to patch, put several strips of tape over the
rip, extending past it a good way, and then anchor the
whole patch in place with a couple of crosswise strips.
That's all there is to it. The amazing thing is that such
patches really work, even for quite big holes and
tears. The idea, of course, is to take the tape off later

56. A hasty patching job with gray tape

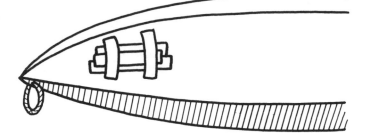

and apply a permanent fiberglass patch. But boaters who are perhaps a little lazy or who hate the smell of resin often put off this permanent patching job for months while they just accumulate more and more gray-tape patches on the bottom of their kayaks. A certain amount of wear and tear is inevitable with fiberglass kayaks; it doesn't mean that you're a poor boater. But naturally beginners are going to snag a lot more rocks and patch their kayaks far more often then experienced river runners.

The permanent patching job that you do at home is a bit more complicated. You'll need a well-ventilated place to work, preferably outdoors; a couple of saw horses or the equivalent to prop your kayak on; resin and catalyst; fiberglass cloth and scissors; and brush you can throw away; a painter's paper bucket or coffee can in which to mix up a batch of resin; some old clothes that you won't mind ruining; and sandpaper.

Prepare the area around the break (or tear, or crack) by first cutting away any jagged half-attached pieces, sanding off the typical cosmetic surface (gelcoat) on the outside of the kayak, and smoothing the remaining cracked or splintered fiberglass beneath. This is real drudgery, but many patches look crummy, and are weak too, just because the kayak's surface wasn't cleanly and smoothly prepared. Heavy-duty industrial sandpaper (supplied by Phoenix kayaks in their patching kits) is the best stuff for sanding your breaks by hand. But it's far easier to use a special sanding-disc attachment for a standard electric drill, with the grittiest sanding discs you can find, to prepare the patching area.

Next, cut out the patches themselves from the *fiberglass cloth*. Ten-ounce fiberglass cloth (a moderately heavy-feeling, medium-coarse weave) is the standard for both building and repairing kayaks, and one large patch of this stuff will usually do the job. But you can obtain much better looking and stronger results by using several overlapping patches of a lighter, finer fiberglass cloth (4—or 6—ounce). In any case, cut the basic patch in a rectangle (oval patches tend to unravel while you're working with them) that extends several inches past the damaged spot in all directions. Then, if you're using multiple layers of light cloth cut two more patches, each one a couple of inches bigger, all around, than the last. For convenience, you're going to apply the patches on the outside of the boat, although fanatics who want to preserve their kayak's appearance try to make most patches from the inside—an awkward space to work in, to say the least. Nonetheless it's important that no jagged fiberglass edges be left inside the boat, to cut or puncture your flotation bags, so you will often have to slap on at least one patch from the inside. If you've broken off part of the nose plug of your kayak through too vigorous an eddy turn into a rock, then instead of using a flat patch you'll want to fill up the hole with a kind of glop made by cutting up the fiberglass cloth into tiny strands, or cutting up nonwoven fiberglass mat. In any case, once the patches for the entire kayak are all cut out, you are ready for the messy part of the job.

Most boats are made of fiberglass and polyester resin, so polyester resin is what you probably want to use for repairs. Epoxy resin boats are rather rare, primarily because of health dangers in the manufacturing process, but if you do have an epoxy boat that needs repair, use epoxy resin. In small amounts the toxic qualities aren't so critical, but epoxy is still a

difficult medium to work with. Probably the best
thing to do is to get a copy of Charles Walbridge's
Boat Builder's Manual and read everything he says
about epoxy resin systems before starting work. By
comparison, working with polyester resins is absolutely trivial, except that they smell terrible, get all
over you if you're not careful, and can ruin clothing.
Any idiot (including the author) can do a good job of
patching with polyester resin. Several types of
polyester resin are available at plastics supply houses,
but avoid "casting" resin and "finish" resin, both of
which have special cosmetic properties and are too
brittle to make good patches.

Figure out how much resin you're going to need
(the fiberglass cloth soaks up a surprising amount, so
at first be generous), and pour it into the disposable
cardboard bucket or old coffee can. Next add the
catalyst, or "hardener." For polyester resin this is a
liquid called Methyl Ethyl Ketone Peroxide (MEKP)
and it's amazing stuff. In most cases, if you follow the
directions carefully, you will only be adding a few
drops (counting them one by one) to activate a
goodly batch of resin. Buy the resin and the hardener
at the same time from the same source and follow the
mixing directions to the letter. Beginners usually get
nervous, think that a little extra hardener can't hurt,
dump it in and then watch open-mouthed as their
whole pot of resin "goes off" in a couple of minutes.
Naturally, if you mix too "hot" a batch you won't have
enough time to apply all your patches. At around
70° F a well-mixed batch of resin will give you over
twenty minutes of working time before it starts to set
up and harden.

Once your resin is mixed, lay the cut patches out
in sequence on a piece of cardboard and, using a
cheap brush, impregnate them with resin. The white
fiberglass cloth will turn transparent as it soaks up
resin. Then, handling them gingerly, put the patches
on the kayak, smoothing them well and pushing any
air bubbles to the outside. Only the fiberglass gives
strength, not the resin, so don't slop it on once the

patch is in place. In fact, the ideal method is to squeegee off all excess resin once the patch is in position. For multilayer patches, apply the separate layers one on top of the other, and then try to brush the excess resin off the whole thing. Try to organize everything so that you can accomplish the whole job with one batch of resin. The stuff is too messy to mix up and apply twice. If you suspect that you may do a lot of kayak repairing in the course of one summer, you can buy a box of disposable vinyl gloves (available at the same plastics outlets for a couple of bucks) and wear them when you work with resin. About the only way I've ever been able to clean resin off my hands is by hard scrubbing with acetone—not fun.

And there you are. Your kayak should be as good as new. There is no real limit to the amount or size of patches you can apply and still have a first-rate whitewater craft. If you patch with care there should be no limit, either, to your kayak's effective lifetime. When you do change boats it ought to be to take advantage of some new design, not because the old kayak is worn out. And it goes without saying that after a number of successful river trips you begin to look on your kayak as an old friend, a trusty companion that's worth taking care of.

Long Trips

Organizing a successful two-week river trip is something to be proud of. A successful trip is one where everyone gets enough to eat and likes the food, where none of the gear gets wet or lost, and where the inevitable little river emergencies don't catch you unprepared. Of course, to do a long trip, you need a long river. There are many, but most of the spectacular and well-known ones in this country are, of necessity, protected, managed, and controlled by one government agency or another. Thus, obtaining permits (and sometimes reservations) often becomes a part of the planning and organizing process.

Once on the river itself most boaters heave a sigh of relief; and really, only the most elementary camping skills are needed to live comfortably on the river day after day, camp after camp, rapid after rapid.

Advance Planning

To be perfectly honest, the best advice for beginning boaters about planning long river trips is, Let someone else do it. That is, try to join a trip that other people, more experienced than yourself, are putting together and leading. It's worth it. During your first season on the river you will have enough to think about, wondering whether you can handle that next big rapid, without troubling yourself about the logistics and organization of a whole group. Besides, by tagging along on a couple of well-run river trips you will get a feeling for what has to be done, as well as make a lot of new friends for future trips. River friendships have a way of lasting.

But here's a brief rundown of what you have to do before you can successfully launch a longer trip. The first step is research: What part of the country will you choose? What river? What degree of difficulty? What water level and what time of year? Some good sources for this kind of information are the regional whitewater guidebooks (many are mentioned in the next chapter), whitewater clubs and organizations, and, perhaps best of all, word of mouth from friends who have already done the trip. Before committing yourself to the river for a week or more, you really want to form a clear idea of the difficulty of a particular run. Knowing the class is often not enough. The best thing is to get your information from someone who knows that particular river and who also knows your level of boating skill. If you're considering a river in some other region or state, try to get your sources to compare it with local whitewater runs that you've already done. There's nothing worse than realizing on your second day out that the run you've selected is too tough but that you can't really turn back.

A good map of the river you want to run can be an enormous help in evaluating the trip. Small-scale USGS topographic maps can give a lot of information about rivers, especially about the gradient of a given stretch. Certain rivers that are included in the National Wild and Scenic Rivers System are covered in handy recreation-oriented maps (showing campsites, permanent toilet facilities, and the like) that are published by the controlling agency—the Bureau of Land Management, Forest Service, and so forth.

The best maps, however, are those made by river runners for river runners, and of these, undoubtedly the most unique are the scroll maps made by Leslie Jones. Jones is a pioneer kayaker who got into mapmaking by accident and kept at it. He has produced detailed maps of about thirty western rivers, and he sells them, literally, out of his basement, more as a public service than as a real business. These maps are long scrolls that the boater unrolls progressively as he proceeds downriver. They can be carried in a plastic bag but are also available in waterproof mylar for an extra charge. For information write to Les Jones, Star Route Box 13, Heber City, Utah 84032.

The Westwater River Guides series includes splendid guide maps in pamphlet form, but to date it only covers the Grand Canyon, the Snake, Dinosaur, Desolation, and Canyonlands. It's too bad there aren't more books in this series. They contain a lot of interesting historical and general information aside from just river-running facts and are also available in waterproof editions.

Once you have focused your attention on a given river and have done your homework—talked to folks who've run it, read guidebook descriptions, looked at maps—there's often one more step before you can start detailed preparations: applying for a permit. The permit system is neither universal nor uniform, but some such system was inevitable with the increased popularity of whitewater river running in recent years. There is still no precise answer to the question, Just how many people can boat down a river before something important is lost? A river may have a certain "carrying capacity" if you just consider available campsites and sanitation facilities, but quite a different capacity if you are trying to maintain a sense of adventure, remoteness, and solitude. The tentative answers that the various river agencies have come up with are all, in some measure, compromises. And like most compromises they offend almost everyone, but whitewater boaters of conscience all admit that totally open access to the longest, the most powerful, and the most beautiful rivers would produce intolerable overcrowding and ugliness. The only real disagreement is over the mechanics and criteria for regulating river traffic, not the need for regulation.

The official ground rules for river running vary greatly in different parts of the country and on different rivers. In some areas only commercial outfitters need a permit, and private trips may put in when and where they like. At the opposite end of the regulatory spectrum is the Grand Canyon where, out of a fixed total of "user days," the vast majority are allocated to commercial outfitters and a private party must take its chances in a lottery system for the remaining few places. This system makes it nearly impossible for skilled amateurs to enjoy running the Grand Canyon, but very easy for a handful of established commercial outfitters to herd their paying customers through the canyon in noisy, unesthetic, outboard-powered *baloney boats,* offending every real river lover they pass with the noise and gasoline smell of their "big rigs." Unfair? You bet! But so far, the Grand Canyon is the only example I know of river regulation gone crazy. The system is so patently unjust that there is every hope it will soon have to be modified. Most of the other big western rivers, such as the Salmon, the Green, and the Colorado through Cataract Canyon, are regulated by pretty reasonable policies. And many west coast and east coast rivers, smaller in scale than the giants running out of the Rockies, don't have any permit systems at all (but usually don't offer such long trips either).

How do you get a permit? You'll find a list of agencies to write to and the rivers they control in Appendix B. Write to the ranger in charge, outlining the dates and length of your proposed trip and adding a word on the personnel and their whitewater boating experience. One positive aspect of the whole permit process is that it keeps inexperienced boaters from getting hurt in rivers that are far too hard for them. So approach applying for a permit with a positive attitude and give the person you're writing enough information to make a fair and accurate judgment of your party's skills.

But don't, please, get the impression from all this that whitewater touring, this free and magical sport, has already become dominated by and submerged beneath a layer of red tape and bureaucratic regulation. The vast majority of rivers in this country are still unregulated, while the longest and most famous really need it. In general, wildwater is still wild. May it always remain so!

Packing

Having received your permit (if you needed one), preparations for the big river trip can get into high gear. Basically you have to assemble all your boating and camping gear, plan and buy your food, and make sure you can pack it all to keep it secure and dry even in the middle of the biggest rapids.

Don't underestimate the thought and care needed to keep your gear and your food secure, dry, and accessible. Fortunately, there are a few time-tested tricks that should make it a little easier, especially at first. Few things are more miserable, after a long day on a tough river, than trying to make camp when everything you've brought has been accidentally soaked. Don't laugh; it happens all the time, especially to naive beginners.

There are really two kinds of trips, requiring different packing methods: unsupported river trips with only kayaks (or other light paddle craft such as C–1s and C–2s), and raft trips or kayak trips with raft support. It's all a question of space. Kayakers by themselves are very much in the position of backpackers, while rafts offer the same cargo-carrying capacity that long, patient strings of donkeys do in the high country—in short, a luxury trip.

A multiday trip with only kayaks is in some ways more of a challenge—to your ingenuity at least if not to your whitewater technique (heavily laden kayaks become rather sluggish, and good judgment dictates that you boat fairly conservatively). To pack for an all-kayak trip, you will have to take out your normal flotation bags, and ethafoam pillars too if you use them, and replace them with special storage/flotation bags. The best ones can be filled entirely with gear, or partially filled and partially inflated, a handy feature as the trip wears on. Usually you seal the storage compartments of these bags by rolling the plastic ends around a dowel and sliding a split plastic tube over the whole thing, like a clamp. In others the plastic ends are rolled up and held in place by a snap-over flap. These closures really work; they are waterproof. But if you want to be doubly sure that critical articles stay dry, wrap them in heavy-gauge plastic garbage-can bags before packing them inside the storage/flotation bags. If you're carrying a down sleeping bag rather than a fiberfill one, or a down jacket to wear around camp in the evening, this is especially important.

Limitations of space in a kayak (one small bag in front of the foot pegs and a larger one behind the cockpit) dictate that you cut your kit down to the absolute minimum. Carry a tarp with which to rig a light shelter, but no tent; an absolute minimum change of dry clothes; and, of course, avoid bulky fresh food. If possible buy low-volume compressed freeze-dried food rather than garden-variety dehydrated food. Although foam pads are standard items with most backpackers, you might try a small air mattress that can be collapsed to save space. Unlike backpacking, you will find that space, not weight, is critical in a kayak—except for trim, that is. A loaded kayak handles badly enough compared to an empty one. Don't compound the problem by putting all the weight on one side, or all forward or aft. Small dense objects go better in front; lighter but larger ones in back. It's easy but you have to remember to think about it.

Perhaps the only advantage you have in packing a kayak is that your load is not likely to escape. Cramming your storage bags in place behind the foot pegs and the seat is sufficient; they won't fall out and, in any case, there's nothing to tie them to. (You wouldn't want the end of a rope hanging loose in the cockpit to tangle your feet.) Just be ruthless in eliminating all nonessentials and you won't have too much trouble packing your kayak. Remember, it can be done. Self-contained kayakers have paddled for over a month, for example, down the headwaters of the Amazon. And although it's a lot of work, there's something terribly satisfying about being free of any bulky support craft on longer trips. For a sense of isolation and remoteness, nothing beats a self-contained kayak trip. Still, for pure whitewater sport, surfing waves, and playing in rapids, you'd better make sure there's at least one raft along to carry the heavy stuff.

Packing a raft is somewhat trickier. You've already learned that in heavy water you want as much weight in the front of your raft as possible to meet each oncoming wave, so naturally you'll stow heavier gear to the front unless you're leaving extra room for a passenger or two. But good packing in a raft really begins with your rowing frame. Rafts themselves are rather squishy things, prone to flexing, buckling, and losing their shape. So ultimately if you want the load to stay put, it must be fastened in some way to the rowing frame. Gear can be put on the frame or else just fore and aft of it in the space between the typical cross thwarts and the bow or stern tubes, but it must always be lashed to the rowing frame as well as to D-rings set in the outer tubes. The ideal thing is to have a rowing frame that's designed to accommodate and hold the carrying containers you'll be using.

Although army-surplus assault rafts disappeared from the market ten years ago, the best waterproof containers are still army-surplus ones, and amazingly they are still readily available today. Most famous is the *black bag.* Many commercial outfitters issue one apiece to their clients for all personal gear, and every serious river runner has a couple of these black bags in the garage, ready to go. Black bags are made of black rubber, and are about a foot and a half wide, a foot deep, and a little over two feet tall. They end in a high sleeve which rolls up over itself and is held in place with a strap. Black bags are incredibly handy and still quite cheap.

The other surplus containers of interest to whitewater boaters are metal cases. Small ones, ammunition cases *(ammo boxes),* are ideal for carrying cameras, spare lenses, wallets and watches, prescription glasses, and that sort of thing. They have a very tough latch and are really waterproof. Then there are big metal cases that look somewhat like modern ice chests only often larger and infinitely more rugged. Who knows what these chests were used for in the military? There are a lot of them around and it's probable that they had diverse roles in their former life. But on the river they tend to become commissary chests, ideal for storing food and cooking utensils. These large chests can best be slipped between two cross members of a rowing frame, and even stacked one on top of the other as long as the bottom one is lashed to something more rigid than a rubber tube. So if you're building your rowing frame, it might be best to get a couple of waterproof chests first and build around them. If you have a ready-made frame, hunt around until you find waterproof chests that are compatible with it. (Some rowing frames are designed to hold modern picnic coolers.) Of course, you don't have to use rigid chests to carry food or gear; a big collection of black bags will do. But the big chests certainly are handy. In any case, the first place to look for containers is in your local surplus store.

57. A waterproof chest stowed securely in a rowing frame

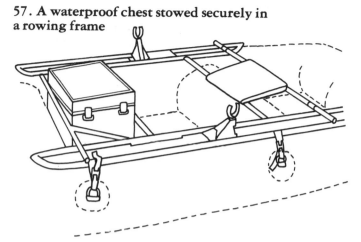

All these containers have to be lashed to a raft. In fact, if you're clever, every single thing on the whole raft will be tied down. Whatever isn't tied on will be lost, inevitably. The best material for tying and lashing loads is certainly 1–inch-wide nylon webbing, available in bulk at any mountaineering and most backpacking shops. Always get and carry more than you think you need; it will all get used. Simple figure-of-eight knots and a little forethought can save a lot of frustration: tie any bags that might be used during the day (lunch, extra clothes, and the like) on the outside or near the top of a pile of gear, where you can get them off easily.

The final step in packing a raft is a kind of safety check. You must make sure that no loose ends of rope or sling are lying about the boat that could catch and tangle someone if, for example, the raft flipped. And you must also take care that no sharp objects are protruding against which a passenger, or even the boatman, could be thrown during the bucking-bronco jolts of a big rapid. It's a good idea to pad sharp metal oarlocks or rowing pins. These last details are easy to overlook in the excitement of pushing off, but they are critical.

What you put in your raft is another story. If a couple of friends are running a river in one good-sized raft, there is no space problem whatever; if one raft is running support for a dozen kayakers, then you're back to a rather cramped situation. But in general there's lots of room and you can permit yourselves any number of extras and even downright luxuries. What the basics are we'll see in the next section.

River Camping

Life along the river has a special quality found almost nowhere else—neither beauty nor exhilaration nor repose, but flow. The daily rhythm of moving on down the river takes over, gets in your blood. You make camp at night with a nomad's appreciation of the spot, heightened by the knowledge that in only a few hours the river will claim you again, pulling you on downstream like a leaf or a log. Lazy mornings in a riverside camp are energized, rendered special by an undercurrent of tension between the river's movement and your own fixity, until finally it's too much and you succumb; the river wins again and swirls you off. If your trip is long enough you will begin to forget that you have ever done anything else: making camp, breaking camp, flowing on through an endless alternation of flatwater and wildwater.

River camping, just as much as whitewater boating skill, makes this day-to-day flow down the river possible. But unlike boating, river camping is neither difficult nor esoteric. There's almost nothing to it. Most river runners tend to be "outdoor people" before they are attracted to whitewater. And if you've ever done any backpacking you can easily cope with river camping. This, of course, is not a text on camping and outdoor equipment. Most of our readers don't need one, but if you do, you can't do better than to read *Walking Softly in the Wilderness: The Sierra Club Guide to Backpacking* by John Hart. Here, we'll only look at what is unique about river camping: the modifications and changes you must make in your normal backcountry camping routine to cope with the riverine environment and to protect it.

Let's start on familiar ground with sleeping gear and shelter. It's not much different; you still need a sleeping bag on the river. But the message here is, Forget down. Down sleeping bags are notorious for taking days to dry out if they ever get wet, and while wet they have all the insulating value of a soaked cotton tee shirt. Fiberfill bags, which have made big inroads into the backpacking market in the last few years, are the only thing to take on a river tour. It doesn't really seem to make much difference which of the synthetic fibers you chose—PolarGuard, Hollofil, Fiberfill II—although every manufacturer would have you believe that their particular fiber is the ultimate. They all work about the same when wet; that is, they don't get very wet, they retain their loft and keep you warm when they are wet, and they dry out with amazing speed. Of course, you never plan on your sleeping bag getting wet, but no precautions are foolproof (even a black bag can get ripped or come unbuckled) and in the river's wet environment, sooner or later you sleeping bag *will* get soaked. If that happens, wring it out as hard as you can and hang it up (preferably in a breeze) to dry. Most of the moisture will wick to the bottom of a fiberfill bag and evaporate, and even if you have to crawl into a soaking fiberfill bag, your body heat should dry it out in less than an hour! If for some reason you wind up taking a down sleeping bag on a river trip, at least wrap it in a plastic garbage bag before stuffing it in a waterproof container, just in case . . . .

When it comes to shelter, one tent is as good as another for river camping. And the sophisticated models—mountain tents designed for high winds, blizzards, and the like—have no advantage whatsoever. In fact, one of the pleasures of river camping is that you can get by with so little. Unsupported kayakers certainly won't have enough room to carry tents complete with poles and flysheets in their tiny boats. Instead, use a lightweight tarp that can be rigged as a kind of lean-to cover over your kayak even if there are no handy trees about. With the fifty-foot length of line that a lot of prudent kayakers carry anyway, one can do wonders rigging a tarp as a rain shelter, which, although less cozy than a tent, is all you need. The same goes double for rafters, because their long oars can be rigged as tent poles in a variety of ways, and a tarp can be slung over them to create a pretty fancy shelter.

So far we have hardly strayed from backpacking orthodoxy, but in two aspects of river camping special conditions do take us away from the norm: cooking and sanitation.

For many backpackers the day of the cheery evening campfire is almost over. This is because in areas like California's High Sierra, generations of hikers have simply stripped away all available dead wood. As a result, and to keep the same thing from happening elsewhere, wilderness travelers of conscience routinely carry small gas or butane stoves wherever they go. On a lot of rivers this is really not necessary, at least not yet, because of a special circumstance— spring floods. In full spring spate, swollen with snow melt, rivers have an incorrigible tendency to lift off, tear out, uproot, and sweep along a tremendous amount of dead and living wood every year. (Dead trees lodged high on canyon walls show awe-struck boaters just how high and powerful the spring-flood stage can be.) So on many rivers there is an abundant and annually renewed supply of dead, dry wood, scattered about and left behind as the river levels drop. There's more than enough firewood, and using it only keeps the river from looking messy (although spiky tangles of driftwood are, in the last analysis, quite "natural"). But if wood is sometimes abundant—and it isn't on arid desert rivers—good campsites are often scarce. Since everyone follows the same trail, the river, you can count on your campsite being used again and again after you've left. Unless you're careful your wood fire can leave terribly unsightly charred remains for other boaters to look at. One of the best solutions, for rafters anyway, is a portable fire box made of sheet metal that fits right into a rowing frame and supports a couple of big waterproof chests during the day. In the evening it keeps white beaches white by completely containing a cooking fire, and it simplifies cooking too by providing support for pots and grates. In the morning the ashes can be washed off to start their long trip to the sea. Such fire pans are mandatory on certain controlled rivers, but they should be used everywhere whether required or not.

The limited number and the fragile quality of riverside campsites really dictate a gentle approach when river camping—the same approach you would adopt toward any lovely, easily damaged land. Imagine a hundred other parties as big as yours camping on the same beach, and then think of returning again as the hundred and first. That will more or less tell you how to behave.

One relatively critical problem on rivers is that of human waste. Everything rather quickly drains and leaches into the water, so you can't just go behind a bush and bury your feces as you might in the high country. Too many whitewater rivers in America are already polluted to the point that boaters don't dare drink from the water around them—real wet deserts—and although most of this pollution is civic and industrial, large groups of boaters on popular rivers can have a big impact.

On many permit-controlled rivers all large rafting parties (or all rafting groups, period) are required to carry portable toilets and to float their waste out with them. This is a reasonable and necessary regulation, and we can only urge boaters to comply a hundred percent. But what about unsupported kayakers who barely have room for a sleeping bag and a few days' food? Portable toilets are out of the question, but if you care about the river, expend some energy and hike as far as you can from the riverbank to do your business. Bury feces and burn the toilet paper. On popular rivers managed by the Forest Service or similar agencies, the only reasonable long-term solution is to install permanent toilets at designated camping spots. To some folks this completely destroys the feeling of running a "wild" river, a treasured feeling even if it's sometimes only an illusion. Personally, I look at it differently. If you're willing to forego the most popular river runs, travel a bit further, and work a little harder, there will always be true wilderness rivers to run—or at least for a few hundred years more. But the "wilderness experience" we treasure most in whitewater boating is our own emotional response to dynamic and elemental forces in the river itself. In the middle of a beautiful rapid, any river is a wild river. And permanent toilets and designated campsites, where user pressure demands them, may be the only way to keep some of these "wild" rivers runnable. Let's keep them *all* runnable.

When you see the amount of gear piled high on some whitewater rafts, it's hard to think of river running as a low-impact sport. But rafts and kayaks, unlike skis, don't even leave tracks on the medium through which they flow. When we break camp each morning, why leave any more traces on the bank than our boats do in the water?

CHAPTER 10

A REGIONAL GUIDE: WHITEWATER AROUND THE COUNTRY

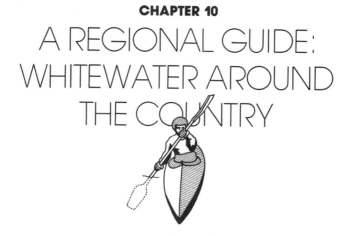

It would be unfair as well as unrealistic to attempt detailed descriptions of even a dozen representative whitewater runs around the country. Several authors have already done just that in whole books (the best of which is *Wild Rivers of North America* by Michael Jenkinson). And to give even a passing nod to every interesting, exciting, famous, or just plain beautiful whitewater river run in the States would take not one, but a whole series of volumes.

But perhaps this chapter can give you a feeling for the type of rivers and the type of wildwater adventures you can expect to find in different regions— your own or others you may someday visit—as well as some background on the local whitewater *milieu* and the local styles and traditions of whitewater boating.

Regional divisions are somewhat arbitrary, and certain rivers are so important that they probably deserve a section of their own. But for simplicity we'll divide this whitewater survey into the West Coast, the Northwest, the Southwest, and the East Coast. This leaves a lot of blanks on the map and neglects some fine rivers (for example, in the North Central states, which are a canoeist's paradise), but it does cover the major whitewater regions. Our maps locate the rivers mentioned in the text and other notable whitewater in each region.

The West Coast

Whitewater boating on the West Coast begins just a few hours' drive north of Los Angeles in the Sierra foothills along the Kern River, and extends north through the High Sierra, the interior counties of northern California, the long coast range, and up through the coastal rivers of southern Oregon. West Coast rivers are clearwater rivers, steep, tumbling mountain and foothill rivers, not big in volume but big in character. Where each major rock, each rapid has a name and a unique shape. Where the boater isn't hypnotized by long stretches of large rhythmic waves but rather is intrigued and provoked by constantly changing river features. West Coast rapids tend to be as much intellectual challenges as physical workouts.

If you live on the coast or are planning to visit the area for a whitewater holiday, two guidebooks are "must" reading. The first, Charlie Martin's *Sierra Whitewater,* covers literally all the good whitewater in the High Sierra. It's written in a light and personal style, and all the river descriptions are scrupulously documented. The other book, *West Coast River Touring* by Dick Schwind, takes up where Martin's book leaves off, covering the northern coastal drainage from the Rogue River to well south of San Francisco. Like *Sierra Whitewater,* this is a model guidebook and has a superb chapter discussing the hydrology of coastal rivers—when they flow best for touring, how to understand the water cycle and tables, and information to help predict when rivers will be at optimum condition. Schwind's book is absolutely the best treatment of this subject I've seen anywhere, both scholarly and accurate yet clear and accessible to the layman.

California has been the scene of a number of pitched battles between environmentalists and recreational boaters on the one hand, and dam builders on the other. Sad to say, the defenders of free-flowing rivers have suffered some cruel defeats (the latest as of this writing, over the New Melones Dam, which is destined to flood out the most popular whitewater in the state, the Upper Stanislaus River). But ironically, the Sierra Nevada is a kayaker's paradise precisely because of the numerous dams. The most popular whitewater rivers are found on the western slope of the Sierra and most are dam-controlled to some extent. This means that water releases continue all through summer and well into fall, turning a short spring run-off season into year-round boating. This is a case where shades of gray triumph over black and white, since every wildwater enthusiast who has run High Sierra rapids in August is forced to admit that if dams are bad, they're also good. It's all a question of degree and moderation, which is a hard lesson for many of us boaters to learn.

And what of the runs? The two most popular whitewater rivers in California are the Stanislaus and the South Fork of the American, superb Class 3 to 4 runs, but on weekends the kayaker must be willing to share these rivers with hundreds of rafters on commercial trips. Just south of the Stanislaus drainage is the Tuolumne, perhaps the fiercest regularly run whitewater on the coast; Clavey Falls is the toughest drop on the Tuolumne, and a clean run in a kayak at any water level qualifies you as a real expert. Further south, the Kings and the Kern Rivers offer challenging whitewater: while to the north, on rivers like the Mokulumne, the consumes, and the Truckee, as well as the North Fork of the American, the boating is less consistent but still good when the water's up. On the eastern slopes of the Sierra there are really only two whitewater rivers: the South Fork of the Carson and the West Walker, which is technically the most continuously difficult whitewater in the Sierra when it comes into condition. The Carson, in contrast, is an easygoing Class 2 to 3 ramble amongst snowy peaks. Since neither of these two rivers are dam-controlled and both are small, you must get there early in spring. As a matter of fact all West Coast rivers are relatively small. Every whitewater river in the Sierra and many of the northern coastal rivers can be run in a long day. A "long" boating trip on the West Coast seldom lasts more than two or three days, although the Rogue is so scenic that it's worth four or five.

Traveling north of San Francisco to run the coastal rivers, one encounters a different scene: fewer actual mountains but more forests, fewer boaters but generally more water, fewer dams but still a very long season and great runs. Here we have the Eel, the Trinity, the Klamath, and the Smith, and finally just across the border into Oregon the remarkable Rogue. And those are just the major rivers. A host of smaller, lesser known rivers, forks, and tributaries dot the northern coastline and coast ranges. I don't think anyone could do all the runs described in Dick Schwind's guide to this area in three or four years of serious whitewater kayaking.

And a word about the boaters themselves. Just as earlier Sierra Club rock climbers pioneered new routes and almost invented modern American rock climbing on the walls of Yosemite Valley, so too Sierra Club river tourers introduced and pioneered whitewater sport on the West Coast. Different Sierra Club chapters scattered throughout California have their own river touring sections, and their members are about the friendliest, most helpful boaters you'd ever want to meet. The *Paddlers News Bulletin,* published by the River Touring Section of the Loma Prieta Chapter of the Sierra Club, contains the best information available on month-to-month whitewater activities, competition, and conservation issues in California. For addresses of boating groups and some

58. West Coast whitewater

ROGUE

SMITH

KLAMATH

TRINITY

EEL

TRUCKEE

CONSUMES

NORTH FORK OF THE AMERICAN
SOUTH FORK OF THE AMERICAN

MOKULUMNE

SOUTH FORK OF THE CARSON

STANISLAUS

WEST WALKER

TUOLUMNE

KINGS

KERN

very helpful phone numbers that you can call to get water level information, consult the two guidebooks to this region.

The Northwest

While the network of boatable coastal rivers actually extends right on up to the Canadian border, Northwest whitewater conjures up a different image. It has a mystique built almost exclusively on the big-water boating of central Idaho. Splendid rivers such as the Owyhee in southeastern Oregon, the Grande Ronde in northeastern Oregon, or the Skagit in Washington just don't fire the imagination of wildwater enthusiasts the way the Salmon or the Selway always have. Actually there are four major and classic whitewater runs fairly near each other in Idaho: the Main Salmon River, the slightly tougher Middle Fork of the Salmon, the fierce and remote Selway, and Hells Canyon on the Lower Snake. They are what wildwater in the Northwest is all about.

These are mountain rivers, rising in the Sawtooth and Bitterroot ranges and flowing through some of the ruggedest country in the West. But this is also big water, with more volume and more power than most West Coast whitewater, comparable during high-water spring run-off with some of the big desert rapids. Yet Idaho water is clear, not muddy, and although river features tend to be big they have definition and scale: rocks are seen, not submerged, and waves are well-defined barriers rather than confused monsters. These are clean-cut, chiseled-out rivers, and in the crisp mountain air their whitewater virtually sparkles.

And these rivers are long. This is touring country where you will spend a week on the river, not an afternoon. This means advance planning and, of course, writing away for permits long before your trip (at least on these major rivers, although there are lots of smaller rivers and tributaries in the Northwest where

59. Northwest whitewater

SKAGIT

JOHN DAY

GRAND RONDE

HELLS CANYON

SELWAY

MAIN SALMON

MADISON

MIDDLE FORK OF THE SALMON

OWYHEE

UPPER SNAKE

GREYS

you can just put in and go).

The Middle Fork of the Salmon (96 river miles long) and the Main Salmon (also known as the "River of No Return"), which is a 79- to 153-mile run depending on how you do it, are both very well described in Scott and Margaret Arighi's book, *Wildwater Touring,* which covers a number of other Northwest rivers including the John Day, Grande Ronde, Rogue, and Owyhee. Salmon River runs take at least a week, and, as the water is fairly serious (a lot of Class 4 at normal water levels), this is no place to learn how to kayak or how to handle a raft. Learn at home and travel to Idaho to enjoy yourself.

The Selway is considered even harder than the Middle Fork, and feels a lot more isolated and re-mote, particularly since commercial operations on the river are severely restricted and the number of parties allowed at one time is very low. The Snake River, although it lacks some of the colorful boating history of the Salmon, is probably the most exten-sively run river in the northern West—not only the Lower Snake, through Hells Canyon, but the Upper Snake, just south of Yellowstone Park where it flows through the Teton country around Jackson Hole. This part of the Snake is admirably described in one of the Westwater series of folding guide maps, the *Snake River Guide* by Verne Huser and Buzz Belknap. There is no real local whitewater scene here, since the local boater in this region is the excep-tion rather than the rule. Wildwater buffs from all over the country consider the long drive to central Idaho's mountain rivers well worth it.

The Southwest

Geographically the Southwest can be taken as the four states that meet at Four Corners: Utah, Colorado, Arizona, and New Mexico. Climatologi-cally it embraces the cold, snow, and high altitude of the Rockies as well as the more typical baking desert heat. The area is a wildwater paradise, and there are enough great rivers and rapids here to keep you excited for a lifetime. But the story of whitewater boating in the Southwest is ultimately the story of one river, the Colorado.

The Colorado River basin is enormous and complex (naturally so, even before modern Americans began hacking it up into one of the most complicated and controversial water-delivery systems in the world), and virtually every other river in the region eventually flows into the Colorado. In the whitewater world the Colorado is "the big one," and the Grand Canyon of the Colorado is to wildwater adventure what El Capitan in Yosemite is to rock climbing—the ultimate symbol and, even today, the ultimate experience. For this reason, let's leave the Grand to the end of our brief survey of the Southwest and see what else this region has to offer.

The image of southwestern water is one of power and sweep—big-volume rapids where the surge of moving water even more than the configuration of canyon, boulders, and bank creates the boating challenge. And, of course, this water is a dull brown, muddy and opaque, frothing rather than sparkling. That's generally true, but even the Colorado starts as a mountain stream, fed by other mountain streams which are not all big, not all muddy. There are two centers of kayaking interest in Colorado: Denver and Aspen, and most Colorado boaters spend at least half their time in clear, high mountain rivers. Aspen in particular is uniquely situated as a whitewater center. It sits on the Roaring Fork, a small but fierce upper tributary of the Colorado with numerous distinct sections of every class of difficulty. Downstream from Aspen is the confluence of the Roaring Fork with the Crystal, a really spectacular mountain river full of steep, narrow, boulder-choked drops, threading its way down between the sort of brilliant red-rock walls that gave Colorado its name. Thirty miles or so below Aspen both these rivers (now joined) enter the Colorado at Glenwood Springs. Although the Colorado is only a baby giant at this point, there are fine runs both up and downstream from Glenwood. Just over the pass from Aspen, in the opposite direction, is the Arkansas River, a whitewater classic with almost every kind of boating in easily accessible stretches; it is frequently the site of major kayak races including national championships. Thus, Aspen boaters find themselves at the hub of an extensive whitewater circuit; not surprisingly there are several whitewater schools and a great number of local paddlers in the area.

Moving toward the desert basins, we find a distinct change of character in rivers on the western slope of the Rockies: a mingling of mountain and desert characteristics. The country is more arid, the rivers more muddy, but you still see high, snow-covered mountains on the horizon in spring. The Gunnison used to be one of these magic rivers as it flowed through the Black Canyon in southwestern Colorado—a marvelous run recently swallowed by a dam. *Requiescat in pace!* But others are still free and flowing—rivers such as the Dolores, which winds out of the San Juan Mountains to become a true desert river, and the Animas, a rugged stream high in the San Juans with the most unusual shuttle in the West. After an exciting run of about 25 miles (with two hair-raising Class 6 drops) the Animas canyon closes in to form an unrunnable death trap, dropping 250 feet per mile! Solution: take out and board the historic narrow-gauge railroad that plies between the mining town of Silverton and Durango (prior arrangement needed).

Another western-slope favorite is the Westwater Canyon of the Colorado, just inside the Utah border. This is an exciting run through an impressive (and to some, oppressive) gorge with a lot of good Class 4 water. It's also the only difficult desert water I know of that can be conveniently run as a one-day trip, although many parties break it into two. Westwater Canyon makes a fine "safety valve," or test run, to see if you're ready for other longer desert trips.

60. Southwest whitewater

CANYON OF LODORE

YAMPA

DESOLATION CANYON

CROSS MOUNTAIN CANYON

GREEN

ROARING FORK

CRYSTAL

LABYRINTH CANYON

WESTWATER
CANYON

CATARACT CANYON

GUNNISON

ARKANSAS

DOLORES

SAN JUAN

COLORADO

CONEJOS

GRAND CANYON

ANIMAS

RIO GRANDE

SALT

Below Westwater Canyon, the main Colorado is a good deal less exciting for whitewater purists until its confluence with the Green River, just above Cataract Canyon. The Green is a kind of left-hand or western branch of the upper Colorado system and has some marvelous stretches of water.

Whitewater boating on the Green begins just below the Flaming Gorge Reservoir where, after floating across a park-like area called Brown's Hole, you enter the "Gates of Lodore" and are soon surrounded by the high rock walls of the Canyon of Lodore. This is a run of some 90 miles through Dinosaur National Monument, with great scenery and only moderate whitewater except for three really big rapids which can all be portaged. Partway down this run, the Yampa River enters from the east, and the Yampa too offers splendid desert boating. A classic, not overly severe run stretches 45 miles on the Yampa from Deerlodge Park to the confluence with the Green at Echo Park. But upstream of this stretch is a run of another nature altogether—Cross Mountain Canyon. Cross Mountain is regarded as one of the most serious stretches of whitewater in Colorado (or anywhere); how much of it is Class 6 depends on whom you ask, but everyone agrees that there is lots and lots of strenuous, critical, demanding Class 5 water. In short, Cross Mountain is for experts only, and more for a test than for fun. This steep, boulder-blocked run is out of the question for rafts.

Continuing down the Green we encounter a fine five-day run that takes us through Desolation Canyon and all the way to the town of Green River, Utah. This run is an ideal introduction to desert whitewater, for it is sustained but not really very hard. Below Green River is a remarkable section of desert boating; it has not a single rapid, yet is so spectacular that it would probably delight even the most fanatical whitewater buff (if he wasn't in a hurry). This 117 – mile stretch is often called simply Canyonlands, and comprises two major canyon areas, Labyrinth and Stillwater canyons, plus a host of minor ones and some truly amazing rock and desert scenery. This is the ultimate pure "float." But things change at the end of this section as the Green meets the Colorado and the two disappear into Cataract Canyon. Cataract used to be bigger, but now only extends for 47 miles until it's drowned in Lake Powell, the official end of the upper Colorado basin. This is a scorcher of a whitewater run; the key rapids have names like Mile-Long, Big Drop, and Satan's Gut, and they live up to them.

Finally, of course, we have the Grand Canyon itself. The full ride from Lee's Ferry all the way to Lake Mead is over 250 miles—a big trip in every way. The Grand doesn't merely represent, but *is,* the very quintessence of southwestern desert boating, so much so that to many wildwater enthusiasts doing the Grand is as much a pilgrimage to the source as an outing. For every boater, but especially the kayaker, the Grand Canyon is an overwhelming experience. It has everything: complex, subtle rapids; brutal simple ones; above all, big ones, with tons of crashing, muddy water making the simple act of paddling seem a surrealistic defiance of the gods—angry gods at that—and enough stillwater to recover between crises. And then some. No need to talk of the scenery; surely everyone who's read this far has seen numerous color photos of this most wild of all canyons. It's hard to take a bad picture down there, and the Grand is a perennial subject for photographic art books.

Many of the individual rapids in the Grand Canyon are legendary, and Lava Falls, near the end of the trip, is generally considered the fiercest whitewater drop in the whole country. But a new Grand Canyon legend is in the making, and it's a crying shame: the legendary difficulty, almost impossibility, of getting a permit to run this magical river. Anyone who wants to pay $750 (with inflation it will soon be $1,000) can climb aboard a big rubber raft and be hustled down the canyon by a commercial outfitter. If, on the other hand, you've spent years acquiring the whitewater skills to do it yourself in a kayak or a raft, if you boat for pleasure not for pay, for pure love of the river and love of adventure, forget it! An unbelievable 92 percent of all "user days" in the canyon are allotted to commercial outfitters. Why? There is no logical reason except bureaucratic obtuseness, and perhaps lobbying pressures from folks who don't want to lose their bread and butter. The system is so manifestly unfair that it doesn't seem possible that it can last much longer. Hope for the best, and write letters to the Park Service if you care.

Recommended reading on southwestern wildwater begins with a copy of Major John Wesley Powell's *Exploration of the Colorado River of the West and Its Tributaries,* a real historical thriller about the first descent of this amazing river. Try to find an edition (one is available in paperback from Dover; see Appendix C) with the original black and white etchings, masterpieces of early landscape illustration in their own right. The Westwater River Guides series does a good job with several combination map-guidebooks for different parts of this region (Grand, Dinosaur, Canyonlands and Desolation). And Jenkinson gives a fine introduction to the history of river running and exploration in the Colorado basin in *Wild Rivers of North America.* Unfortunately, there is still no published guide for all the fine high-country whitewater in Colorado (mostly kayaking, since many of the rivers are too small for rafts).

We shouldn't leave the Southwest without saying that there are a number of other whitewater playgrounds all the way south right to the border, notably on the Rio Grande. But frankly they're overshadowed by the memorable wildwater runs of the main Colorado basin.

The East Coast

Many westerners seem to feel, quite unjustifiably, that the West has a monopoly on wild and beautiful country. Of course it isn't true, and it's not true with rivers either. Just as a New England autumn can rival the color displays of the Rocky Mountains, so too, eastern whitewater holds its own when compared with that of the West. It's different and it's good. What the eastern states lack in big water they make up for in diversity, richness, number of rivers, and technical boating challenge. The paddling scene is different too. Here modern whitewater paddling in fiberglass kayaks seems to be a natural outgrowth and extension of an earlier fascination with canoeing on gentler river stretches. The sport is older here, has deeper roots, and there are probably more paddling clubs in this part of the country than anywhere else.

When we talk of East Coast whitewater we're referring to an area that stretches from Maine right into the Deep South. The rivers are relatively small, lively, and rocky. Many whitewater runs throughout the region are fed by spring run-off rather than water releases from dams, so in many localities the white-water season is short but intense. A lot of New England streams are considered to be too tight for rafts and thus are the exclusive province of kayaks and other hard-hulled craft (C−1s and C−2s). In the South, particularly in West Virginia and Georgia, the whitewater rivers are bigger, but they are still so tight and rocky that oars are almost never used when raft-ing (they stick out too far) and paddle boats are nearly universal.

It's my guess, but only a guess, that the tight, obstructed quality of eastern whitewater has pro-duced a typical eastern paddling style. A western paddler such as the legendary Walt Blackadar can espouse a *soft* style of drifting sideways into a rapid and waiting to see what happens only because he normally boats in the big, open water of Idaho rivers. Such an approach wouldn't work in the East, where numerous rocks present real, no-nonsense ob-stacles that have to be maneuvered around in time. So if an eastern style of whitewater boating does exist, it involves a lot of quick, powerful maneuvering, anticipating a situation rather than waiting for it. Certainly all the eastern kayakers I've had the pleasure of boating with "out West" in recent years have been quick, nervous paddlers, very good ones indeed, who would rather be doing something with their kayaks every minute than relaxing and enjoying the ride. Then, too, the number of gifted whitewater slalom racers from the East Coast bears out this suspicion. A lot of technical water is to be found in the East, and it develops technical paddlers.

There are too many rivers in the East to list them all, but here are some of the classics. In Maine the big (but not so hard) rivers are the Allagash and the Penobscot; for whitewater try the Dead River and other smaller streams. In Vermont the West River is almost synonymous with whitewater, having been the scene of the national whitewater championships for many years. In New York, the Neversink, a tributary of the Delaware, gained a great reputation by holding off determined attempts to boat it until 1960, rather late in the game for such an "old" region. But the heaviest concentration of whitewater in the East is in eastern Pennsylvania and West Virginia (with a little sliver of Maryland thrown in). Here we find the Youghiogheny, the Cheat, the Gauley, the Savage, and the enigmatically named New River. The New has the reputation of being the only eastern river to offer true "western water": enormous standing waves, giant hydraulics, and the like. It's definitely a big river, and one that everyone talks of with respect. And further south, right on the Georgia–South Carolina border, we find the Chattooga, another marvelous river with an unpronounceable name, which was catapulted to national fame by the movie *Deliverance.* The unfortunate result of such publicity has been a large number of deaths in recent years as totally unprepared canoeists with no whitewater experience attempted to run the river because they'd seen it done on the screen.

These are only a few of the big-name eastern rivers. I'm convinced that the best kayaking in the East

61. East Coast whitewater

ST JOHN ALLAGASH

PENOBSCOT

DEAD

WEST

UPPER HUDSON

NEVERSINK

SAVAGE

YOUGHIOGHENY

CAPACON

CHEAT

RAPPAHANNOCK

GAULEY

NEW

SOUTH FORK OF
THE CUMBERLAND

OBED

CHATTOOGA

CHAUGA

is probably to be found on smaller runs, well-known to locals but unknown to the rest of the country. So the best thing to do is make contact with local paddlers, and a good way to start might be to check the list of clubs in the American Whitewater Affiliation (see Appendix B) to see who's paddling in the area you're interested in. This is, in fact, a good move if you want to contact other paddlers anywhere.

There are many guidebooks to eastern rivers, but most of them are canoe guides to relatively flat water. Two exceptions are Bob Burrell and Paul Davidson's *Wild Water West Virginia,* and Ray Gabler's *New England Whitewater River Guide,* good introductions to eastern whitewater.

And Beyond . . .

Logically, this chapter should have at least a short section on Alaskan whitewater and at least some mention of the wildwater possibilities beyond our borders: classic, even historic river runs in Europe, the first tentative whitewater explorations in South America and Africa, and the still untouched rivers tumbling out of the high Himalaya. But on reflection, it seems clear that the less said of far-off whitewater the better. It's tempting, but also it's unfair. The few boaters who journey from the "Lower 48" up to Alaska or the Yukon do so with the feeling that they are entering another world. And it's true, the Far North is still a place for whitewater pioneers. Here at home wildwater sport is alive and well, but our whitewater is in some measure acquired territory, no longer a blank on the map. And blanks on the map are good for the soul.

So let's end this quick survey of whitewater around the country with the hope that no more of these magic rivers disappear beneath dams before we have a chance to discover them, boat them, love them, and with luck protect them. Whitewater is living water. Long life!

CHAPTER 11

WHITEWATER SPORT PAST & FUTURE

The wildwater enthusiast today often looks at his sport with mixed emotions. What, after all, is progress? And does it make sense to apply this word, or this idea, to the sheer joy of running rapids? From where I stand, it seems that a lot has been gained but something lost too in the evolution of whitewater sport.

As we sit in our sophisticated fiberglass kayaks at the top of a big drop, there's no doubt that we've come a long way. These agile boats, built and reinforced with space-age materials and processes, are far stronger, lighter, and more responsive than the first kayaks. With these modern craft, with a paddling technique that has been developed and refined for years, and with an expanding pool of river knowledge gleaned and shared by an ever-growing whitewater community, we can confidently and safely run rapids that were scarcely dreamed of by the pioneers of the sport. This is progress indeed. And yet when we consider the number of beautiful whitewater rivers that have already disappeared beneath reservoirs and dams, the increasing weekend crowds on certain rivers, and the growing amount of bureaucratic regulation and red tape we must fight our way through to even reach some of the finest rivers, it seems as though this progress hasn't really been free. Progress never is.

The long-range question is, Can the essence of wildwater adventure survive and prosper? More than anything else the answer depends on whether or not in another generation or two any free-flowing rivers will be left for free spirits to boat. No one can answer this question for sure, but we can take a step back and try to put the whole sport into perspective —find out how it all started, how wildwater sport spread and grew—and make a few educated guesses about where it can, should, and will go in the future.

A Short Whitewater History

Whitewater skills existed long before whitewater sport. Rivers were the highways and trade routes of the ancient world and wherever rivers got snarly, steep, narrow, and difficult, primitive people just lashed their logs tighter together or strengthened and reinforced their boats, and somehow made it through.

By an irony of history, the idea of running rapids for fun, of whitewater sport, came to us from Europe, although the crafts we use and much of our paddling technique originated in North America (or in nearby Greenland). But we should hardly be surprised that the magic of whitewater has tempted and delighted people in all corners of the globe, and in all the ages, even if they never got around to inventing kayaks. In the twelfth century, a scholar-poet of the Southern Sung dynasty named Yang Wan-li wrote a poem entitled "Boating Through a Gorge":

*Here turtles and fish turn back
and even the crabs are worried.
But for some reason poets risk their lives
to run these rapids and swirl past these rocks.*

This Chinese scholar would feel at home in the
Grand Canyon today; and what American kayaker
wouldn't jump at a chance to boat the upper gorges of
the Yangtze River. No modern whitewater enthusiast
has the slightest trouble understanding Yang Wan-li
when he writes in another poem:

*The narrow stream twists and turns
     through thousands of rocks;
Our little boat changes direction a hundred times.
All of us laugh
     while we're shooting the rapids.
When we've left them behind
     we start to feel depressed.*

But we must look to Europe at the turn of the
century for the beginnings of whitewater sport as we
know it. From the start, river running seemed to be
an Alpine sport, since the most exciting and beautiful
rivers tumble down out of the Alps. And the
development of whitewater boating in Europe shows
strange parallels with the other two Alpine sports,
mountain climbing and skiing. Whitewater paddling
began almost simultaneously in France and Germany,
and in each country it followed a unique path.

In France, doubtless because of the French fur-
trapping experience in America, the preferred craft
for river running was the open canoe. The first sport
canoe, however, was exhibited in Paris by a French
Canadian with the very un-Gallic name of Smith.
Modeled after Indian canoes, it was, in fact, simply
called *un canadien* or "a canadian." In Germany and
neighboring Austria, the Eskimo kayak was the
model from which whitewater boats were
developed—not true Eskimo kayaks of stretched
skin, but collapsible kayaks of wood and canvas. The
first one was made in 1905 by a student named

62. 1907 advertisement for the original Klepper foldboat

Heurich who copied an Eskimo boat on display at a Munich exposition. Hans Klepper, originally a tailor, saw the student's "collapsible" boat, bought the patent from him, and launched a serious business manufacturing *foldboats*. For the next half-century the name Klepper and the term foldboat would be synonymous with kayaking.

The curious thing about the French going one way and the Austro-Germans another is that they did exactly the same thing in mountain climbing and skiing. For example, climbers from the Eastern Alps have always tied their rope around the chest, and used the front or toe points of their crampons for climbing ice. French climbers in the Western Alps tie on around the waist and have always used the side points of their crampons. In skiing, the French always rotated their bodies while the Austrians counter-rotated. Why? Perhaps because of a temperamental and metaphysical opposition as much as any rational historical answer. Indeed, it's only been in the last ten years or so that this curious split in Alpine sports techniques has begun to disappear on the crags, on the *piste,* and in the river. But this historical oddity definitely marked the development of whitewater sport in Europe.

The Eastern Alps became the center of serious whitewater boating because of one important fact—you can roll up in a kayak but not in an open canoe. Eskimos, of course, used their skin kayaks for hunting in bitterly cold Arctic waters. For them rolling up after an upset was far more than a trick to show off one's paddling skills; it was a matter of survival. As a result, Eskimos, particularly those of South Greenland, became superb paddlers, routinely dazzling European explorers and missionaries who traveled among them with their ability to roll completely over in their boats. It's hard to form a clear picture of the precise technique that most Eskimos used to roll their kayaks, since the early travelers who described this feat used the most extravagant and picturesque language. Today the building and paddling of skin kayaks is virtually a lost art. In a couple of generations the outboard motor has all but eliminated a centuries-old skill. (The first recorded mention of Eskimo kayaks is on a map by the Danish cartographer Clavus, dated 1425!)

But the eskimo roll didn't arrive in Europe overnight. Kayak clubs were founded almost from the first: in 1907 at Linz on the Enns River and in 1912 at Munich. As the sport of river running in these new foldboats prospered, more clubs were formed and a mini-bureaucracy reared its ugly head. (There are always people who would much rather regulate a sport than actively participate in it.) So many people were experimenting with new shapes and designs for "col-

63. Nineteenth century engraving of an Eskimo kayak

lapsibles" that the Austrian Kayak Association
thought it should bring this chaos under control, and
in 1924 laid down a set of standard dimensions for all
such boats. This restriction brought the development
of new techniques and the opening of new rivers almost to a complete standstill for a number of years. A
lesson the International Canoe Federation still hasn't
learned! In fact, kayaking was only rescued from
these doldrums by a young man who didn't give a
hang about boating by the rules. He kept experimenting with new boats, and at the same time pursued
another goal—attempting to roll his kayak up just
like the Eskimos. The young man's name was Hans
Pawlata, and he finally did it.

On 30 July 1927, on the Weissensee, Pawlata
became the first European to do an eskimo roll.
Singlehandedly he gave the sport new impetus, since
paddlers no longer needed to be afraid of capsizing in
difficult whitewater. Although he initially used an
extended-paddle position in his roll (this position,
you'll remember, is still called the Pawlata roll), Pawlata went on to become a real master of "eskimoing,"
as it was called, and was probably the first European
to do a hands-only, no-paddle roll. Naturally, the
kayakers of his generation, armed with this formidable new technique, began looking for new worlds to
conquer, new gorges and new rivers to descend.

The development of extreme whitewater boating
at this time paralleled developments in alpinism
where climbers of the same generation were making

repeated and determined attempts to scale what were then called the "three last problems" of the Alps—the north faces of the Matterhorn, the Grandes Jorasses, and the Eiger. For whitewater enthusiasts the equivalent of the Eigerwand was the Salzachöfen Gorge, a fierce and dangerous slash through steep rock walls below Lueg Pass on the Salzach River. The Salzachöfen was a true Alpine problem. The first to solve it was a young Viennese kayaker, Adolf Anderle, who successfully boated the gorge in 1931, effectively raising contemporary whitewater standards another big notch, and setting off a whole new round of exploration and discovery on streams hitherto considered impossible. Shortly thereafter the one-to-six scale of difficulty was formulated; and with the introduction of slalom racing in Austria and Switzerland (the first slalom was run on the Mühltraisen in 1934) it seemed as though whitewater sport had truly come of age in the Alps.

After the black interregnum of the Second World War, which brought almost all sporting activity to a halt, whitewater sport rapidly revived in Europe and became immensely popular. But even with the introduction of the new synthetic kayaks, few new stretches of water were left to conquer. So after mopping up the last few "unrunnable" gorges, the most active and talented European boaters of the post-war period turned their energies to racing; and that's still pretty much where the sport stands in Europe today. Although the French recently have come on very strong, eastern Europeans still dominate the international whitewater scene.

In America, things are somewhat different. The whitewater scene is more open and less well-defined. Generally, there is less interest in racing and more in river touring than in Europe. A great number of American whitewater fans are rafters, who float rivers rather than paddle them, and this group has no counterpart in Europe. And the history of whitewater boating in this country is a very different story indeed. Some of the most dramatic chapters in the

story of American whitewater were written long
before anyone thought of running rapids for fun.

Canoes have always been very much in evidence
on American waterways. Predating the arrival of
white men, canoes were used in turn by Indians, explorers, missionaries, traders, fur trappers, and ultimately sport fishermen—primarily on the rivers and
lakes of the northeastern and north central parts of
the country, and the adjoining portions of Canada.
While it's undeniably romantic to think of the famous
voyageurs in their birchbark canoes as the first whitewater boaters in America, it simply isn't true. Fairly
conclusive evidence shows that they never ran any
big rapids, but portaged them all, only running what
we might call riffles or very gentle rapids indeed. And
that's been pretty much the story of open canoeing in
this country, just as it was in France in the early years
of this century. Even today, Class 3 water might be
considered the limit for open canoes, and then only
for a few experts. In general, serious rapids have
always been avoided rather than sought out by
canoeists. Nonetheless, the tradition of river travel
for fun, of long enjoyable days moving down a river,
comes to us directly from anglers and hunters and
their guides, who have been canoeing on north-
woods waterways since the nineteenth century.

Whatever indigenous *whitewater* tradition we
have in this country comes from the explorers and
freighters who ran the major western rivers, but not
because they enjoyed rapids. John Wesley Powell is
certainly the most famous and the most significant of
the western explorers who headed down unknown
rivers, and the journal of his exploration of the Colorado (recommended in the last chapter) is still one
of the most gripping adventure stories ever recorded.

But a relatively unsung breed of men, the commercial river freighters who piloted rafts and drift
boats, made the most important contributions to our
native whitewater traditions. The first commercial
outfitters were men like Harry Guleke, who plied the
Salmon River of Idaho in sweep-guided drift boats of

64. Running a rapid in the Grand Canyon, engraving from John Wesley Powell's classic, *The Exploration of the Colorado River and its Canyons*.

his own design, carrying freight of every description to settlers and miners along the river. When city folks, eager for adventure, wanted to be taken down these wild western rivers, they naturally turned to the river freighters, and the freighters said yes. One cargo was the same as another to these men. Guleke took his first paying group down the Salmon in 1896, and thus initiated the most enduring American style of whitewater boating—the commercial trip, in which a boatman shoulders all responsibility and risk. This is, of course, an exaggerated and somewhat unfair statement, and doesn't take into account the shared perils (especially in the early days) or the friendship and personal bonds that can spring up between boatmen and passengers. But the point here is that there has never been a strong amateur tradition of running rapids in this country. Even today, with the real and rapid growth of kayaking, whitewater canoeing, and do-it-yourself rafting, the majority of whitewater trips undertaken in the United States every year are still guided commercial ventures.

We already know about the contribution of Pioneer Utah boatman Nat Galloway, who figured out how to row through rapids facing downstream and pulling back against the current. But despite the innovations and energy of a number of such early boatmen, commercial whitewater trips never really took off until after World War II. Then suddenly the market was glutted by military-surplus pontoons and assault rafts. The techniques for rowing and steering traditional wooden boats (drift boats, cataract boats, double-ended dories) could be used even more effectively with these new inflatable craft, which also were less tippy, harder to destroy, safer, and best of all, carried more people. Today only one company that I know of out of the hundreds that run commercial whitewater trips still uses wooden boats, brave and anachronistic little craft, in a great river gorge like the Grand Canyon.

But what of the paddlers? How did Americans begin kayaking? Until the fifties, kayaks meant foldboats. The few "Kleppers" seen in this country were usually used for tandem paddling on long and gentle rivers. There was no real attempt to push the whitewater limits of these sturdy wood and canvas boats as there had been in Europe—doubtless because the sense of remoteness on the many semi-wilderness rivers was adventure enough. The few people who tried to run serious rapids in foldboats were considered real kooks who were just asking for it.

Then, still in the fifties, the first fiberglass kayaks appeared from Europe, and with them a handful of European paddlers, such as Roger Paris, a French whitewater champion who was to influence the emergence of modern kayaking first in California and then in Colorado, where he settled. Americans, of course, have a special fondness for applying technology to recreation, and the idea of fiberglass must have been especially appealing because before long these kayaks were available everywhere. By the early sixties whitewater kayaking as we know it was an established sport, albeit a small one, in this country. Just how long whitewater sport can continue to flourish here is another subject altogether.

River Politics and the Future

This is not a book on conservation but on whitewater river touring. Yet the two subjects are inextricably linked. Free-flowing whitewater streams and rivers are both a scenic and a psychic resource, but they have become, in modern times, a diminishing resource. Where do we stand today?

Through most of the first half of this century, it was all the vogue to equate dams with progress, hydroelectric power with the good life, and to see the "taming" of savage rivers as a natural expression of the restless American spirit. This rather naive period is now over, but we're still trying to cope with its creations. On the one hand we are left with a large number of extravagant and carelessly thought-out water projects—the most boggling of which is the whole Colorado River basin system. The water of this project has already been overapportioned (more acre-feet allocated than actually exist), its dams have never yet generated power at anywhere near their planned capacity, and there is a growing salinity problem that no one knows how to solve, technically or financially! On the other hand, a large and powerful bureaucratic apparatus—the Bureau of Reclamation and the Army Corps of Engineers—is dedicated to self-preservation and to the building of even more dams. Add to this a political "pork barrel" tradition that is still alive and well in the seventies, and you get a situation that bodes ill for free-flowing rivers everywhere.

Until the late fifties and early sixties few Americans had actually run and experienced whitewater, so it had few committed advocates up to then. But the number of people who treasure whitewater as a playground for the body and the spirit has grown ever since, and the number of battles fought to protect it has increased likewise. River conservation groups have scored some signal victories and suffered some tragic defeats, and still the fight goes on.

The most important single victory for river conservation was the passage by Congress in 1968 of the *Wild and Scenic Rivers Act.* Initially, sections of only eight rivers were protected under this act: the Rogue, the Middle Fork of the Salmon, the Clearwater, the Rio Grande, the Wolf, the St. Croix, the Eleven Point, and the Feather. Other rivers have been added since, and many others are now under study for possible inclusion under the Act. The Wild and Scenic River designations are great in themselves, but many river lovers fear that it is a case of too little too late. In the first place, these protective designations generally apply only to stretches of river and not to its entire length. Several categories are provided and a government booklet on the Rogue River in Oregon describes them in the following language:

The Wild River *classification requires that the river be free from impoundments and generally inaccessible except by trail, with watersheds and shorelines essentially primitive and waters unpolluted. The objectives of this classification are to provide river-oriented recreation opportunities in a primitive setting and to preserve the river and its immediate envi-*

ronment in a natural, wild and primitive condition essentially unaltered by the effects of man.

The Scenic River *classification requires that the river be free of impoundments with shorelines or watersheds still largely undeveloped, but accessible in places by roads. Management in this area is to maintain or enhance the condition of high-quality scenery and provide opportunities for river-oriented recreation dependent on the free-flowing state of the river consistent with the primitive character of the surroundings.*

So far so good. But there is a third and much weaker designation.

The Recreational River *classification applies to those portions of the river readily accessible by road that may have some development along their shorelines. This river class is managed to provide a wide range of outdoor recreation opportunities on the river in its free-flowing condition.*

While this last category doesn't look reassuring, we must say that so far it's been used only in recognition of existing conditions along a stretch of river, and not as a loophole designation through which further development can be squeezed. And, clearly, even a little protection is better than none at all.

It's my feeling that the Wild and Scenic Rivers Act is the best hope for safeguarding and maintaining most of the country's high-quality whitewater. Some people are disappointed, believing that the Act doesn't protect enough, and fails because it mostly applies to portions rather than whole rivers. Even more disappointing is the slow rate at which the system has been developed and expanded; it really should cover more rivers than it does at present. But it does provide a legal and social bulwark against the dam builders, the power mongers, and the special interests who would like to replace every moving stream with a so-called recreation lake. The more rivers this generation can include within the Wild and Scenic Rivers System, the more whitewater there will be for the next generation. As individuals or in a group context, we should lobby for the extension of this system whenever possible. Every letter helps.

Naturally, the Wild and Scenic Rivers Act protects rivers with no whitewater too. This is good in itself, and it offers a valuable lesson to the whitewater enthusiast: *There are very few of us—too few perhaps to save our favorite rivers from impoundment, pollution, or development. Too few, that is, if we fight these battles alone.*

Wildwater sport is a fine and rather special madness, and I've tried to be candid in pointing out that it's really not for everyone. Whitewater enthusiasts are not only few in number, they're also loosely organized; they don't have large "war chests" to spend on lobbying and political campaigns, and *by themselves* don't have the votes to make politicians sit up and take notice. It's critically important, therefore, that the "whitewater community" cultivate as many friends and alliances as it can in the fight to preserve as much whitewater as possible.

The recent struggle over the damming of the Stanislaus River in California was a bitter defeat for river lovers, but it provided an object lesson in the realities of river politics. Dams are big business in every sense, and money has a way of being heard in the public forum. To defeat the critical Stanislaus referendum, the pro-dam forces simply outspent the conservation forces by an incredible margin to wage and win one of the more deceitful campaigns in recent years.

On the other hand, a few years back the Sierra Club was narrowly able to head off a proposed dam in the Grand Canyon itself, but only by taking the issue to the people in a nationwide campaign. The Canyon was seen and understood as an American symbol by enough people—people who had never run the Grand and probably never will—so that this disaster was averted. And this is our ace. A wild river, a whitewater river, an untamed river is indeed a symbol, as much a thing of beauty in the mind's eye as from the seat of a kayak. And the public, it seems to me, is willing, even eager, to preserve important symbols in the American landscape. But this implies sharing information and experience, and forming alliances that must reach far beyond the world of whitewater enthusiasts and whitewater clubs. Let's not be too selfish or too elitist about the wild water we love to paddle. If we can find ways to share this wildwater magic with enough people, we may still succeed in keeping our favorite rivers white.

CHAPTER 12

A WILDWATER ALBUM

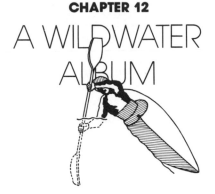

In our whitewater adventures there are certain moments—not necessarily the hardest—which are so special, so unique, that for days or weeks afterward we can't get them out of our minds. Moments we'd like to share with others but generally can't because there's no way to relate them—no words to express the quality of light bouncing off the water, the way the spray from a big hole hung suspended in midair, the form and color of rocks, the impossible line your boat followed, all on its own, just when a flip seemed certain. . . .

Good photographs of these ultra-special whitewater moments are rare. But photos may still be the best way to attempt to express such inexpressible events. So here's a wildwater album to end this book and to keep you dreaming until your next trip.

Slalom race on the Truckee River, California. Photo by Lito Tejada-Flores.

Roger Hazelwood dropping into a hole, East River, Alaska. Photo by Carrie Dondero.

Keith Childs in the Pine Creek Rapid, Arkansas River, Colorado. Photo by the Aspen Kayak School.

Peter Looram surfing on the Lieser River, Austria.
Photo by Terry Killiam.

Kirk Baker entering Lava Falls, Grand Canyon,
Colorado River. Photo by Luzon Birdsong.

1973 World Slalom Champion Norbert Sattler
running a rapid on the Lieser River, Austria. Photo
by Terry Killiam.

Playing in Shoshone Rapid, Glenwood Canyon,
Colorado River. Photo by Karen Miller.

Cully Erdman surfing in Upset Rapid, Grand Canyon, Colorado River. Photo by Luzon Birdsong.

Kirk Baker surfing across the Colorado River on a high brace. Photo by the Aspen Kayak School.

Keith Childs playing in the Arkansas River, Colorado. Photo by the Aspen Kayak School.

Paddle raft in Snaggletooth Rapid, Dolores River, Colorado. Photo by Steve Miller.

Rubber raft in Lava Falls, Grand Canyon, Colorado River. Photo by John Blaustein.

Alan Bierly in the endo hole in Rapid #4, Arkansas River, Colorado. Photo by Steve Miller.

GLOSSARY

BLACK BAGS: Waterproof military surplus containers, very popular with river runners.

BLIND DROP: A rapid where one cannot see the end of the whitewater from the top of the rapid.

BOW DRAW STROKE: A variation on the draw stroke, used in eddy turns. Sometimes called a *Duffeck stroke*.

BROACHING: Washing up sideways against a rock or other midriver obstacle.

CFS: The volume of flow in a river expressed in cubic feet per second.

DOWNRIVER KAYAK: A specialized racing boat designed for straight-line speed at the expense of maneuverability. Downriver kayaks are long and narrow with a deep V-shaped keel and no rocker.

DOWNRIVER RACING: A long-distance race with no control gates or mandatory maneuvers, the sole object of which is to paddle a given stretch of river as fast as possible. Often called a *wildwater* race.

DRAW STROKE: A stroke in which the kayaker pulls his boat toward the paddle "planted" in the water; sometimes called a "hanging" stroke.

EDDY: An area of water that is relatively motionless or flowing in a reverse direction to that of the main current. Often called a *back eddy*.

EDDY LINE: The line of demarcation between the main current and the reverse flow within an eddy; sometimes marked by turbulence and small whirlpools. In violent cases this line of demarcation may be referred to as an *eddy fence*.

EDDY TURN: A maneuver used to enter or leave an eddy. The kayaker drives across an eddy boundary, letting the opposing current turn the nose of his kayak smartly around.

ENDO: Standing the kayak momentarily on end (vertically upright) while surfing. Also called an *endover*, *nosestand*, *tailstand,* or *pirouette* (if the kayak turns in midair).

ESKIMO ROLL: A maneuver by which the kayaker rights his overturned kayak, bringing it and himself back into an upright position. Several versions are possible.

EXTENDED PADDLE ROLL: A roll in which the paddle is slid forward in the kayaker's hands to obtain a longer lever arm and hence more leverage to roll with. Often called a *Pawlata roll*.

FEATHERED BLADES: Two blades (as on a kayak paddle) set at right angles to each other.

FERRYING: Moving laterally across the river by paddling diagonally against the current. When facing and paddling upstream, this is called an *upstream ferry*; when facing downstream and paddling in reverse, it is called *back ferrying* or *setting*. The whole maneuver is sometimes referred to as *ferry gliding*.

FOLDBOAT: An early form of collapsible kayak, consisting of a wooden frame covered by waterproof canvas.

FOOT PEGS: Part of a kayak's internal bracing system; two pegs, often adjustable, against which the kayaker braces his feet.

FRP (*Fiberglass-reinforced plastic*): The technical term for the construction commonly used in modern kayaks; i.e., woven fiberglass cloth embedded and held rigid in a matrix of resin, either polyester or epoxy.

GRAY TAPE: Common duct tape used to repair boats on the river.

HAYSTACKS: A regular succession of large standing waves.

HIGH BRACE: Another so-called "hanging stroke" in which the kayaker levers the upper part of the paddle shaft up and away from him, while supporting himself on the power face of the paddle blade in the water.

HIGH SIDING: Moving to the high side of a raft which is being lifted by a large wave in order to avoid flipping.

HIP SNAP: More accurately, a movement of hips *and* knees which tends to flip a capsized kayak back upright.

HOLES: Depressions in the river's surface where a portion of the current is "recirculating" or falling back in on itself. Also called *souse holes*, *suck holes*, *stoppers*, *keepers* or simply *reversals*.

HYPOTHERMIA: A serious medical condition resulting from extreme loss of body heat and consequent lowering of the body's core temperature. Can lead to death if not treated in time.

KAYAK: A small, streamlined craft paddled by one or two people. Initially a skin boat used by Eskimos for hunting in open arctic waters, the kayak has evolved over a long period into a sophisticated fiberglass craft for whitewater sport.

LINING: Letting one's boat, raft, or kayak down an unrunnable stretch of river on a rope.

LOW BRACE: A bracing stroke in which the paddler pushes down into the water with the back or nonpower face of the paddle blade.

PADDLING JACKET: A waterproof, anorak-like jacket often worn by kayakers.

PILLARS: Reinforcing structures of foam which support the top deck of a kayak in rough water.

POGIES: Waterproof mitts that attach directly around the paddle's shaft and protect the paddler's hands in conditions of extreme cold.

PORTAGE: Carrying one's boat, kayak, or canoe around an unrunnable section of river or between two waterways.

POWER FACE: The concave side of a paddle blade —the one with which you scoop or stroke water most effectively.

POWER STROKE: The basic stroke to move a kayak forward.

RECREATIONAL SLALOM KAYAK: A design which shares many of the slalom kayak's high-maneuverability characteristics, but which is of larger volume, making it more stable and forgiving in big water.

REVERSE SWEEP: Exactly like a normal sweep stroke except that it starts in the rear of the boat and arcs widely out toward the front; executed with the nonpower face of the blade.

RIFFLE: A stretch of shallow water producing gentle, even surface wavelets or turbulence; not a technical problem at all.

RIGHT- AND LEFT-CONTROL: Applied to kayak paddles, the term right- or left-control indicates which hand is fixed during the normal forward stroke cycle.

RIVER LEFT: The left side of the river, looking downstream.

RIVER RIGHT: The right side of the river, looking downstream. The terms *right* and *left bank* are also used in the same sense.

ROCK GARDEN: A stretch of river heavily obstructed by boulders.

ROCKER: The amount of upward curvature in the hull of a kayak from the center toward bow and stern.

ROWING FRAMES: Wooden or metal frames lashed to inflatable rafts to provide rigid support for a pair of oars.

SCREW ROLL: An eskimo roll performed with the paddle shaft held in a "normal" position, that is, without changing one's grip on the paddle.

SCULLING: A continuous "figure-of-eight" stroke to one side of the boat which supports the paddler while "pulling" the boat to that side.

SHUTTLING: Arranging transportation or return transportation for a whitewater run; taking one or more vehicles from the put-in point to the take-out point or vice versa.

SLALOM KAYAK: A specialized racing boat designed for quick-turning maneuverability at the expense of straight-line speed. Slalom kayaks are short and often of low-volume with a rounded bottom and lots of rocker.

SLALOM RACING: Whitewater competition in which the contestants must maneuver their kayaks (or canoes) through a course defined by gates suspended above the water.

SPRAY SKIRT: A neoprene or nylon cover (also called a *spray deck* or *splash cover*) which hooks over the cockpit rim and fits snugly about the kayaker's waist, sealing the kayak's cockpit.

STANDING WAVES: Permanent waves in the river formed when water flows over an obstacle.

STRAINERS: River obstacles such as submerged trees or bushes through which current may continue to flow, possibly trapping an unwary boater.

SURFING: A playful exercise in which the kayaker balances his boat on a standing wave in the river.

SWEEP STROKE: A widely arcing forward

stroke that provokes a strong turning motion to the opposite side. Often used as a corrective stroke in forward paddling.

TONGUE: The final clear water entering a rapid; usually a V-shaped patch of smooth water protruding down into the turbulent whitewater of the rapid.

VOLUME: In a kayak, a measure of the total enclosed volume within the boat's shell. Small volume is preferred for "sneaking" through slalom gates; large volume is an advantage in heavy water and big waves.

WET EXIT: The way a kayaker gets out of a capsized kayak while underwater.

WRAPPING: An extremely dangerous situation in which a broached craft is bent sideways around a rock by the force of the current.

IMPORTANT
ADDRESSES

Whitewater Clubs
and Organizations

The following clubs and groups are all members of the
American Whitewater Affiliation, a national organization
for river runners which is both an active voice for river
conservation and an effective communications link
between whitewater enthusiasts in different parts of the
country.

Alaska

Knik Kanoers & Kayakers
Ed Swanson
3014 Columbia
Anchorage, AK 99504

The Peninsula Paddlers
c/o North Peninsula
   Recreation Dept.
Box 7116 NRB
Kenai, AK 99611

Arkansas

Adventures, Inc.
Gary Morgan
2905 N. Taylor
Little Rock, AR 72207

Arkansas Canoe Club
Carla Freund
1408 Rockwood Tr.
Fayetteville, AR 72701

The Bow & Stern
Joel S. Freund
440 Mission Blvd.
Fayetteville, AR 72701

Ozark Mountain Canoe Club
Les Long
Star Rt. 1
Russellville, AR 72801

California

Southern California Canoe
   Assoc.

Ron Ceurvorst
3906 S. Menlo Ave.
Los Angeles, CA 90037

LERC Voyageurs Canoe &
  Kayak Club
Leon Hannah
12814 Arminta St.
N. Hollywood, CA 91605

Lorien Canoe Club
J. A. Rose
Box 1238
Vista, CA 92083

Chasm Outing Club
Box 5622
Orange, CA 92667

Sierra Club
  Loma Prieta Paddlers
Kathy Blau
2710 Ramona St.
Palo Alto, CA 94306

National Friends of the
  River
Marcel M. Hernandes
1964 Menalto Ave.
Menlo Park, CA 94025

Idlewild Yacht Club
Bob Symon, Rep.
800 Market St.
San Francisco, CA 94102

Sierra Club River Touring
  Bay Chapter
Tom Allen
1943 Napa
Berkeley, CA 94707

Antioch Whitewater Club
Max Young, Pres.
40 N. Lake Dr.
Antioch, CA 94509

Whitewater Voyages/River
  Exploration, Ltd.
William McGinnis
1225 Liberty St.
El Cerrito, CA 94530

The Bear Boaters
Philip C. Lang
6925 Wilton Dr.
Oakland, CA 94611

Tomales Bay Kayak Club
Mike Eschenbach
Box 468
Pt. Reyes Sta., CA 94956

RAFT Kayak School
Mike Snead
Box 682
Lotus, CA 95657

Alpine West
Tom Lovering
1021 R. St.
Sacramento, CA 95814

Colorado

C.S.U. Whitewater Club
James Stohlquist
Activities Center, Box 411
Colorado State University
Ft. Collins, CO 80533

Otero Junior College
  Recreation Club
I. B. Rikhof
La Junta, CO 81050

Connecticut

Appalachian Mountain Club
  Connecticut Chapter
John Kotchian
50 Meadowbrook Rd.
Hamden, CT 06517

Water Works
Box 111
Cornwall Bridge, CT 06754

Greenwich High School
  Kayak Club
David J. Moxhay, Advisor
10 Hillside Rd.
Greenwich, CT 06830

Delaware

Buck Ridge Ski Club
Mark Fawcett
R.D. 1, Box 426 E
Arthur Dr., Wellington
  Hills
Hockessin, DE 19707

Florida

Indian Prairie Farm
Ramone S. Eaton
Box 395
Anthony, FL 32617

Georgia

Georgia Canoeing Assoc.
  Cro's Division
William Bubba Crochet
2127 Desmond Dr.
Decatur, GA 30033

Camp Merrie-Wood
3245 Nancy Creek Rd.
  N.W.
Atlanta, GA 30327

Idaho

Idaho State University
  outdoor
Ron Watters
Box 9024 I.S.U.
Pocatello, ID 83209

Northwest River Supplies
Bill Parks
Box 9243
Moscow, ID 83843

Illinois

Chicago Whitewater Assoc.
Pamela Allen
5460 S. Ridgewood Ct.
Chicago, IL 60629

Belleville Whitewater Club
Linda Seaman Tansil, Rep.
No. 3 Oakwood
Belleville, IL 62223

Wildcountry Wilderness
  Outfitters
516 N. Main St.
Bloomington, IL 61701

Southern Illinois Canoe
  & Kayak
Aldon Addington
R.R. 1, Box 263
Makunada, IL 62958

Indiana

Hoosier Canoe Club
Don Halper
5815 Crittendon Dr.
Indianapolis, IN 46224

Kentucky

The Viking Canoe Club
Halsey Sanford
622 Maryhill La.
Louisville, KY 40207

SAGE—School of Out-
  doors
209E High St.
Lexington, KY 40507

Louisiana

Bayou Haystackers
Susie Latham
1829 Casa Calvo
New Orleans, LA 70114

Maine

Mattawamkeag Wilderness
Park
Robert Kelly, Park Manager
Box 104
Mattawamkeag, ME 04459

Penobscot Paddle &
Chowder Society
William F. Stearns
Box 121
Stillwater, ME 04489

Maryland

Terrapin Trail Club
Box 18, Student Union
Bldg.
University of Maryland
College Park, MD 20742

Potomac River Paddlers
Sea Scout 1775
Jim Hill
18505 Kingshill Rd.
Germantown, MD 20767

Baltimore Kayak Club
David Rodney
3201 Chapman Rd.
Randallstown, MD 21133

Monocacy Canoe Club
Box 1083
Frederick, MD 21701

Mason-Dixon Canoe
Cruisers
Ron Shanholtz
222 Pheasant Tr.

Hagerstown, MD 21740

Massachusetts

Hampshire College
Outdoors Program
Deborah Cole
Hampshire College,
West St.
Amherst, MA 01002

Experiment with Travel,
Inc.
Box 2452
281 Franklin St.
Springfield, MA 01101

Appalachian Mountain Club
Boston Chapter
5 Joy St.
Boston, MA 02108

Kayak & Canoe Club of
Boston
Phil Temple
Bolton Rd.
Harvard, MA 01451

Michigan

Raw Strength & Courage
Kayakers
Jerry Gluck
2185 Mershon Dr.
Ann Arbor, MI 48103

Minnesota

BIG Water Associates—
North
Ralph Beer
565 W. Sandhurst Dr.
Roseville, MN 55113

BIG Water Associates—
South
Rick Gustafson

10009 Oxborough Rd.
Bloomington, MN 55437

Cascaders Canoe & Kayak
  Club
Linda Jensen
4925 Emerson Ave. S.
Minneapolis, MN 55409

Mississippi

Paddle Pushers Canoe Club
c/o Miss Ike Thomas
All Saints School
Vicksburg, MS 39180

Missouri

Arnold Whitewater Assoc.
John J. Schuh, Pres.
490 Pine Ct.
Arnold, MO 63010

Central Missouri State
  University Outing Club
Dr. O. Hawksley, Rep.
Warrensburg, MO 64093

Ozark Wilderness Water-
  ways Club
Box 16032
Kansas City, MO 64112

Montana

Studies in Recreation
Joel Meier
Dept. of HPER
University of Montana
Missoula, MT 59801

New Hampshire

Ledyard Canoe Club
Steve Ruhle
Robinson Hall
Hanover, NH 03755

Coos County Cruisers
c/o Weeks Memorial Library
Lancaster, NH 03584

Nulbegan Paddle Co.
David Hawkins
Box 381
N. Stratford, NH 03590

Mt. Washington Valley
  Canoe & Kayak Club
Doug Armstrong
Box 675
N. Conway, NH 03860

New Jersey

Murray Hill Canoe Club
V. E. Benes
Bell Labs, Rm. 2C-360
Murray Hill, NJ 07974

Mohawk Canoe Club
Dartery Lewis
455 W. State St.
Trenton, NJ 08618

Rutgers University Outdoor
  Club
RPO 2913
New Brunswick, NJ 08903

New York

Appalachian Mountain Club
  New York Chapter
Emilie Pentz
145 Sheridan Ave.
Roselle Park, NJ 07204

Kayak and Canoe Club of
  New York
Ed Alexander, Rep.
6 Winslow Ave.
East Brunswick, NJ 08816

N. Y. Whitewater Club

Roy G. Mercer
110 Bleecker St.
New York, NY 10012

Sport Rites Club, Inc.
K. T. LeClair
Brayton Park
Ossining, NY 10562

Northern New York
    Paddlers
Box 228
Schenectady, NY 12301

Adirondack Mountain Club
    Schenectady Chapter
Betty Lou Bailey
Schuyler 16, Netherlands
    Village
Schenectady, NY 12308

Niagara Gorge Kayak Club
Doug Bushnell
41–17th St.
Buffalo, NY 14213

Adirondack Mountain Club
    Genesee Valley Chapter
John A. Robertson, Jr.
581 Lake Rd.
Webster, NY 14580

North Carolina

Carolina Canoe Club
Tom Erickson
Box 9011
Greensboro, NC 27408

Watauga Whitewater Club
Richard Furman, M.D.
State Farm Rd.
Boone, NC 28607

Haw River Paddle Shop
211 E. Main St.
Carrboro, NC 27510

River Runners' Emporium
3535 Hillsboro Rd.
Durham, NC 27705

Nantahala Outdoor Center
John P. Kennedy
Star Route
Brayson City, NC 28713

Ohio

Columbus Council, AYH
Joe Feiertag
1421 Inglis Avenue
Columbus, OH 43212

Keel-Haulers Canoe Club
John A. Kobak, Rep.
1649 Allen Dr.
Westlake, OH 44145

Cuyahoga Canoe Club
Chuck A. Tummonds
Box T
Mantua, OH 44255

Oregon

Oregon Kayak & Canoe
    Club
Box 692
Portland, OR 97201

Sundance Expeditions
14894 Galice Rd.
Merlin, OR 97532

Southern Oregon Kayak
    Club
Chuck Schlumpberger
8890 Rogue River Way
Rogue River, OR 97537

Pennsylvania

Slippery Rock State College
L. H. Heddleston, Director

Student Activities & Recreation
Slippery Rock, PA 16057

Allegheny Canoe Club
Walter Pilewski
755 W. Spring St.
Titusville, PA 16354

Penn State Outing Club
John R. Sweet
118 S. Buckhout St.
State College, PA 16801

Eastern River Touring Assoc.
Greg Derco
Box 451
State College, PA 16802

Harrisburg Area Whitewater Club
Box 2525
Harrisburg, PA 17105

Harrison Area Community College Outdoor Club
3300 Cameron St.
Harrisburg, PA 17110

Conewago Canoe Club
George F. Figdore
2267 Willow Rd.
York, PA 17404

Allentown Hiking Club
Bill Bevan
124 S. 16th St.
Allentown, PA 18102

Appalachian Trail Outfitters
29 S. Main St.
Doylestown, PA 18091

Appalachian Mountain Club Delaware Valley Chapter
Fred Cox
476 Kerr La.
Springfield, PA 19064

Dauber Canoe & Kayak
Walter Daub
Box 59
Washington Crossing, PA 18977

Tennessee

Tennessee Scenic Rivers Assoc.
Box 3104
Nashville, TN 37219

Sewanee Ski & Outing Club
Doug Cameron
University of the South
Sewanee, TN 37375

The Baylor School
Chattanooga, TN 37401

Tennessee Valley Canoe Club
George M. Marterre
Box 11125
Chattanooga, TN 37401

Footsloggers
Box 3865 CRS
2220 N. Roan St.
Johnson City, TN 37601

East Tennessee Whitewater Club
Mike Holland
Box 3074
Oak Ridge, TN 37830

Chota Canoe Club
Box 8270 University Sta.
Knoxville, TN 37916

Bluff City Canoe Club
Box 4523
Memphis, TN 38104

Texas

Great Fort Worth Sierra
  Club
River Touring Section
525 N.W. Hillery
Burleson, TX 76028

Texas Explorers Club
Bob Burleson, Rep.
Box 844
Temple, TX 76501

Explorer Post 425
A. B. Millett
708 Mercedes
Ft. Worth, TX 76126

Kayaks Limited
Larry A. Dailey
4110 Markham St.
Houston, TX 77027

R & M Outfitters
Maurene Hufford
2534 Teague
Houston, TX 77080

Whole Earth Provision Co.
2410 San Antonio
Austin, TX 78705

Texas Whitewater Assoc.
Thomas B. Cowden
Box 5264
Austin, TX 78763

Utah

Wasatch Whitewater Assoc.
Chris Arthur Spelius
161 South 11 East
Salt Lake City, UT 84102

Wasatch Mountain Club
Jim Mason
511 South 9th East
Salt Lake City, UT 84102

VTE Alpine Club—River
  Trips
Randy Frank
Union Bldg., University of
  Utah
Salt Lake City, UT 84112

Vermont

Marlboro College Outdoor
  Program
Malcolm Moore
Marlboro, VT 05344

Johnson Whitewater Club
Pamela C. Peckham
Box 649
Johnson State College
Johnson, VT 05656

Brattleboro Outing Club
Donald L. Kinley
1 Deacon Pl.
Brattleboro, VT 05301

Northeast Canoe Manufac-
  turing
Ed Parenteau, Sr.
284 Indian Point St.
Newport, VT 05855

Virginia

Blue Ridge Voyageurs
Harry W. Patch, Jr.
1610 Woodmoor La.
McLean, VA 22101

Canoe Cruisers
John C. Hefti
1515 N. Buchanan St.
Arlington, VA 22205

Coastal Canoeists, Inc.
Larry & Hope Gross
Box 566
Richmond, VA 23204

Explorer Post 999
R. Steve Thomas, Jr.
3509 N. Colonial Dr.
Hopewell, VA 23860

Washington

Washington Kayak Club
Dave Hamilton
17318 30th Ave. S., ŒM2
Seattle, WA 98188

Pacific Water Sports
Lee A. Moyer
1273 S. 188th
Seattle, WA 98148

University of Washington
Canoe Club
Intramural Activity Bldg.
Seattle, WA 98195

White Water Sports
Larry Jamieson
6820 Roosevelt Way N.E.
Seattle, WA 98115

The Tacoma Mountaineers
Kayak & Canoe Commit-
tee
Bob Hammond
3512 Crystal Spring
Tacoma, WA 98466

Desert Kayak & Canoe Club
Larry E. Thomas
450 Mateo Ct.
Richland, WA 99352

West Virginia

West Virginia Wildwater
Assoc.
Idair Smookler
2737 Daniels Ave.
S. Charleston, WV 25303

Wildwater Expeditions Un-
limited, Inc.
Box 55
Thurmond, WV 25936

Canoe Assoc. of West Vir-
ginia
Herbert C. Rogers, Pres.
111 - 18th St. East
Wheeling, WV 26003

Wisconsin

Sierra Club
John Muir Chapter
Rosemary & David Wehnes
2604 N. Murray Ave.,
#107
Milwaukee, WI 53211

Wisconsin Whitewater
River Runners
Dennis Slater, Jr.
5530 W. Cold Spring Rd.
Milwaukee, WI 53220

Wisconsin Hoofers Outing
Club
Wisconsin Union Direc-
torate
800 Langdon St.
Madison, WI 53706

Fond Du Lac Voyageurs
Canoe Club
114 Harrison Pl.
Fond Du Lac, WI 54935

Canada

Edmonton Whitewater
Paddlers
Box 4117, S. Edmonton PO.
Edmonton, Alberta
Canada T6E 458

Ontario Voyageurs Kayak
    Club
J. G. Shragge
116 St. Germain Ave.
Ontario, Canada M5M 1W1

New Zealand

Canoe Camping Ltd.
112 Ohiro Bay Parade
Wellington 2, New Zealand

Nelson Canoe Club
Box 793
Nelson, New Zealand

Peru

South American Explorers'
    Club
Robert Cook
Casilla 3714
Lima 1, Peru

Switzerland

Kanu Club Zurich
Otto Kosma
Dufourstr. 3
8008 Zurich
Switzerland

River Regulatory Agencies

The following are the principal agencies that amateur river runners must contact in order to obtain permits for major western rivers (as mentioned in the text, most of the best eastern whitewater is as yet unregulated). Some rivers are tightly controlled with regard to commercial trips but as yet uncontrolled for private parties; the agencies which oversee these are not included here. Of course, it's possible that as river use (and user impact) grows, more and more rivers will become subject to some kind of permit process. For a complete listing of all the river regulatory agencies in the U.S., see the June 1970 issue of *Down River*, the whitewater enthusiast's monthly magazine.

Arizona

Grand Canyon National
    Park
Box 129
Grand Canyon, AZ 86023
602-638-2411

*The Grand Canyon of the
    Colorado.*

Colorado

Dinosaur National Monu-
    ment
Box 210
Dinosaur, CO 86040
303-374-2216

*The Green and Yampa,
    within the monument.*

Idaho

Challis National Forest
Challis, ID 83226
208-879-2285

The Middle Fork of the Salmon.

Nez Perce National Forest
Kooskia, ID 83539

The Selway and the Middle Fork of the Clearwater.

Nez Perce National Forest
White Bird, ID 83554

Parts of the Salmon and Hells Canyon of the Snake.

Salmon National Forest
North Fork, ID 83466
208-865-2382

The Salmon River Canyon.

Sawtooth National Recreation Area
Stanley, ID 83278
208-774-3511

The Upper Salmon River.

Utah

Canyonlands National Park
446 South Main
Moab, UT 84532
801-259-7165

The Colorado and the Green, within the park.

Grand Resource Area
446 South Main
Moab, UT 84532
801-259-7231

Westwater Canyon of the Colorado, and the Dolores.

Flaming Gorge National Recreation Area
Dutch John, UT 84032

The Green River, immediately below Flaming Gorge Dam.

North Vernal Resource Area
Box F
Vernal, UT 84078
801-789-1362

The Green River from Little Hole to Brown's Park.

Price Resource Area
P.O. Drawer AB
Price, UT 84501
801-637-4584

Desolation and Gray Canyons of the Green River.

Equipment Manufacturers and Suppliers

The following list is neither complete or exhaustive, but it does contain many of the leading suppliers of quality whitewater equipment. An important criterion in the selection is that every firm listed offers a catalogue, brochure, or other description of its products at no cost. While it's logical to begin shopping for whitewater gear at a specialty shop if there is one in your area, the information in these catalogues can be a great aid in comparison shopping.

Bart Hauthaway
640 Boston Post Rd.
Weston, MA 02193

Canoes, kayaks, accessories.

Camp-Ways, Inc.
12915 S. Spring St.
Los Angeles, CA 90061

Inflatable rafts.

Dayton Marine Products
7565 E. McNichols Rd.
Detroit, MI 48234

Sportyaks.

Easy Rider Fiberglass Boat Co.
Box 88108, Tukwila Branch
Seattle, WA 98188

Kayaks and canoes.

Extrasport, Inc.
Box 22
Halesite, NY 11743

Canoes, kayaks, wooden paddles, accessories.

Hurka Industries
1 Charles St.
Newburyport, MA 01950

Molded Kevlar paddles.

Hyperform
25 Industrial Park Rd.
Hingham, MA 02043

Lettman- and Prijon-designed kayaks, canoes, and accessories.

Iliad, Inc.
55 Washington St.
Norwell, MA 02061

Fiberglass paddles.

Kayak Specialties
Rt. 1, Box 83
Buchanan, MI 49107

Wooden paddles.

Hans Klepper Corp.
35 Union Square West
New York, NY 10003

Kayaks and foldboats.

Mitchell Paddles
Canaan, NH 03741

Wooden paddles.

Natural Designs
2223 N. 60th St.
Seattle, WA 98103

Kayaks.

New World Paddle Co.
Rt. 8, Box 112A
Easley, SC 29640

Wooden paddles.

Nona Boats, Inc.
977 W. 19th St.
Costa Mesa, CA 92627

Kayaks, canoes, cartop carriers, accessories.

Northwest River Supplies
Box 9243
Moscow, ID 83843

Rafts and accessories of all kinds; also kayaks and related gear.

Old Town Canoe Co.
Old Town, ME 04468

Kayaks, canoes, wet suits, accessories.

Perception, Inc.
Box 64
Liberty, SC 29657

Kayaks, canoes, cartop carriers, accessories.

Phoenix Products, Inc.
Box G, Route 421
Tyner, KY 40486

Kayaks, paddles, accessories.

Rocky Mountain Kayak
Supply
Box 8150
Aspen, CO 81611

Whitewater accessories.

Rogue Inflatables, Inc.
8500 Galice Rd.
Merlin, OR 97532

Inflatable rafts, frames, and oars.

Seda Products
Box 997
Chula Vista, CA 92010

Kayaks and canoes, paddles, helmets, vests, and flotation.

Sevylor
6279 E. Slauson Ave.
Los Angeles, CA 90040

Inflatable kayaks (Tahitis).

The Ski Hut
Box 309
Berkeley, CA 94701

Kayaks, canoes, accessories.

Summit, Inc.
Lower Churchill Rd.
Washington Depot, CT
  06794

Wooden paddles.

Whitewater Boats by Dick
  Held
Box 483
Cedar City, UT 84720

Kayaks and canoes.

Wildwater Designs
Box D
Penllyn, PA 19422

Life vests, wet suits, paddling jackets, etc., in kit form.

APPENDIX C
A WILDWATER BIBLIOGRAPHY

This is a selective list of books and periodicals about white-water sport in general; it does not include guides to specific rivers and regions. Several guidebooks are recommended in Chapter 10, and many others are available. But reliability varies, so it's wise to consult with experienced boaters in your area before buying.

Arighi, Scott and Margaret S. *Wildwater Touring*. Macmillan Publishing Co., Inc., New York, 1974. 334 pages.

A not too technical introduction to river touring in general, with descriptions of nine Northwest river tours.

Evans, Jay and Robert R. Anderson. *Kayaking*. The Stephen Greene Press, Brattleboro Vermont, 1975. 192 pages.

The first complete American book devoted to kayaking; numerous photos.

Hartline, Bev and Fred. *A Sketchy Introduction to Whitewater and Kayaking*. Published by the authors, 1974. 20 pages.

A light-hearted and witty collection of very basic instructional sketches and tips on kayaking.

Huser, Verne. *River Running*. Henry Regnery Company, Chicago, 1975. 294 pages.

A volume devoted exclusively to river running in inflatable rafts; offers extensive information on equipment.

Jenkinson, Michael. *Wild Rivers of North America*. E. P. Dutton and Co., Inc., New York, 1973. 413 pages.

Nine classic wild rivers described in great detail with notes on 106 more; well-written.

McGinnis, William. *Whitewater Rafting*. Quadrangle/The New York Times Book Co., New York, 1975. 361 pages.

A comprehensive, well-illustrated guide to all aspects of rafting, including descriptions of runs down two dozen rivers.

Norman, Dean (editor). *The All-Purpose Guide to Paddling: Canoe, Raft, Kayak*. Greatlakes Living Press, Matteson Illinois, 1976. 218 pages.

A collection of short chapters by different authors on such esoteric subjects as canoe poling and kayak surfing, as well as more basic river touring topics.

Powell, J. W. *Exploration of the Colorado River of the West and Its Tributaries*. Dover Publications, Inc., New York, 1961. 400 pages.

A reasonably priced softcover edition of Powell's classic, with the original engravings reproduced.

Ruck, Wolfgang E. *Canoeing and Kayaking*. McGraw-Hill Ryerson Ltd., Toronto, 1974. 95 pages.

A simplified, well-illustrated introduction to both flatwater and whitewater paddling; somewhat better for classical flatwater canoe technique than for whitewater.

Steidle, Robert and Walter Pause. *Alpenflüsse-Kajakflüsse*. BLV Verlag, Munich, 1969. 175 pages.

Contains descriptions of the 50 best known whitewater runs in the Alps. Although published only in German, this book is a must for anyone planning a European whitewater vacation. Beautifully illustrated.

Urban, John T. (editor). *A White Water Handbook for Canoe and Kayak*. Appalachian Mountain Club, Boston, 1974. 77 pages.

This well-written little pamphlet was for many years the standard instructional material on whitewater paddling.

Walbridge, Charles. *Boatbuilder's Manual*. Wildwater Designs, Penllyn, Pennsylvania, 1973. 70 pages.

Must reading for anyone considering building his own fiberglass kayak or canoe.

Periodicals

River World (formerly *Down River*). Published seven times yearly by World Publications, 1400 Stierlin, Bldg. C, Mountain View, CA 94043.

An exciting, well-illustrated, and wide-ranging publication aimed at the whole spectrum of river-touring enthusiasts: kayakers, canoeists, and rafters; flatwater as well as whitewater; competitive as well as recreational.

Canoe. The magazine of the American Canoe Association, published bimonthly by The Webb Company, Inc., 1999 Shepard Road, St. Paul, MN 55116.

Oriented somewhat more to the open canoeist than to the whitewater buff, this magazine nevertheless appeals to paddlers of all descriptions.

American Whitewater. The journal of the American Whitewater Affiliation, sent to members quarterly.

A very serious, always interesting, definitely nonslick and noncommercial compendium of what's happening in whitewater boating around the country. Join the A.W.A. or one of its member clubs to get this journal (see Appendix B).

INDEX